Kaleidoscope

of Stories by a Free Spirit

James Lockett Malony

Front Porch History

2012

James Lockett Malony is a graduate of West Point 1945, and is currently the latest member of a line of graduates starting in 1854 plus one Naval Commodore in 1807, which was the highest Naval rank at the time. James served as an Infantry Unit Commander in 1945 Philippines and Japan before returning to the United States and starting his own consulting company, serving U.S. Clients in Europe, West Africa, South America and Russia. He also continued to serve the U.S. government in providing training services.

ISBN-13: 978-0-9855969-2-7

Contents

Introduction

I am sure that there are numerous people who have had lives far more exciting than mine, and probably more humorous, so I have no claim for originality on these scores. I guess that I may be one who finds life as an adventure with many humorous episodes, as well as those less so. I have written for my own enjoyment a number of these episodes which occurred during my lifetime—some, I think are funny; some are unusual; and some which happened to others have true historical value, but also show an unusual ability to survive and succeed against overwhelming odds.

My stories cover a kaleidoscope of situations and geographical locations both domestic and overseas and cover several wars, two assassinations, four coups, assignments in the Philippines, Japan, Germany, Italy, Liberia, Nigeria, and Russia, as well as being involved in big league U.S. Government contracts.

So to those who read these renderings, I hope that you will not be too critical of my writing style and my somewhat questionable moral standing, to which I can only reply "Mea Culpa."

Foreword

Everyone has stories, but I consider Jim Malony to be the best story teller I have ever met. In this book, Jim tells us his tales in such a way that you feel he is there with you. I read some of his stories years ago and persuaded him to publish and share them with the world. With the help of a world class editor and friend of many West Pointers, Remy Benoit, Jim's stories are finally compiled and published in *Kaleidoscope.*

There are many things I like about Jim's stories. They are funny. They are short. They cover a kaleidoscope of subjects and thus the name of the book represents a multitude of events spanning over 80 years of Jim's life. My mother was a newspaper reporter and was able to capture the details of an event. Although Jim was not a reporter, he too captures the details and I think you will appreciate them as I did.

Jim has led an exciting life. Writing the stories was easy for him. He has traveled and lived around the world. He has a wealth of experiences—many more than most of us. He is still working and adding to his experiences at the tender age of 89.

One of the themes you will detect as you read this book is the ability to survive against all odds. Jim has the ability to succeed when most would give up. He does not jump over the hurdles and obstacles put in his way. He simply uses the classic military maneuver of flanking them. That perspective shows through in the stories.

Jim's style of presenting real life circumstances holds your attention. His stories transport you to many of the countries in which he has lived, sharing their history and geography. You will not put the book down until you finish the stories.

I consider Jim a dear friend. The bonds of being fellow West Pointers (Class of 1945 and Class of 1968) tie us together for life as brothers; we have grown and strengthened that bond in the time we spend together whether on the golf course or in doing business...

It is an honor to have helped Jim to get this book to press. Enjoy it as I did.

—Chuck Giasson, Colonel Ret. U.S. Army

Editor's note: These stories are representative of oral history. They are representative of their times and do not represent the beliefs of the editor, publisher, or any one other than their respective authors.

Part I

Odd Occurrences at West Point

Overview: West Point 1941–45

As many sons of West Point graduates who moved from Army Post to Army Post while they were growing up, our focus was on being a West Pointer because we were creatures of our own environment as our exposure to the outside world was rather limited. In my case I was in a long line of graduates; in fact I was sixth generation—my father (Malony) Class of 1912; my Uncle (Lockett) Class of 1908 (didn't graduate); my grandfather (Lockett) Class of 1879; my great-grandfather Class of 1852; and Commodore James Barron of the U.S. Navy circa 1807 who was my great-great-uncle. I am sure that if my ancestors would turn over in their graves over my sins at West Point, they would be called the "Whirling Malonys, Locketts, and Barrons."

Well, as luck would have it, I won a competitive exam from 36th Congressional District in upstate New York, and after a nip and tuck battle with the Surgeon Generals Office over a slight deficiency of my true height—5'6" was passing (see my story entitled "An Inch in Time saved Mine")—and entered the portals of West Point on July 1, 1941. My father had never really encouraged me to go there, and believe me, if I had known that a somewhat lackadaisical attitude towards being disciplined was not tolerated, I might have looked elsewhere for an education. But the damage was done and there was no turning back and I spent the most miserable year of my life due to my resistance to the hazing that went on, as naturally, this attracted a lot of attention from the Upperclassmen which made matters even worse.

I certainly wasn't a star at the academics either and in June 1942, after twelve tumultuous months, I failed the mathematics course and had to take a re-examination to re-enter the Academy as a Plebe again. This time I got through all of the courses and was graduated June 1945. I always loved soldiers and being in the field, and considered myself a good leader, but I was never considered a good "company man." I must admit, however, that my thirst for adventure, and the challenge of the unusual led to some interesting situations in life. My West Point stories are, as they used to say in the movies, a *Preview of Coming Attractions.*

Cadet James Malony with parents, General and Mrs. Harry Malony, at his West Point graduation in 1945.

A Half Inch in Time Saved Mine

To get selected as a student at West Point is no easy task. First, only a limited number of candidates could be selected most of which had beaten out a number of candidates from his congressional district through a competitive Government Employees exam sponsored by his Congressman.

In my situation I had to beat out over 250 competitors for just one appointment. The situation was exacerbated by my lack of academic brilliance, but I was 1/2 inch short of the minimum of 5'6" in height.

How all of this was overcome is covered in this story.

Getting into West Point in 1941 held many hurdles for me. The first was to win an appointment to the Academy, which could be won by several methods one of which was by Presidential decree—these appointments were usually awarded to the winners of a competitive examination held nationwide. These appointments were small in number and one had to be near genius to win. Other appointments could be won by honor graduates of West Point Prep schools, but in 1941, one had to be enlisted in the Army for 3 years in order to attend. The main source of appointments was from Congress itself. Each Senator had two appointments per year to give, and each Representative also had a number each year to award. The size of our pre-WWII class was about 450, smaller than many community colleges today.

Very few applicants to West Point were given appointments outright by the congressmen—most required the applicant to take a competitive exam against other applicants within a particular congressional district; the winner got the appointment and the runner-up was designated as First Alternate. In my particular case 250 others competed for my congressional district, the exam incidentally was the standard Civil Service exam that others took to qualify for Civil Service jobs.

I was notified in early March that I had won the appointment; now all that I had to do was top the entrance and the physical examinations. Since I had studied diligently for the entrance exams, I had no qualms about passing the academic part; but the physical part could be a problem (to a small guy). In 1940, minimum height was 5'4", but in 1941 the minimum was 5'6" and I was stuck almost in the middle at 5'5-1/2". As the day arrived for both examinations to be held at Walter Reed Army Hospital in Washington, D.C. I conceived a diabolical plan to grow that one half inch the details of which follow:

Step one Receive a bump on the head, which would create some improvement of my height.

Step two Place chewing gum on top of the aforesaid bump.

Step three Place pre-stiffened hair over the chewing gum, thus growing the critical one half inch.

Sounds very simple and straightforward doesn't it? Well, here is what happened that day at Walter Reed and the events that followed.

I had found a half of a split duck pin at the Post bowling alley at Fort McNair where my father was stationed—just the thing for a bump on the head, I thought. When we arrived for our physical we were required to remove all of our clothes and wear a hospital gown as a cover, so here comes strike one: a person walking around naked with a portion of a bowling pin is sure to attract attention. I was sure that if I was caught trying to artificially grow that elusive one half inch, I would be disqualified on the spot and live in perpetual disgrace.

I decided to go through with step one and then dispose of the bowling pin. I nudged the candidate next to me and spoke in a *sotto* voice "Hey buddy, do me a favor and hit me on the head with this," and handed him the bowling pin. His reaction was almost immediate—his face became frozen with fear and I am sure that his heart was beating at many times its normal rate. "Whaaaat!" he replied in a voice rising in panic. I am sure that he thought I was a homicidal maniac who wandered out of the woods surrounding the hospital and saw a line and joined it.

Desperately I looked around and saw no one seemed to have noticed. Through gritted teeth, I growled, "Keep your voice down, you stupid shit; hit me on the head, hard! And, if you tell anyone, I'll have to hurt you."

At that I drew myself up to my full 5'5" and stared maniacally up to his 6'3". His eyes were assuming the size of two billiard balls and God only knows what he was getting ready, to do. "Hit me! Hit me!" I cried. Suddenly as if it was self defense—whammo! He struck and I saw stars. I staggered over to an adjoining bench where I disposed of the old bowling pin. All candidates avoided my stares. "Oh well," I thought, "you clever little bastard, everything is going like clockwork. Let's feel the bump." As I reached up to see how much I had grown, I felt absolutely nothing, not even a skin abrasion—apparently my hard Irish head had absorbed a blow that would fell an ox without even a ho hum.

"Well, so much for step one," I thought, "let's move on to step two and three." I had already taken care of step three by literally spreading Crisco, a particularly yucky cooking grease, on my head before leaving our quarters for the trip to the hospital.

Step 2 was accomplished by chewing a particularly vile brand of bubblegum. It was red in color, had the consistency of an old rubber tire, and a truly horrible sickly sweet cloying flavor that remained on one's taste buds days after application. Fortunately, I slipped the bubble gum onto the very highest point of my head; sculpted it in a lovely pyramid; combed my hair over my work of art, and off I went to the physical.

The exam itself consisted of testing at various stations, the last of which was the height and weight station. Confidently, I stepped on the scale and weighed in at 130 pounds of pure rippling muscle. As they moved the rod for measuring height, I strained upward until I thought I felt the chewing gum compress; triumphantly I went to the same bench from which I started and the other occupants of the bench were all a buzz over something that happened at the last station. My heart, leapt into my mouth. "My God," I thought, "they've found the chewing gum and I'm dead." My total concentration was to get rid of the incriminating evidence when suddenly, I saw my salvation, for here was what appeared to be an orderly in a white coat sitting not over 20 feet from me with a pair of scissors around his neck. Since orderlies are enlisted men, and my father was a General, I assumed an imperious manner and addressed him: "Hey, Chief, do you want to use them?" "Look," I replied, "come off the shit, just, give them to me—now!" Chief handed me the scissors and I cut off the chewing gum in front of him, and handed them back, and walked off.

Later that day, we had to individually go before a board of offices to be discharged from the hospital; and to be informed of the results of our respective physical examinations. When my time came, I walked confidently into the room where the Board was convening and was stopped dead in my tracks by the sight of "Chief" in full uniform shifting in the position of head of the Board. "Chief" had two stars on his shoulders signifying the rank of Major General. "Chief" was Major General Harmeling, Chief Surgeon whose turf was Walter Reed Army Hospital.

Upon seeing me, Chief smiled wolfishly saying, "Mr. Malony, that chewing gum didn't increase your height any did it?" At that I failed the test and my hard earned appointment to West Point evaporated. But wait! Wasn't there a clause in the Army regulations, which allowed me 60 days for a re-examination?

Yesss! Hooray! The game wasn't over yet! All I had to do was to grow one half inch in 60 days and I was in!

The regulation also stated that the examination could be held at Army installations other than Walter Reed—this then removed me from the clutches of Chief. I then consulted the Surgeon at Fort Meyer, Virginia, across the Potomac River from Fort McNair, who gave me a series of exercises designed to stretch my spine enough to met the 5'6" standards.

The principal exercise consisted of tying my feet to the bottom of an old iron bed issued by the Army Quartermaster and grabbing the rungs at the top of the bed and sleeping that way. Well it worked like a charm. I would wake a veritable giant of 5'7", but after an hour or so, my vertebrae would collapse like an old accordion and I would revert to my former shriveled status.

Once again the same brain that concocted the bubble gum scam went into action. My step-mother owned an old LaSalle touring car with a large backseat, and the soldier who was assigned to the care and gardening around our quarters was authorized to drive the car. His name was Private Nelson. The solution to my problem was obvious—Nelson, and the soldier who performed similar duties next door, would pick me up bodily, carry me out to the LaSalle, whisk me out to Fort Meyer, stand me up to be measured while I was still 5'7"; the Surgeon would sign the exam papers—and I would be a future West Point Cadet. The brilliance of my plan was not appreciated by my father, who not only responded to my proposal with a loud *no*, but also with a louder *hell no*! My alternative plan was to just plain stand on my tiptoes until I felt the measuring standard touch the top of my head—simple, but since it was so outrageous, it could work.

Dutifully, I reported to Fort Meyer on the appointed day to be measured. The Surgeon placed the standard at 5'6" and I stood on my tiptoes and everything went according to plan. The Surgeon pronounced that I had passed and signed the exam form. As I started to breathe a sigh of relief, the Surgeon turned to a brand new 2LT who was to serve as a witness. "Just sign here" said the Surgeon (a full Colonel in rank). "No, Sir," replied the 2LT, "this man stood on his toes." The Surgeon said very pointedly, "Well, we'll measure him again." The scene repeated itself. The 2LT didn't get it! The Surgeon wanted me to pass. A moment later, a soldier who had passed out on the Fort Meyer polo field was brought in. The Surgeon, ordered the reluctant 2LT to attend the stricken soldier, hastily signed the 2LT's name as the witness, and whispered in my ear: "Take these papers to Walter Reed, and get the hell out of here." Hence I entered West Point on July 1, 1941 as the shortest man in my class, a distinction I held for the next 4 years.

Epilogue

In June 1942 I had some difficulties with the Academic Department, which resulted in having to retake the final exam which I had failed, but as a civilian out of the Academy. Once again we had ninety days to get smarter and, if I passed, I would re-enter as a Plebe again. I scored almost perfect on the re-exam, which made me wonder how I ever failed it in the first place. Once again all of us who passed had to take the standard physical examination to include height and weight at Walter Reed. I assumed that since I had passed the height part a year ago I would get a free pass this time. The group of us who were scheduled to re-enter the Academy were gathered near the examination room, when an officer strode up to us and genially inquired about our status and our enthusiasm about going back to West Point. Upon the officer coming into view, I froze in my tracks—it was Chief again. Chief, with that same wolfish smile reminisced about physical exams in general, and then said "You know fellows, last year some applicant to the Academy put chewing gum in his hair so that he could pass the exam, isn't that funny?" I did my best to resist the impulse to sink to my knees and crawl on my belly like a reptile unnoticed out of the room. Whether he knew I was in the crowd I'll never know.

What I did know was that I failed again! My position was that I was 5'6" in 1941, and that if I had shrunk as a result of the physical pounding I took during that year was not my fault, it was the Academy's fault. This gained me an audience with a newly drafted Major who probably had not been in the Amy for more than a month. While he was groping for a solution to the dilemma of a shrinking cadet, I remembered that the 1940 regulations stipulated that 5'4" was the minimum, but had been changed to 5'6" in 1941. Seizing the 1940 regulation from the bookcase behind him, and hastily turning to the section on height and weight. I covered up the date with my hand and loftily informed the Major that the hospital was mistaken as I only had to be 5'4" so what was all of the fuss about? Apologetically he signed off on the exam form and sent me on my way back to West Point to serve my second Plebe year.

I hope that when I reach the Plebe gates in Heaven, St Peter doesn't have Chief at his side with a tape measure.

Misadventures in Mah (My) House

The villain in this story had been an All American linesman for a southern college before he came to West Point. Since he was ineligible to play for Army, his temper and impatience grew almost daily. To make matters worse, in his fourth year as a cadet, he became our First Captain, which was closely related to having a message from God, and even his own classmates avoided him as if he had some strange, contagious social disease.

During my first Plebe year at West Point in 1941, we had a Cadet Officer (God's other son), who was an animal to say the least. He was an ex-All American at Vanderbilt before coming to West Point, but was ineligible to play for Army.

The recipients of all of this pent up hostility generated by not being able to play football were his classmates, as well as the rest of the Corps of Cadets. Cadet Officer took no nonsense in the Mess Hall; and he let everyone within earshot know that it was *Mah House.* No one, but no one, broke the rules there. There were no pranks, no loud talking, or breaking things in *Mah House*, and those who did suffered severely, at the time physically. Cadet Officer was a Confederate through and through and took no slurs on the South; any suspicion on his part brought an instant reaction. The sight of this beetle browed, All American with a build like a water buffalo advancing on a terrified victim was enough to keep even the bravest cadet toeing the line

For the Mess Hall there were certain rules which Plebes had to follow. Namely, each table had a Table Commandant, usually a First Classman seated at the head of the table. At the end of the table sat the unfortunate Plebes whose job was to serve the food, handle the beverages, answer trivial questions, and eat basically at attention. One mistake, such as dropping a beverage glass thrown to the Plebe whose assignment was that of Water Corporal, after banging on the table to get the attention of the Plebe, resulted in all the Plebes at that table "sitting up." This meant no more food, sometimes the duration of the meal.

So, as you can see, being in the Mess Hall was closely akin to what I imagine the Christians might have felt like in the Roman Coliseum. Our Table Commandant during this incident was a skinny, hook wormy person who came from deep Mississippi, who took great delight in torturing the Plebes at his table with ingenious ways to prevent us from eating. The culmination of his torture on that particular day was to ask each Plebe the significance of it. As each of us in turn gave the wrong answer, we were told to "sit up" so there went another meal! Finally, with about five minutes to go before the end of the meal, *Hookworm* relented and told us to eat. If you can appreciate bolting down helpings of baked beans and brown bread, you can well imagine that enough gas was generated to float the *Graf Zeppelin* with appropriate side effects. While gorging ourselves, *Hookworm* proudly announced that the day was the anniversary of the birth of the Confederacy, and that all Plebes were to bring something appropriate to the table that evening to celebrate the occasion. That afternoon we had Cavalry instruction. In 1941 the Army was still not convinced that horses were obsolete, so dutifully we had to learn how to ride and maneuver a group of thoroughly bored and mean animals. Seized with an overwhelming desire to offer something appropriate for the Confederacy celebration, I found an old brown paper bag, filled it with the droppings from the horses, tied a ribbon around the top of the bag, and placed it on our table, along with the ice cream and cookies brought by the other Plebes (all of whom probably made general in their later lives).

Unfortunately *Hookworm* was not at the table when Cadet Officer approached and addressed the first Plebe. "Well, ah say, wot have we here?"

"A celebration, Sir," said Plebe number one. Cadet Officer's beetle brow came together giving him an even more ominous aura. "Who in the hell does some sumofabitch think he is—having a celebration in mah house!" Plebes numbers one and two in unison said, "Sir, we are celebrating the birth of the Confederacy."

Cadet Officer said, "Well that's different. Let's see what we have here. Ah, that's nice, ice cream, and yes cookies to go with the ice cream; that's mighty considerate of you Plebes."

"You brown nosing bastards," I thought, "but please God, make Cadet Officer vaporize before he looks into the brown bag." As Cadet Officer advanced on my brown bag, I could hear the bells of doom tolling in my ears and my life flashed before my eyes. Why had I been so mean to my three sisters? Why did I put that horned toad down Macy Dodd's back in the 6th grade? Oh why, did I skip Sunday School and spend my dime on candy which was for the collection? An everlasting monument to bravery was that I managed to hold my bladder as he held the brown bag in his hands. Beaming with pleasure because his beloved Confederacy was being so honored he then asked, "Who brought this nice present?" No answer. Some of the amiability was slowly dropping from his demeanor. "Ahm[1] gonna ast[2] one more time—who brought this nice present?" Again a painful silence followed. Seeing that this was rapidly deteriorating into total disaster, I piped up, "I did, Cadet Malony, Sir."

"Well Cadet Malony, what's in this nice brown bag?" he growled. "Something appropriate for the occasion, Sir," I babbled. As Cadet Officer fumbled for the ribbon I stood frozen with horror as he peered into the nice brown bag and saw its contents, his face turned a bright vermilion; veins stood out of his neck; and I swear his eyes turned red. He opened his mouth several times to inhale and, finally out came such a thunderous noise that the Mess Hall became quiet. The Officer of the Day (Commissioned) hung over the parapet to locate the noise which was gathering the strength of a runaway locomotive.

"It's horseshit," he cried, and the walls trembled! Slowly he turned to me, incoherent with rage. "You little sumbitch ahm[3] gonna kill you," he roared as he advanced holding before him his hands which resembled two very large hams. I prayed to God again, vowing to mend my wicked ways, when suddenly *Hookworm* appeared pleading, "For God's sake don't hit him." One punch to the chest sent *Hookworm* ass over tea kettle into an adjacent wall where he collapsed in a heap. By this time both the Officer of the Day and a large portion of the Corps of Cadets were watching the course of events with deep interest. Much to Cadet Officer's credit he, with great difficulty, contained himself and vowed to me his full attention to my disciplinary deficiencies until he graduated in June, 1942. The meat wagon came and took *Hookworm* away with broken ribs.

Epilogue

Cadet Officer was not punished.

While I was a momentary hero to my classmates, and the members of the Corps of Cadets who were not red necks, I spent the remainder of my first Plebe year doing push-ups and other forms of torture in the

---

[1] I am

[2] ask

[3] I am

Cadet Officer's room during my spare time, resulting in a spectacular set of muscles, for which, to my dying day I will credit the Confederacy.

Breakfast in Bed

I still giggle hysterically when I envision the chaos which ensued upon execution of this plan by the Plebes at our summer camp in 1944.

During my first Plebe year at West Point, pre-WWII in 1941, we were still being trained with the 1903 Springfield Rifle; clothed in old leggings instead of modern day combat boots; and protected by old World War I helmets which resembled an upside down bedpan.

Instead of a combat oriented training program which West Point adapted in 1942, we were sent to "summer camp" after a very arduous "beast barracks" where we were hazed and yelled at for six weeks—day and night. The summer camp was very genteel in the style of the old Army. Tents were lined up by surveying instruments so that not one tent pole was out of line. These tents held from two to four occupants. All occupants displayed their white trousers and coats on racks located near their cots. Socks, shirts and so forth were neatly stored in footlockers at the foot of their cots.

Through the encampment ran a main thoroughfare, at the end of which was a 75mm cannon and a guardhouse housing the various members of the guard, including Officer of the Day, Officer of the Guard and Sentries who patrolled the circumference of the encampment. The Sentries, of course, were Plebes, and they patrolled for two hours and were off for four, but had to remain in the Guardhouse when not on duty.

Our Guardhouse food consisted of hot coffee and sandwiches made of two day old bread sliced about one half inch thick and stuffed with a monstrous chunk of Spam, liberally smeared with some sort of grease that looked and tasted like something out of a Mack truck crankcase. Eating one of the guard sandwiches was a Herculean task and digesting it was akin to swallowing a sixteen pound shot put. To further enhance its charm, one sandwich was guaranteed to raise enough gas to float the *Graf Zeppelin* as we had previously experienced by eating an entire meal in five minutes in *Mah House*. The environment in the Guardhouse was deadly to say the least.

As time passed on our tour of duty, and when no one was looking, the Plebes would smuggle these sandwiches under their shirts, and during the hours of darkness, would also place coffee in strategic locations for later enjoyment while walking the post. As each guard detail was posted they would stuff their leftover sandwiches down the muzzle of the 75mm cannon, pour the coffee after the sandwich and pack it tightly with the rammer staff used to clean the barrel after use. After enough sandwiches had been packed and mixed with coffee, a monster slug had been created, designed to create havoc in its wake.

As part of the Reveille ceremony, an enlisted soldier would blow a bugle to signal that all personnel should wake up, shave, have breakfast, clean their tents, and be ready for the day's activities. While the bugler was bugling, another enlisted soldier would load a 75mm blank into the cannon and the second soldier would pull the lanyard and the cannon would rattle the tent poles with a hellava bang.

All of the Plebe Sentries who knew of the surprise the Upperclassmen would have when the great slug of sandwich was blown down the street, were gathered at the windows of the Guardhouse in anticipation. Unfortunately, they were unaware of the Safety aspects of stuffing the cannon in the first place, and also, had no idea of where the great slug would go.

As the lanyard was pulled, instead of the usual loud bang, there was a dull *flub* sound, and clouds of acrid smoke enveloped the Guardhouse, the cannon, and the surrounding area. As the smoke cleared before the horrified eyes of the Plebe Sentries, they saw a scene of complete shambles. The First Classmen who had the block of tents closest to the cannon were sitting up groggily in their cots, with brown coffee stains with pieces of Spam plastered on their tents and bedding; and worst of all, big splotches of brown stained their beautiful white uniforms which were hanging within cannon range. The path of the great slug had carried about fifty yards down the broad thoroughfare, and the devastation was complete. Spam was hanging from tree branches, the axle grease the cooks had used on the sandwiches had formed phlegm-like puddles on the frames of the tents and for about thirty seconds one could have heard a pin drop. Once the shock had worn off, shrill cries of outrage could be heard as the Upperclassmen emerged from the chaos. The Plebe Sentries in the Guardhouse were busily engaged polishing their shoes and brass, and the ones whose turn it was to walk the guard posts, were busily trying to assist the enraged Upperclassmen, while valiantly trying to keep from rolling with laughter on the ground. Fortunately the Honor Code forbid the asking of questions which would serve to self-incriminate, so we escaped unscathed, and the victims were never really sure who the culprits were.

For those cadets Class of '41 who always wanted to be served breakfast in bed, the Class of '44 was only too happy to oblige.

Off to the Races

When I entered West Point as a Plebe in July 1941, I was positive that nothing has changed from 1908 when my father had entered also as a Plebe. The academics were basically the same almost, with a few courses in English and a foreign language thrown in. As a matter of fact, upon rummaging through the potpourri which most Army families collect in their many moves around the world, I found some of my father's textbooks and they were identical with mine.

As part of our peacetime training we had lessons in table manners, etiquette, ball room dancing for which we were issued patent leather dancing shoes, and horsemanship, the courses which were held indoors in the winter, and outside in the cavalry plain in the spring.

As a group, we handled most of the efforts to civilize us in good spirit with perhaps the exception of ballroom dancing during which we had to learn dancing by dancing with each other. If you can use your imagination, you can picture two Plebes sweat soaked in their woolen uniforms in the middle of July struggling to the tunes played on an upright piano by a motherly "Cadet Hostess"—this was one of the *most* degrading experiences of one's life, except Horsemanship. This was just a minor inconvenience, as compared to the ordeal of learning to ride in the approved Cavalry style. Many of the Plebes in my class in 1941 were from the various cities in the U.S. and had only seen *pictures* of horses, so we all started out from the lowest level.

For our first lesson, we were led into the indoor riding hall and were greeted by the meanest, leathery skinned First Sergeant imaginable. He wore a perpetual scowl which was designed to turn an errant cadets knees to jelly. The Sergeant stood in the middle of the riding ring with a solitary horse on a halter.

After calling us to attention, he stationed himself in the middle of the ring and barked out "This, Gentlemen, is a horse 'M1-A2' issued from Fort Riley, Kansas Remount Station."

He then named each part of the horse from head to toe and its function. For example: "These are called legs, they allow the horse to stand."

Those who were not familiar with horses took in every word as if they were listening to Moses' Sermon on the Mount; while those of us who had grown up with horses, while being afraid to laugh out loud, were hysterically giggling to ourselves. The Sergeant finished up his lecture by holding up the horses tail and saying "This, gentlemen, is called a dock." In later life, I always smiled to myself when one would address a Ph.D. as "Doc." Some of them really lived up to the name.

Well, the Sergeant wasn't through with us yet as the class always lasted an hour and a half. Having introduced us to "The Horse," he then directed us to a picket line, which is a rail held up by a post on each end to which was attached a group of the meanest looking beasts I had ever seen. Even more ominous was that while these villainous looking animals had bridles there were no saddles. I and my classmates, who were experienced with horses, knew what that meant! And we knew that the results of riding without a saddle was an experience which a "tenderfoot" would never forget. Riding without a saddle at a slow walk was OK but, when the order was given "Slow trot ho!" an unsuspecting rider would have the most painful experience of his life and would be absolutely convinced that his ability to conceive children would be irreparably damaged. The lucky ones would be so stiff and sore that navigation was extremely difficult.

Once we had learned how to manage the rudimentary elements of staying on a horse, and making him go where directed, we then were able to use saddles bridles and that's where the fun *really* started. Hour after hour we learned trot, canter, and gallop and a number of Cavalry movements. All of this time the old Sergeant was reminding us "Don't be afraid, show no fear, the horse is your friend." Sergeant lied!! The horse is not only smarter than you are, but there are no mutual interests between you. Here are damning examples of my claim.

1. The main interest of the horse is to get back to the stable in the shortest period of time possible to expedite this he has a number of options.

    a) Clamp the bit between his teeth so that you can't pull the reigns in and bolt for home.

    b) Buck you off and run for the stable.

    c) Suddenly roll over, thus scraping you and the saddle off and thunder off.

d) The same goes for rearing up on his hind legs.

2. Horses have a disposition in accordance with colors. My roommate and I devised the color code for various dispositions which was as follows:

    a) Grey or white horses are lazy, slow moving, have mouths like iron, and are stubborn. They are safe, but will subject you to yelling by your instructor.

    b) Black horses are "hot," evil tempered, prone to buck, and run away—stay away from them.

    c) Brown horses, especially light brown, are like riding a rocking chair; have a nice even temper and are eager to please. However, the more towards black in color they are, the more likely they are to behave like their black brothers.

    (Of course this is all baloney, but we all believed it anyway, especially the city boys who didn't know any better.)

3. Horses don't need to observe good manners, while you are touring the stables with your very proper date from an elite Eastern woman's college, he may suddenly emit a thunderclap of a fart which blows her hat off. A feeble rendition by you, quite by accident, sentences you to oblivion.

4. Horses can poop on the ground—you can't.

5. Horses can have carnal knowledge with other horses in public—you try it and you get ten years in jail with all the other perverts.

6. Horses love carrots and other weird vegetables, the same ones your mother used to jam down your throat.

7. Horses are psychic; they know when you are afraid. Armed with this knowledge they will try to disobey your every command, and head for the stables every chance they get. One of their tricks, if they know you are a pushover, is that they will scrape you off against a fence or a tree and head for home. The solution to hiding your fear was *never, never look your horse in the eye* when you went to the picket line to return him.

The horses we rode were old and wise and pity the cadet who showed fear or was a clumsy rider. As we received various Cavalry commands, the horses would execute the movements by rote no matter what you did. In a minute, I'll show you what I mean, but first, let's for a moment envision what our riding hall at West Point looked like.

It was an innocent looking building. Upon entering, one would see three sections, each separated by a heavy canvas curtain. The floors were tanbark and dirt. Each section formed a riding rink with its own instructor and our maneuvers were performed in each independently.

One afternoon in which all instructors in the individual rings were in full cry, the instructor in the furthermost ring, which was adjacent to us, gave the command "Gallup Hoaah" and the air was full of the thunder of hooves from the adjacent area.

We in turn were responding to the command "Slow Trot Hoaah" and were sedately trotting in our circle, when suddenly, bang! The canvas curtain flew up and a black horse from hell burst forth, eyes red, and froth flying in all directions, energized at a dead run. Holding on for dear life was a city boy from Brooklyn who we always teased about his funny accent. He had lost his stirrups, his saddle had slipped to one side, and he was assuming the posture of a Pony Express rider fleeing from Apache Indians who had gotten out of the wrong side of the bed that morning. The cadet was screaming at the top of his voice, "Stop you son-of-a-bitch!"

As the runaway horse ran through the riders in our ring, pandemonium reigned, and the runaway proceeded to burst through the next curtain.

In the third ring, our horses also were trying to run in every direction imaginable; the scene was chaotic. Cadets were brushed off: some chasing their own runaway horses; some just to get off the ground. From a horse's point of view it was a chance to even the score for the hours spent with cadets who were beyond redemption as far as ever learning to ride with any degree of skill.

Some were just bucking in place, while others followed the runaway through the second canvas with the same result. The scene was straight out of Dante's *Inferno*. Fortunately, there was no canvas curtain at the end, so the bulk of the runaway horses gave up the chase—but not the original one who, frustrated by the wall, turned with the rider still clinging for life. (Why he didn't just fall off I'll never know, his eyes as big as hard boiled eggs as he started to run back over his original route.)

Once again the cry went out, "The sonofabitch is coming back!" the retreat was on. Cadets who were intact after the last charge through their ring, plus the walking wounded, scuttled like crabs for safety; some getting their horses back to the picket lines; others chasing their horses to no avail; and the instructors screaming like banshees trying to bring some degree of control to their assigned ring. On the way back, the runaway had to slow down because of melee caused by so many unattended horses running around, and was finally subdued by one of the Sergeants. They had to pry "Brooklyn's" hands off the saddle and to lead him, crestfallen to a safer place. I am sure that the horses, when they returned to the comfortable stables, and over their oat bins, had a good horselaugh over the events of the day. "Brooklyn" never lived it down.

The Laundry Bag

This was a true story about which several ribald jokes can be made. The hero was one of our highest ranked cadets.

At West Point, the Cadet Officer ranks just below God in terms of respect, fear, intimidation, and all the rest of the privileges of being holy. Cadet Officers never swear, drink, ogle the fair sex, and think only the purest of thoughts. This particular Cadet Officer had all of these attributes. But he was known to provide some attributes of his own, namely an active affection of the fair sex.

During the war years of 1941–1945, all social activities for cadets in the flesh pots of the big cities were severely curtailed, and we had to be content with several hours of freedom when we were fortunate enough to be transported *en mass* to attend Army football games away. In these treasured hours, drinking and public display of affection were indulged in only with a full appreciation of the punishment inflicted on the poor soul who was apprehended; six months of walking punishment tours, plus reduction in rank to zero, and confinement to quarters for six months except to go to class, or exercise, was the reward for the detection of the use of spirits.

Thus, as anyone can see, four years of this builds up certain tensions which may cause some rather ill conceived actions on the part of the afflicted cadet. If the fable were true, that all male institutions served generous portions of saltpeter to cool the ardor of certain high-strung males, and since it was one of the ingredients in gunpowder, I wouldn't have been surprised if the entire garrison at West Point didn't go up in smoke at the slightest occasion.

As one can imagine, any source of female companionship was fully appreciated, and the most available, besides the Army nurses at the Post Hospital who were officers and ranked us, were the ladies who worked at the Post Laundry. These beautiful dainty things usually weighed in at

170 pounds on the hoof and the figure of measure was "ax handles." Thus, the dimensions of their buttocks was the number of ax handles measured across this massive expanse of quivering, bouncing, rolling, bulbous flesh was the figure of merit. As can be imagined, a four ax handle lady was a thing to behold! However, in our stressed condition some of us resolutely forged ahead. I sometimes suspect that the old field artillery song "Over hill, over dale, we hit the dusty trail," was not about the field artillery at all, but was composed after a trip to the Post Laundry.

Well, everyone knows that in the Army, "Rank hath its privileges," and so it was with the Cadet Officer.

He had attracted the most comely of the laundry ladies (one ax handle across) and with lust in his heart escorted her along "Flirtation Walk," a footpath along the banks of the Hudson, which was off limits to non-cadets, to include officers. Unfortunately, a particular Tactical Officer (one assigned per company to enforce discipline among other things) was walking along this footpath when he heard a rustling in the underbrush and innumerable shrill cries.

Thinking he had heard a wild animal in distress, he came upon the Cadet Officer fully mounted on his escort galloping at a fast pace, without moving more than a foot. The Tactical Officer, knowing that he must do his duty, informed Cadet Officer that he must be punished and that the punishment would be grave—indeed, to include reduction in rank; many, many hours on the area (quadrangle); and perhaps the rest of his life confined to his room—decided as a matter of dignity to let him write up his own offense, which then would be considered by a Board of Officers. Depending on the seriousness of the offense, and the appropriate punishment would be metered out, and announced from the "poop deck" which is an elevated balcony overlooking the Mess Hall. These announcements occurred during the supper hour to impress possible culprits the futility of breaking the rules.

As could be expected, the entire Corps of Cadets had heard by the grapevine of Cadet Officer's adventure and was expecting to witness the penultimate, namely the fall of Cadet Officer. Several weeks passed with no announcements from the poop deck. On Fridays all demerit lists were posted in one of the entrances to the "area" (quadrangle). These lists included minor offenses, as well as the major ones, which we felt would include Cadet Officer adventures in erotica. A quick scan of the major offense list revealed nothing. Finally, as we worked our way down the minor offense list, low and behold, was the offense, which Cadet Officer had written up on items on himself at the command of his Tactical Officer.

It read "Cadet Officer, *for unathorized article in laundry bag*, 5 Demerits."

Hunting the Lurking "Lucky Tiger"

Apprehension for possession of alcohol at West Point is a sure road to nine months confinement to your room, plus punishment tours; walking the quadrangle in the Central Barracks area, under blouse and trousers, belt, and rifle every Wednesday and Saturday afternoon.

Many cadets, upon becoming new Second Lieutenants, embark upon years of hard drinking just to catch up with four years of this enforced abstinence. Some of us try to get a head start in the drinking department by developing ways and means of obtaining and imbibing in "spirits." This undertaking is with full knowledge of the onerous punishment which is described above. Additionally, if the culprit has a cadet rank, he is unceremoniously stripped of that as well. This is like being drummed out of the Foreign Legion.

All of us in my Company, A-2, were blessed with three years of iron discipline applied by Lieutenant Colonel L and Major B who were our Tactical Officers; both of whom viewed my scalp as a real trophy.

My roommate, who shared my proclivities, took great pleasure in trying to outwit these two terror-striking martinets, and even by today's standards, our campaigns included acts of sheer genius. For example, we found that by removing the mirror and cabinet above our wash basin, we were able to hide booze, hams, and so forth, without fear of detection. Removal of the cabinet was facilitated by having only two screws actually holding the cabinet; the other four were dummies having had the body removed by a sharp file. Both our Tactical Officers knew we had things hidden, and it became a game to try to outwit us. The dynamic duo made up for their frustration by making sure I kept my unbroken string of punishment hours on the area, so in retrospect, my defiance reaped just rewards.

At the start of my first class year, my roommate and I decided that the cabinet removal method was clumsy and time consuming. Compounded by the fact that our dates, who provided our source of supply by smuggling the "spirits" through the gates, were becoming increasingly unreliable, we had to reorganize our operation.

I immediately established, through our waiters in the Mess Hall, a pipeline straight to the liquor store in Highland Falls, a small town adjacent to the Academy. I would imagine I was one of the few cadets who was served alcohol during supper. Having solved the logistics problem, we were confronted by the dilemma of where to hide the contraband. Our solution was not to hide it at all. We simply took a bottle of Lucky Tiger hair tonic, which had a dark brown color, and replaced the contents with "spirits."

Cadets must display their clothing and toiletries in their metal lockers with nothing concealed—ever! Obviously, being very conscious of West Point regulations concerning displaying everything, I displayed my Lucky Tiger hair tonic bottle up front and on the top shelf. Our Tactical Officer must have looked at that bottle every week we were in barracks, and although he knew we had our inventory someplace in the room, he never found it. This was in 1944–45, at this writing it is 2011, sixty-seven years later and I still look upon that particular cat and mouse game with relish.

Fortunately today West Point is much more liberal; they even have lady cadets, but, think of all the fun they're missing.

Showdown at Beechie Howard's

Most of you Ivy League or Staff Officer types would never fully appreciate a true Southern roadhouse. Usually it has a long bar, sawdust on the floor, country music, and country girls who do not have "tight knees" (as they say). Some of the bigger roadhouses had gambling in the back room and *femmes de joie* upstairs for the young men with raging hormones. If there weren't accommodations upstairs, the parking lot would do.

This created a need for a great deal of cautious footwork when proceeding towards the entrance: "Eyes straight ahead was the order of the day." Accompanying all of this was usually a set of rather large hostile bouncers, complete with brass knuckles and "saps" to subdue the usual wildman, or someone with a Yankee accent who quickly became very unwelcome.

Beechie Howard's in the 1940's was everything described above in spades. It was located in Phoenix City, Alabama, on the banks of the Chatahoochee River, which separated Columbus, Georgia, from Phoenix City. Every Sunday morning there reportedly were one or two bodies floating in the vicinity of Beechie's, dead from knife wounds. Obviously, one was well advised to keep one's bowels open and his mouth shut in Phoenix City. Phoenix City, incidentally, was the subject of a documentary, called *Sin City*, made by one of the big TV networks back in the 70's.

My West Point class in 1943 and 1944 spent a lot of time during July at Fort Benning, running our asses into the ground and sweating quarts in the process. We were not allowed to drink beer, or socialize with *anyone*; this included Red Cross girls, Army brats, and WACS.[4] Generally we were so damn tired that we were rendered absolutely harmless anyway. We had heard stories about Sin City and one of my classmates and I vowed to visit Beechie Howard's and drink all the damn beer in Alabama, regardless of the fact that we would be AWOL (absent with out leave). If caught off the post we would be punished when we returned to West Point with six months confinement to your room, with only attendance

[4]Woman's Army Corps

allowed to classes, and trips to the gymnasium for exercise, plus, as mentioned above, hundreds of hours walking off demerits in the "area," a quadrangle made of the hardest cement—one hour for each demerit.

This seems to be a high price to pay for a few beers and feminine company, but the fact was that there was a war on and we were not allowed to leave West Point except for scattered weekends and football games. However, the powerful surge of hormones, which accompanies periods of prolonged isolation overcomes all caution.

Having heard about Beechie Howard's from the GI's at Fort Benning, we succumbed to our obsession, and after supper call on a Saturday evening, hitched a ride to Phoenix City with two of our non-com instructors. We made our grand entrance into what we hoped was the palace of sin (Beechie's).

As we stood at the bar savoring our first beer in over eighteen months, we noticed that the place was bustling with paratroopers from the "jump school" at Fort Benning, and soldiers from the 1st Armored Division—the same Division which had been badly battered by General Rommel's Africa Korps at Kasserine Pass in North Africa. The 1st Armored was being reconstituted at Fort Benning and would later be part of the invasion force in Europe.

Many of the non-coms of the original 1st Armored stayed with the Division when it returned from Africa and were not inclined to engage in friendly conversation with outsiders. They had that "look" about them that combat soldiers often get. On the other hand, here were the paratroopers—boots polished so you could see your own reflection in them, brass polished so that it gleamed, trousers pressed so that one could cut his fingers on the creases, hair cut short, clean shaven, and demonstrating all, the good things a soldier should be.

There was only one thing wrong with this picture: they thought they were tough and were not bashful about trying to show it. After many beers, and fending off questions about our peculiar uniforms, we noticed that the volume of noise from that paratroopers side of the bar was rising and the 1st Armored people were becoming ominously quiet.

Casually, a 1st Armored soldier sidled up to a particularly loud paratrooper and asked in a conversational tone, "Are you a paratrooper?" To which the paratrooper said in a loud voice, "You're damn right I am, want to make something of it?" The 1st Armored soldier slowly put down his beer and said, "Well, let's see you open your parachute before you hit the ground," and at that he hit the trooper right between the eyes and down he went.

At that, the entire bar and the adjoining tables erupted and what a grand fight it was. My classmate and myself ran for the door, barely getting by the M.P.'s. coming the other way. Safely out on the sidewalk we didn't waste any time getting back into our barracks.

The next day the non-coms who were our instructors were telling us of the mass arrests at Beechie Howard's. We, of course, expressed shock and dismay that our armed forces would behave in such a barbaric manner, and at the same time shuddered at the thought of our fate if we too had been arrested.

Classmates Stick Together

In 1945 Chiang Kai-Shek and the Nationalist Army were on the run in mainland China, and the countryside was filled with bands of deserters and the remnants of the private armies of the War Lords whose allegiances switched from time to time between Mao and Chiang. Part of this maelstrom of people were wealthy Chinese families seeking to escape to Taiwan with as much wealth as they could carry in their pockets and on their backs.

While they were awaiting boats to help them escape the on-coming Red Army, their expenses mounted. They had to sell many of their heirlooms and valuables, which subsequently appeared in the shops along the main thoroughfare. It was indeed a shoppers paradise with gold, silver, and ivory pieces available at bargain prices, in addition to objects of art which probably are priceless today.

My two classmates, Lieutenants D and T, who were starters for Army's football team, respectively, suggested that we would participate in this future bonanza by hitching a ride from Atsugi airport in Tokyo to Shanghai on one of the Military Air Transport Service (MATS) aircraft on one of their "milk" runs to the China mainland.

One fine weekend we arrived in Shanghai, supplied with our meager pay and cartons of cigarettes for trade and ready for any bargains we could find, or anything else for that matter. Later, after having exhausted our resources acquiring various transportable objects, we went to Harry's Bar, an expatriate watering hole, and consumed a number of cocktails. While we were enjoying the benefits of Mr. Johnny Walker's best product, in walked a very rough customer from the West Point Class of 1942. He was an All-American tackle for Army and a very rough customer, indeed. After more cocktails were consumed, it was suggested that we convene later at another location where the entertainment was "outstanding" and that he would join us.

Amidst clouds of Scotch whiskey fumes, we finally arrived at our destination and were admitted by a striking platinum blond, blue eyed lady, obviously Eurasian. Buoyed by the prospect of the evening, we entered into a well-decorated living room, the centerpiece of which was a gold, lacquered piano. Suddenly it dawned on all of us that we were in a Eurasian house of ill repute, as all the occupants were young, nubile, blond, and blue eyed. Our "Hostess" had seated herself at the golden piano and was well into a classical rendition of *Claire de Lune*, when her efforts were interrupted by someone trying to break down the door.

Upon opening it the "Hostess" was swept aside by a squad of the most ill kept, filthy, smelly soldiers I have ever seen. Their uniforms were all different and in tatters, and their odor would knock down a horse. They were obviously the scraggly remains of either the Nationalist or a War Lord's Army. While the girls shrieked and scattered in a dozen different directions, the soldiers were waving their weapons, looking at us with venom and shouting at the "Hostess" who was shouting back at them in staccato Chinese.

The three of us stood in shock while all of this was going on, realizing that it was us the soldiers were after, probably to hold for ransom. This then posed a number of problems for us, the least being unauthorized transportation using government assets; leaving a theater of operations without clearance; bartering in the black market; and being found in a house of ill repute.

The last issue, being that from the looks of the Chinese soldiers they would probably have shot us without a single qualm or kidnapped us for ransom, and either option was unacceptable. As we stood there pondering our fate, a huge figure appeared in the doorway. Closer inspection revealed Robin had come to join the party. Upon surveying the situation involving three immobilized 2LT's, a shrieking Hostess, and 10 very ugly Chinese soldiers, Robin declared that the odds seemed OK and started to take off his coat.

The three of us (Class of '45) quickly changed the odds to 10 to 1 by thundering down a hallway, and out of a window; elbowing each other trying to fit two football players and myself (5'5" and 137 pounds) through a small window. After dropping to the ground with a thud, we ran pell-mell for what seemed to be an hour to safety.

After we had regained our composure and caught our breath, we realized that Robin had not joined us, and was undoubtedly having a very serious discussion with the Chinese irregulars. On the way back, we picked up reinforcements from a nearby services bar and a few weapons and "stormed" the Eurasian establishment only to find all the women gone, all the soldiers gone, and Robin gone. *Now that was scary!*

Time passed, and through our classmates in the Air Force, we learned that Robin had appeared for duty none the worse for wear. However, to this day we all say in our prayers, after we have asked for blessings for various items on our agenda, "... and please God, don't ever let Robin find us!"

We all take solace in knowing that through good times, bad times, Eurasian Cat Houses and bad Chinese alcohol, the Class of '45 sticks together.

Corporal Punishment

The story of my downfall.

Being made a Cadet Corporal as a Yearling (2nd year) was an honor, and since there were only four per company in those days, I was ranked in the top four militarily among my classmates. The chances of becoming a high ranking cadet officer were excellent, unless, of course, you committed some heinous act upon execution of which you were unceremoniously stripped of your rank, and punished by confinement to your room except for classes, meals, and exercise.

After surviving a very hot July and half of August introducing Plebes (freshmen) to the rigors of military life, we Corporals were sent to Camp Popolopen (now Camp Buckner) to rejoin our classmates and participate in field maneuvers and general weapons training

One day following a Corporal's meeting, I was walking back to my company barracks, swollen with self-importance, when I noticed several of my classmates whispering to each other and saying "Look out! Here comes Malony!"

My curiosity was piqued, and judging from their furtive looks, I wondered, "Could it be a party that I would be missing?" As I approached I heard George Troxell, our starting fullback before Doc Blanchard, saying "Don't tell him, don't tell him." I assured everyone that in spite of my exalted rank, if it was party time, I would be honored to join them. Their secret would be safe with me.

Finally, with much cajoling, they informed me they were planning a break out that evening, and that four girls would be waiting on an adjacent road outside the camp boundaries. Then we would all go to the Bear Mountain Inn, around twelve miles down the road for dancing, beer drinking, and perhaps other *ad hoc* activities. I agreed since I would be the fourth man, and who am I to disappoint the extra girl. This agreement was completed provided that I, as a Corporal, would plan the escape over the guard posts manned by Plebes, and lead the way through the woods to the road where the girls were waiting in their cars.

I also answered that I, as the Corporal, would mark the trees so that we could easily find our way to our rendezvous. After Taps and darkness fell we rendezvoused at our starting point on the guard boundaries which encircled the camp. We were perfectly camouflaged in our dark fatigues, and with a feeling of exhilaration, I led them across the guard post without a hitch. It was then that the nightmare started!

At this point, let me digress for a minute. My story is in the 1943 era, and sometime in the spring of that year a German submarine anchored just off Long Island, had sent ashore a group of spies and saboteurs to disrupt the aircraft and armament factories in the area. During the time of these nocturnal adventures, we at West Point were placed on a general alert, because the Germans had not been found yet.

They could have been anywhere. Hence, all military installations on the East Coast were acutely aware of the dangers the saboteurs represented.

Now back to the crossing of the guard patrol and our plunge into the woods under my fearless leadership.

We immediately became lost because it was dark and we couldn't find the trees that I, the Corporal, had marked so carefully. It seemed like hours were spent crashing around in the woods; running blindly into trees; tearing our clothes; pulling out brambles which were in our skin. We were just plain lost and disoriented.

With the curses of my classmates ringing in my ears, I suddenly saw a clearing in the distance and in the middle of the clearing was a well lighted building. With a sigh of relief, I crawled towards the cleaning. I commented to Troxel, "Gee, this building looks familiar." Suddenly I was seized not only with instant recognition, but, paralyzing fear as I found myself looking down the barrel of an M-1 A-2 Garand Rifle held by a terrified Plebe who thought that we were German saboteurs sneaking through the woods.

The familiar looking building was the Central Guard House for the camp. I had led our doughty party in one great circle, back within fifty yards from where we started. I withdrew my head from the foliage from which I was peering. The four of us were running panic stricken into each other, when the nervous Plebe complicated things by firing just over my head and I could feel the pine needles falling down my neck.

At that, we hit the deck again still disoriented as to where we were. In the meanwhile, the Plebe was still firing into the woods calling for the Officer of the Guard. Troxell and one of the others decided to make a break for it, and amid another volley from the Plebe, charged out of the trees. I heard this loud crack as Troxell ran into a parked truck. "God," I thought, "they have killed poor George!"

An inspection of the truck in the daylight revealed that the truck had gotten the worst of the encounter. By the time I recovered and was ready to make my break for it, the woods were full of Sentries hunting for us, hence, all hope of a direct escape were killed. Using the wiles of a soon ex-Corporal, I arose from my hiding place and joined the search party looking for me.

Unfortunately, my Tactical Officer, was leading the search party as Officer of the Day, and quickly identified me as not one of the Sentries. In answer to his query, "Why, Mister Malony, what are you doing out here?" I could only mumble, "Sir, I am doing botanical studies of the Foxglove, a flower that grows only at night." Obviously I lost any shred of credibility which remained and I was placed in confinement to barracks until my punishment was meted out.

Two weeks later, I turned in my beloved Corporal's stripes and spent the next six months walking punishment tours and confined to my room except for classes and exercise. The Plebes whom I had hazed in July and August smirked.

Epilogue

This incident set off a two year vendetta between the Tactical Department and myself, with my roommate being an accessory after the fact. As a result, I spent the bulk of, my next two years walking punishment tours and suffering confinement. In retrospect, if I had not gotten lost in the woods that night, I would have been a Cadet Officer and later on a Lieutenant General, but then again, I have met Lieutenant Generals who are still lost in the woods.

Oklahoma Football: "Boomersooner"

Biff Jones takes on Huey Long, Governor
of Louisiana, Oklahoma wins.

As a kid growing up in the dust bowl of Oklahoma, we all worshiped almost as icons, the University of Oklahoma football team. They used to labor mightily just to break even in the tough "Big Six" Conference, which was made up of Nebraska, Missouri, Kansas University, Kansas State, Iowa State and Oklahoma State. During the depression years, many Universities couldn't afford capable coaches and a few smart ones discovered that many ex-West Point football players and assistant coaches could be assigned as ROTC instructors at the colleges—and act as full-time coaches at no cost. Many of these became very successful in creating major football programs for the University to which they were assigned. Some of these coaches were Major Robert Neyland at Tennessee, Major Ralph Sasse at Mississippi State and Major Lawrence (Biff) Jones at Louisiana State.

As the fortunes fell for the Oklahoma football team, the patience of the University kept apace until, finally, the coach was fired thus leaving a vacancy, which all concerned sought to fill without success. I remember, almost as if it were yesterday, my father and I were sitting on our front porch in Norman, Oklahoma, when a car drove up to our curb and from it stepped one of the biggest men I had ever seen. He strode up our steps two at a time, embraced my father, (all five foot seven inches of him) in a bear hug and thanked him profusely for sending for him. Upon being introduced to him I realized that here was the famous Major "Biff" Jones, coach of Louisiana State, one of the leading teams in the U.S. at that time.

Silently I listened to Biff Jones' story as he recounted it to my father who, at the time, commanded the ROTC unit at the University of Oklahoma. The major rival of Louisiana State was Tulane, a privately endowed college that was viewed with a mixture of hate and envy by the state college students and alumni; the most vocal of which was Governor Huey Long. For non-students of history, Huey Long was a red neck, racist demagogue of the worst kind, who was not only the most powerful man in Louisiana, but in the whole South, and was very dangerous in every respect. His undying hatred for President Roosevelt kept him in the headlines constantly; and if the truth be known, he probably caused the lynching attitudes of many of the rural people in the state to take form in the actual act.

Obviously, he was a very dangerous man. If you studied American history, you would appreciate the "must win" pressure that Huey Long would place on the head coach of LSU to win at all costs. From the lowliest life form in the Louisiana swamps to the highest ladies in the State House in Baton Rouge, LSU held up its head to the "Damn Yankees," which included privately endowed schools no matter where they were located. Tulane, on the other hand was, at the time, and is today one of the leading colleges in the U.S. and possessed a major medical school. Since the amount of money needed to attend over four years was far more than many people could afford, Tulane was a natural target for Governor Long.

Obviously Tulane vs. LSU was always the "big game" rivaling Notre Dame vs. Southern California, Army vs. Navy, etc. In Louisiana, feelings ran high on the annual game. In actuality it polarized the old "depression" attitude of "haves vs. have-nots." Huey Long was at his best politically rooting for LSU. It was along about this time when he stated that while his people in Louisiana were cutting sugar cane in the fields, doing "stoop" labor digging up turnips, potatoes, etc., that "up in the North," Franklin B. Roosevelt was eating fish eggs (caviar) and toast, and drinking Champagne.

With all that going on, Biff had LSU behind at the half and sucking wind with the score at 6-0 in favor of Tulane. As he gathered his team in the locker room to try to set up a wining strategy, Huey Long invaded the locker room with his bodyguards in order to give the team a pep talk, Biff addressed the Governor in the most respectful tones and suggested that his team would not receive his little pep talk. At that time Huey Long threatened Biff with bodily harm if he was not allowed to talk to the team. Biff refused, and Huey started to push him, assisted by his bodyguards. At that, the whole team arose and threw the Governor and his bodyguards out of the locker room and with a roar, ran out and beat Tulane 13-6. Biff stayed behind! When the locker room was cleared, he called his wife, and instructed her to not ask any questions—get the dog, children, and any valuables in the car and meet him at one of the gates at the stadium. They then headed across state lines, as Biff was convinced that he would be assaulted by Huey Long.

Several days after this he appeared at our house.

POSTSCRIPT

Under Biff Jones, Oklahoma started a revival, which yielded several Big Six championships and a national ranking. Oklahoma played Tennessee in the first Orange Bowl. I remember Biff Jones complaining afterward that Tennessee was the "dirtiest team he had ever played" and that "Damn" Bob Neyland was the cause of it.

Tennessee now has its home stadium named Neyland Field. Biff Jones later went on to Nebraska, which appeared in the 1941 Rose Bowl against Stanford, which introduced the T formation to college football. Biff Jones later was appointed as Athletic director at West Point and was instrumental in recruiting Colonel Red Blaik, and embarked Army football to new heights. His son Larry, with whom I grew up, became a two Star General.

It was in the capacity as the Athletic Director at West Point in 1943 almost twelve years after he fled Louisiana and appeared on our front porch at Norman, Oklahoma, that I saw him next. My role was as a scheming cadet who saw a chance of spending a weekend in New York, if he would just give me permission to act as an assistant coach of our varsity boxing team. I couldn't make my weight of one hundred twenty seven pounds for feather weight, so I was grounded while the team went to New York. Hoping that he would recognize the little kid from back in Oklahoma, and that he would have the goodness in his heart to let me go with the team, I made an appointment to see him.

Full of confidence, I strode into his office, saluted smartly, and said, "Colonel Jones do you remember me, Jimmy Malony, listening to your stories about Huey Long?"

With a tired glance he replied, "Yes, how are you?" knowing full well that I was about to do something outrageous. I didn't disappoint him. I was into the first sentence of my pitiful story about why I should go to New York with the team, when he said very firmly "No!" Not pausing to catch my breath, I switched to my back-up story about his coaching at Oklahoma, and our family's pleasure at his success. This time he interrupted me in my most flowery phrases and said even more firmly—"*No*!"

Now I was well into my pitiful story, totally ignoring the first two "No's," when Colonel Jones, much to my horror, rose slowly from his desk and started to advance around it. I am sure he would have "frog marched" me not only out of his office but out of the building. To me he looked as big as a house. With as much dignity as I could muster, I saluted smartly and left with what remained of my decorum. That night I tried to summon the spirit of Huey Long, but he never showed up. He too didn't want to tangle with Biff.

Forty Leagues Under the Sea

The engineering courses at West Point constituted the major part of our curriculum and for the most part hadn't changed much over the years. The courses, for the most part, were designed for officers on the frontier, or remote posts overseas, and of course, combat. One course, which was constituted with what I considered of very little value, was surveying which was primarily used in map-making, road, and bridge building. Being near the bottom of my class, I knew that I was foredoomed to be an Infantry Unit Commander where I would be too busy dodging bullets to worry much about surveying; but the classes did have merit in that they allowed us out of the classrooms to commune with nature. Before proceeding further let me explain what surveying is all about.

Surveying is done by a team of two people, the idea of which is to plot straight lines, and to measure the changes in elevation along these lines. The equipment consists of a Stadia Rod, which is a numbered pole about 10 feet in length, and a pair of binoculars mounted on a tripod. The binoculars have lenses marked vertically and horizontally for references. If I remember correctly, there is a copper weight attached to the center of the tripod by a cord, and I suppose there must be level bubble devices to keep the optical platform level.

One person selects a spot along the path of the survey and plants the Stadia Rod while holding it erect. The other person levels the instrument, reads the number from the Stadia Rod, and records that number. For map-making applications, measurements are taken so that one surveys in a giant circle which begins and ends at the same point —readings taken are recorded in a survey book. Where the survey is started at that point, will be the same place where the survey is finished.

My survey partner was, like I, pushing the bottom of our class, so as well can be imagined, it was the blind leading the blind. We all started on the boat dock on the Hudson River and our ultimate goal was to survey up to Fort Putman near Michie Stadium, which had an elevation of, maybe, a thousand feet above the river. If I remember correctly, we worked for eight or so classes to finish the survey—sweating profusely because it was spring; stomping through brush; around trees; and generally working like dogs. Our day finally arrived upon which we took our last reading at our original site. Much to our dismay, our readings didn't quite check out—we had a *slight* deficiency of 40 feet, which meant we were 40 feet under water.

This happens to be a very precise description of my entire experience with any kind of Engineering, and as you can see from my story, *The Major's Toilette*, this was truly a preview of coming attractions.

Army Nurses I Have Known

Stories which I can personally attest—my kind of women.

Being an Army Brat, from circa 1922 to my current age of eighty-nine, I have had exposure to Army Medics for a number of years; and for the most part Army Nurses, who if there were such a thing as "mean pills," they must have taken them every day at breakfast. There are a number of instances pre-WWII, and shortly after, upon which I rest my case.

Walter Reed Hospital 1938

I was sent to Walter Reed as a sixteen year old victim of Lobar Pneumonia, and was subjected to thirty days treatment with Sulfa drugs which left me as weak and limp as a wet dishrag.

Normally sixteen year old males fell victim of various desires, among which were those involving a wild mix of sexual performances involving the opposite sex, accompanied by a variety of unattractive rashes and pimples. This affliction rendered the victims definitely unattractive. Fortunately I had taken enough medicines to forgo these attacks, but unfortunately also rendered me totally unable to respond to my sex ridden day dreams of love making with the nurses who tended me daily with body washes, muscle massages for my very high fever, and the weeks in a hospital bed.

Finally after a month in the hospital I began to feel some very tentative signs of life in my nether regions as I started thinking of wild parties, etc., with the nurses.

The end of my fantasies came one day as I was having my final body bath, I was in the midst of my erotic dream when I realized that slowly rising much to my horror was my "best friend!"

At last, I was on the road to complete recovery—*Hooray*, I thought, *I was getting well!* My dream suddenly turned into a nightmare—would the nurse notice? Would she turn me into the attending doctor, who would then advise my parents that I was a sex maniac, and attempted to attack my nurse?

My panic-stricken eyes followed every move she made. Slowly she raised her hand to her face, pulled out a pencil tucked behind her ear. Suddenly I heard a loud crack and felt the worst pain that I ever had up until that time. She had struck my offending member, and I shrieked in pain. She never changed expression, put the pencil back behind her ear, put the covers back on me and left the room expressionless.

Now that is a mean nurse.

Discipline at Walter Reed General Hospital

While recovering from Pneumonia in 1938, I noted that there were many field grade officers at Walter Reed for many reasons. The nurses were all in the Army also. The younger nurses were either enlisted, or in some cases lieutenants. These nurses were prone to either passes by higher ranking male officer patients, or subjected to them sullenly refusing to take their medicines or to do exercises prescribed by the surgeons. I am sure these officers were used to having their way through throwing their weight around. The one threat the nurses had was one of the funniest I have ever witnessed, which was:

Colonel if you don't take your medicine I will come at night and give you a high enema!

It worked every time. Army nurses are smart!

Venereal Disease (VD) has always been an area of concern in our Armed Services because of miscreants who are too dumb, or too lazy, to use the protection measures readily available. Any officer or enlisted man who turned up with VD was sent immediately to a hospital or care center for treatment which generally consisted of shots and pills lasting a week or more, and believe me it was no picnic.

This was impressed upon me as one of my duties as a new Second Lieutenant was to visit soldiers from our squadron (a Cavalry designator). I duly reported to the 42nd Gen. Hospital in Tokyo, Japan very early in the occupation in 1945 to visit soldiers of our regiment. I entered the VD ward which was full of "losers" many of them combat veterans, and all in all very tough guys, and very combative to young officers like myself. While I was getting ready to do a very unpleasant duty, the door to the rooms burst open, followed by a very large red headed Army nurse holding a group of needles which looked as big as as ice picks. At first sight there was a rush of even the toughest to areas the furthest from the door; some tried to hide under the beds to no avail. Both entrances to the room were blocked off by the orderlies leaving the occupants no recourse but to succumb to the inevitable.

"O K boys!" beamed the large nurse as she roared "assume the position! Sunny side up!" At this command, all of the patients obediently went to their cots, dropped their pants revealing a parade of shiny buttocks to the mercy of the large nurse. Methodically she punctured each with the contents of the needles. I felt sure that many had faced the enemy with less fear that the large nurse engendered.

Army nurses are tough.

Our regiment, the 7th Cavalry, was known far and wide as a hard fighting, no nonsense, and was liberally sprinkled with old line Irish senior officers who were always ready for a fight or a drink. When these two characteristics were combined, there was hell to pay! To add an even more explosive element to this volatile mixture, was the fact that many of these officers had a total lack of female companionship for up to two years while running around various parts of the Pacific jungles chasing the enemy.

Our squadron (Cavalry for Battalion) had a uniquely talented Special Service Officer we nicknamed "The Duke." Duke was a genius at producing "things" and activities for our amusement, but the pinnacle of his success was his announcement that he had arranged for around twenty-five Army nurses just up from the Philippines to join us at our officers club for a reception in their honor. To celebrate our good fortune, our Commander decided that an early start was permissible, so several hours before the nurses were to arrive we toasted our good fortune with Japanese Suntory whiskey.

Our Squadron Commander who, in typical South Boston Irish behavior was doing yeoman work at the bar and was singing *Garry Owen*, our regimental song, in full voice when the Army trucks which had transported the nurses from the ship at Yokohama to our location in Tokyo pulled up to our officers club and the nurses started to disembark.

As we rushed to finally meet our guests, a shocked hush fell over the officers who walked to greet them, for there stood the scariest bunch of women I had ever seen in one place.

All were still dressed in khaki, and the skin of each one was colored deep yellow from the Atabrine tablets which were to ensure resistance to malaria which most of us had taken while in the Philippines. Nevertheless, the appearance of yellow skinned females, who hadn't been to a hair dresser for a long time, or used little or no makeup, gave the appearance of Maori wild women.

This group of women were led by a rather large nurse with the leaves of Major on her shoulder and the appearance of being of lovable as the rock of Gibraltar. As we started to lurch forward to get acquainted, our fearless leader shouted out "This one is mine!" as he ran and lifted the large nurse over his shoulder to carry her upstairs to the officers club.

There followed, to put it mildly, a very sad scene as the large nurse started to beat our leader about the head and ears. With each blow, our leader's knees would buckle and he would sink a little lower. Officers and nurses all stood paralyzed at the sight closely resembling a pig in a slaughterhouse; and for the most part secretly enjoyed it as our leader was not the most loveable person. The nurses rooted for their leader on with her endeavors so pandemonium reigned.

Finally, our leader fell to his knees from the application of more punishment from the large nurse. "Duke," who was a horrified witness to our leader's downfall, hastened to lead him, bleeding and drunk, to his quarters.

A hushed silence hung over the scene. Finally Duke addressed the nurses saying we were deeply sorry of our breach of etiquette; that our leader wasn't himself; and that we would have the drivers take them to transient quarters in Tokyo before returning to Yokohama the next day.

Head Nurse surveyed us with feigned hostility and said, "Yokohama, kiss my ass! Come on girls let's party!"

We partied.

Army nurses are tough, but great!

Part II

Adventures in the Far East

Overview: Philippines and Japan 1945–1948

As young officers right out of West Point, our first assignments were to various overseas assignments—some went to Europe and the rest went to the Pacific. Those of us who were sent to the Pacific, went consequently to an Infantry Replacement Depot near Clark Field on the main Island of Luzon, an hour or so drive from Manila.

There was considerable Huk[5] activity around as well as some isolated Japanese who had not yet surrendered. There was no immediate danger from either. Nevertheless, it was a distinct change of environment for all of us.

We were all scattered to different assignments—some stayed where we were, and others went to various parts of Japan. Some unlucky ones to Okinawa. I went subsequently to the 7th Cavalry Regiment whose claim to fame was that they were slaughtered at Little Big Horn by Chief Sitting Bull and his warriors.

The Commander of the 7th Cavalry was Irish, and most of the officers were Irish, as he seemed to have collected them as time passed in the various Pacific campaigns. These officers were not just Irish—they were "Southie." For your information, "Southie" means South Boston, which is the port area of Boston. There is nothing wilder than their activities, which are drinking, singing, and fighting—not necessarily in that order. These "qualities" were apparent in the 7th Cav in spades. It was one of the gloriously great times in my career.

The following stories barely scratch the surface.

---

[5]The Hukbalahap, the military arm of the PKP (*Partido Komunista ng Pilipinas*) formed to fight the Japanese.

Jitterbug

One of my heroes, an All American football player out of Texas A&M and a wild man run amok.

In early September 1945, my classmates and I were summarily plucked from our furloughs upon graduation from West Point; put on a transport, the *S.S. Lurline*, along with Army nurses, and were dispatched to Manila, Philippine Islands. We sadly said good-bye to the female contingent, debarked in Manila which had been reduced to rubble by the invasion of the 1st Cavalry Division and the 37th Infantry (Buckeye Division) from Ohio.

Rizal Avenue, *Avenida Rizal*, the "Broadway" of Manila, was just a collection of tin shacks and rubble. Having been in transit for three weeks, my friend and I sought the nearest bar, which was the nearest tin shack adjacent to where we disembarked.

From there we started a sociological survey of sources of sinful things, like wine, women and song. The safest thing we could think of to drink was San Miguel beer, which my friend, who had been an enlisted man there in 1940, said was okay. As we were having a tasting "orgasm" as it was our first drink since leaving Camp Beale in the Mojave Desert in California, three black soldiers ran into the bar and tried to hide. They were followed by three Filipinos carrying captured Japanese Army Arisaka '98 rifles with which they executed the three U.S. soldiers.

Having been just off the boat for perhaps thirty minutes, we were somewhat taken aback when the Filipino owner dragged the U.S. soldiers, dead as proverbial door nails, out of the door and onto the sidewalk, and placed sheets of corrugated tin over them. The owner, in response to our panicky suggestion to call the M.P.'s, said that these soldiers had violated the wives of the three Filipinos and the dead soldiers would serve to teach a lesson to other U.S. soldiers.

This illustration of frontier justice was being mulled over by us when the part of the class that was going north was summoned to get into the trucks to take us to the Infantry Replacement Depot near Clark Field.

We reported to the 24th Replacement Depot, and among the "greeters" was "Jitterbug" Henderson, an All-American End at Texas A&M, who was part of the permanent cadre.

Jitterbug was long, lean, laconic, full of BS, and an absolute wild man. We all took to him like flies to honey and since all of us had literally been confined at West Point for three years (me for four years), we felt we had found a soul brother. Jitterbug had a tent mate who was named "Pappy." Pappy had been a saxophone player in a big dance band somewhere and his claim to fame was that he had a sad basset hound expression, a head as bare as a cue ball, and a picture of his wife naked as a jay bird posing with his favorite saxophone. Obviously, the picture had been viewed by thousands of eyes and was quite well worn—how she could play the saxophone in that position we will never know!

About fifteen miles from camp was a Barrio, which although primitive, held dances for the people every now and then. Jitterbug had made friends with the village elders through gifts of cigarettes, etc., and was viewed as a good friend who would be welcomed at their dances with his friends.

One Saturday evening Jitterbug and Pappy appeared in front of our tent in the encampment and announced that my classmate and myself were going to the dance at the Barrio. Pappy and Jitterbug had buoyed their spirits with *Aeroplano* whiskey, a skull-popping distillation of sugar cane and molasses. With the thought in mind of finally having at least some female companionship, we gratefully joined the expedition to the Barrio. As we sped along with Jitterbug driving, Pappy stood up in the back of our vehicle, a command car, proclaiming like General McArthur that he had arrived. No sooner had the words gotten out of his mouth than a pig scurried across the road, where upon Jitterbug applied the brakes, and I saw Pappy sail majestically over the front of the car, arm still upraised, and skid face downwards for five to ten yards on the black volcanic dust which constituted much of the back roads in the Philippines. Concerned that we might be late for the dance, we hurriedly dismounted, and upon turning Pappy over on his back, we could only see two white eyeballs staring out at us through a coal black face—all other features were obliterated. He still had his right arm extended like McArthur, like a true patriot. We dusted him off, loaded him unconscious into the backseat, more a victim of *Aeroplano* than his inaugural flight, and proceeded to the dance.

I should have known that this inauspicious start was only a preview of darker things to come, and they did.

The dance hall was nothing but a large room on stilts under which garbage, excrement, etc. was allowed to fall through openings on the floor. The odors from this exotic mixture would decompose the bricks from the Chinese walls. This was counteracted by the mind clogging perfumes from the ladies on the dance floor. Leaving Pappy happily snoozing in the back of the command car, we climbed up the ladder leading to the dance hall and I will never forget the sight that I saw.

First there were the old women whose lips and teeth were stained with betel juice: the lips were bright crimson, and the teeth blackened with decay and stains. The old men were in similar shape.

Alert for a sign of danger because this seemed to be a bad dream, I saw the young men, muscular, stocky, some with scars on their faces, and a look that was definitely hostile. But we weren't too concerned as, after all, we had Jitterbug, all six foot four inches and two hundred thirty pounds of him. A look at the "girls" didn't improve the outlook of things too much.

The standout disappointment was the band: an accordion player: a snare drummer; and a saxophone player—all over 60 years old, minimum. Their repertoire was five or six unrecognizable 1930's tunes, which they played over and over (where was Pappy when we needed him?)

There was no way we could beat a hasty retreat without insulting the hospitality of the Barrio, and while we could in a short while be going north to Okinawa or Japan, or south to Malaysia, poor Jitterbug was part of the permanent party at the 24th Replacement Depot and would have to live with our bad manners—so we stayed by the bottle of *Aeroplano* provided by Jitterbug.

We fought our way through the fumes emanating from the ladies perfumes and the "perfume" coming from underneath the dance hall. As the dance wore on, Jitterbug became more energetic and the joint was really rocking. I mean literally! In spite of our pleadings Jitterbug lurched towards a particularly flimsy portion of the floor, which gave way, thus causing the entire band and equipment, along with Jitterbug, to disappear in the murk below the stilts which held the dance hall.

We dashed down the ladder leading to ground level and there, among the struggling band members and their equipment, lay Jitterbug along with the souvenirs left over the years by the occupants of the dance hall above. Our evening was climaxed by putting Jitterbug next to Pappy in the back of the command car and speeding back to our encampment with our senses clouded by *Aeroplano*. Pappy was immediately awakened by Jitterbug's odoriferous presence, but it was either that or walking back. Pappy promptly retaliated by throwing up.

Post Mortem

The next day, after breakfast, we went over to the permanent party section to find Pappy and Jitterbug. Jitterbug was as bright as a silver dollar, but Pappy was a shivering wreck (even glimpses of his naked wife with the saxophone failed to revive him). Closer inspection revealed that in addition to his pale green complexion, he had a series of scabs complete with ground in volcanic dirt stretching from forehead to chin. Since he did not remember how he had acquired them, we offered our sympathy and support on any charges that might be entered by the Colonel he beat up and injuries to the M.P.'s who came to assist the Colonel during the incident. Since we had helped him escape, we wanted him to know that he had our best wishes. Of course we made up the story, but he lived in terror for the next week. God will punish me, I know!

My First Encounter With an Enlisted Man

In the West Point of the 40's, we really didn't have much contact with enlisted men. Sure they helped train us, and, during WWII we did some platoon training with them, but not very much. Certainly not enough to wonder about our first test under fire when we would have to deal with some pretty tough characters, one-on-one. Our private burning question was, "What do I do when a soldier goes out of control and tells us to 'stuff it'?" My introduction to solution of this issue was, as usual in my Army career, unusual!

In the late summer, early fall, of 1945, some of us aspiring infantry leaders were unceremoniously bundled up and shipped to the Philippines on a converted Matson luxury liner, the *S.S. Lurline*, along with one hundred or so Red Cross girls and nurses—an auspicious start for an illustrious Army career! From the boat we were shipped up to an infantry replacement depot where, until the war was ended, they stashed away their cannon fodder—Infantry Second Lieutenants, until needed. This depot, the 24th Infantry Replacement depot, was surrounded by razor sharp barbed wire. I am still not sure whether it was to keep us in, or the Japanese Army out.

Next to the depot stood an old sugar mill, which the Japanese had converted to a distillery that made a skull popping concoction labeled *Aeroplano* of which our buddy Jitterbug was so fond. I was particularly taken with the label itself, which proclaimed the contents as being *Aeroplano* Gin, Rum, or Whiskey, the only discriminators being the color of the liquid inside. The straight sugar cane product was clear, so naturally this was declared to be gin; add a little caramel and the color becomes brown, whiskey; add more and it becomes black, rum. The effects of the drinking of this absolutely amazing concoction were often spectacular. It was not uncommon to see a formerly very dignified officer crawling on his belly like a reptile and baying at the moon.

A hangover from *Aeroplano* was truly awe inspiring. The minimum penalty was three days of the dry heaves and the shakes. I will always remember the picture on the label, which was from an old Jules Verne illustration in one of his books. It was a picture of a dirigible like balloon being propelled by a man riding a bicycle hanging underneath driving the propeller.

Well, I digress from my story, but as you can see, any sort of U.S. type beverage was worth its weight in gold. As luck would have it, one of the permanent cadre at the 24th was from "Petunia Blossom's" (my first wife) small hometown in North Carolina and in celebration of meeting, he invited me over to the Bachelor Officers quarters located over a ravine outside the only entrance to the compound. I noted, however, that to get back into the compound, one had to negotiate his way over the chasm via a rope bridge, followed by a half mile walk to the only entrance.

My newly found friend and I energetically celebrated with numerous toasts to all of Petunia Blossom's family of at least three generations back. Unfortunately, my new friend, LT Cox was rendered immobile, so I was forced to wend my way across that damnable swinging rope bridge, and then walk halfway around the encampment to the only entrance. To complicate matters, I was presented with two cases of real U.S. beer for my consumption by LT Cox who had access to the permanent party stores not available to us replacements. This was like finding pure gold.

Wearily, I wobbled my way across the rope bridge, which seemed to be swinging with an alarming arc, while precariously balancing my golden load, one case of beer under each arm. I envisioned the fun I would enjoy with my replacement type friends who would wonder how on earth I had managed to find U.S. beer in this far off hellhole. My self-congratulations ended abruptly as I came to the barbed wire fence, and I pictured an exhausting trudge of one half mile to the entrance, and then an explanation about the beer to the guard. After all, the wire didn't look too high, and I was in decent shape, so why not save all that hassle and just jump over the fence? No problem!

Hadn't I soared over the obstacles at the Advanced Infantry course at Fort Benning? Of course! No problem!

With great detail, I marked off in the dirt my take off place and visualized the height of my jump; and so with a case of beer under each arm, and a full load of *Aeroplano* aboard, I charged the fence as fast as my five foot five inch on a good day legs would carry me. I hit my mark perfectly and soared like a bird—a flightless Kiwi—right into the middle of the barbed wire; head down; my ass waving in the breeze; but both cases of beer clutched tightly. The more I struggled, the more I became enmeshed. Seeing that I was stuck, with no way out, I became resigned to throwing myself on the mercy of a real live enlisted man. Thus, all of my fears about the first confrontation under unfavorable circumstances with the enlisted sector were about to be realized. I had reflected that facing this first encounter with both feet planted firmly on the ground lent at least some dignity to the confrontation. Being upside down, with my ass in the air, stripped away my last refuge of even looking like an officer. The scenario that followed went something like this:

MALONY: Corporal of the Guard! Corporal of the Guard! [*Silence*]
MALONY: Corporal of the Guard! Corporal of the Guard! [*Silence*]
[*Finally—crunch, crunch, crunch.* SOLDIER *walking on gravel path.*]
SOLDIER: Well, I'll be a sumbitch, what the hail we got here?
MALONY: Get me out! Get me out!
SOLDIER: Lootenant, what you doin' down there?
MALONY: Never mind, just untangle me!
MALONY: Now Lootenant, whatcha a got under yore arms?
MALONY: It's beer.
SOLDIER: Lootenant, that beer looks might heavy from here. Iff'en you keep holdin' it like that yore gonna sink all the way down and then I'll never, be able to get you out, and then I'll have to call the Officer of the Day for hep.
MALONY: [*To myself*] Not the Officer of the Day! We were forbidden to leave the compound. I could be in real trouble, here. [*Aloud*] Tell you what, you take a case and I'll keep a case.
SOLDIER: I always did say that our Yankee officers were reasonable men.

FINIS

On that night I developed an appreciation for soldier humor, their craftiness, and their mentality. A lesson I carried as long as I remained in the Army and it enabled me to truly lead men. Being in that situation stripped me of any illusions I might have had about being a West Point hot shot.

The Surrender: A War Story As Told to Me by a Signal Officer

An absolutely true account of the first formal surrender of a intact Japanese Infantry Unit to a single U.S. Officer at Atsugi Airport, Tokyo, Japan.

I was assigned by the 8th U.S. Army under General MacArthur to join the 7th Cavalry Regiment of the 1st Cavalry Division stationed in Tokyo and other areas, both north and south. The war had just been over, so there were still many Army units which were staffed by many officers who had served in wide areas of combat under difficult circumstances.

While awaiting my orders to clear to my unit and transport to my Regimental HQ, which would take a day or so, I reported to the Officers Club in Yokahama to partake in an "adult beverage" or two where I made the aquaintance of a solitary drinker who was bedecked by a number of campaign ribbons and awards which we called "fruit salad" and he had the rank of Captain.

Although I had heard my fill of "War Stories" while I was stationed in the Philippines for several months, the story which follows was verifiable, and was absolutely appropriate in the confusion caused by the surrender of Japan to the Allied Forces. His true story was as follows:

"I was assigned as a Signal Officer by the 8th Army Chief of Signal Officer, Major General Charles Willoughby, General MacArthur's Executive Officer through 8th Army Signals to fly to Atsugi Airport in Tokyo, Japan from HQ Manila to assist in setting, and to operate an intitial communications site in Manila to guide in the initial occupying forces for 8th Army Staff, and other assets, until full strength was obtained.

"We flew up from Manila in a rickety DC-6 which included, among others, myself as the Signal Officer, a Nisei Japanese speaking non-com, a cadre of installers and mechanics, and a fat, overweight Colonel who was Senior Signal Officer in charge of the project, and who was nicknamed *Col. Fatass*; and whose main contribution was a constant stream of complaints.

"The flight up from Manila, including one stop in Okinawa, was uneventful, until we made the vicinity of Atsugi, when we heard the pilot shriek, 'Holy Shit!' Looking down as we approached the airfield we saw what appeared to be a fully staffed Japanese Infanty Division. The soldiers were standing at attention, with their weapons stacked at their feet; there were no heavy weapons in evidence, but their mobile assets were parked in perfect line at one side of the airfield.

"At the site of the enemy *Col. Fatass* screamed, 'Turn around' and instructions to 'Go back, go back!' Leaving *Col. Fatass* in the rear of the aircraft, we gave the pilot instructions to land. He cleared it with the Japanese Commander of the unit who approached us with his sword outstretched in his hand. Since *Col. Fatass* was the Senior Officer of our detail, protocol demanded that he accept the surrender.

"I went to get the Colonel, who refused to come out of our plane, so the Nisei and I accepted the sword, where upon the Commanding Officer of the Japanese unit said to me, as translated by the Nisei, 'I surrender to you, please inform me as to the location of your prison camp as that I can march my troops there.' I responded that there was no prison camp, but I will give you your *orders* now!

"An expression of fear crossed his face as he replied, 'I want your order.' My reply was, 'Go Home' in my my loudest voice. All of the Japanese soldiers and officers looked at each other in alarm. '*Go home, and leave your weapons here*!' I shouted. It took almost thirty minutes to clear the areas with the soldiers leaving by riding trolleys, buses, railroad cars, ox carts.

"We set up the communications assests within hours and were ready for incoming traffic in record time. That is how a Junior U.S. Officer and an Enlisted Man received the surrender of an entire enemy division, and dispersed them to their home in thirty minutes."

Japan: A Young Man's Dream

About twelve hours after being assigned to the 7th Cavalry Regiment in Tokyo in September 1945, I found myself responsible for the affairs of a large section of the city with the mission to locate hostiles and weapons. Instead, I discovered in my sector the Suntory Whiskey Works, which made a good product of pot distilled ersatz Scotch.

I immediately, as taught at West Point, assumed command of the situation and aggressively started production and transferred the inventory for safe keeping. The inventory turned out to be the Emperor's private stock. Suffice it to say, we liquidated that particular asset with dispatch. It took us about a week to sober up, at the end of which the Colonel politely suggested that if I didn't get my ass back out to my sector, I would be given some very aggressive career counseling. Ever the intrepid explorer, I ventured out into my sector, hangover and all. This time I met my true calling because I found the largest Geisha area in the Pacific Rim; five square city blocks of all flavors of Geisha. It wasn't exactly a red light district, but we soon fixed that! Picture this conversation (it's true).

MALONY: [*over the* SCR *300 radio*] Sir, Sir, It's me, Lieutenant Malony.

SIR: You little bastard, I told you never to call me after lunch.[6] This had better be damned important.

MALONY: Oh, yes Sir, it is, it is.

SIR: Well, It better be good, Chinko[7] is waiting.

MALONY: Sir, I have found the largest Geisha area in the whole world and I am closing it down [*pridefully*].

SIR: Malony, report back to regiment, pack your Val Pak, and report to Atsugi Airport at 0600 tomorrow.

MALONY: For what, Sir?

SIR: I am reassigning you to Korea, perhaps for the rest of your life.

---

[6] He usually was with his *Tomadachi* Japanese girlfriend at that time

[7] His girlfriend

MALONY: Sir, this radio isn't working too well, let me repeat my message. I have found the largest Geisha district in the whole world...

SIR: Careful!

MALONY: and I am going to close it down...

SIR: Get your ass back here and start packing!

MALONY: [*without hesitating*] and no one but the 7th Cavalry can come in.

SIR: Well done! Captain F[8] will be down to assist you in the organization.

Within twenty four hours we had things well organized, coupon books were printed which were comprised of Short Time tickets and Long Time tickets which the customers purchased from the Mamasans. The application of the tickets is self explanatory.

So, at the age of twenty-two, I fulfilled all of a young man's dreams—I ran a distillery and five city blocks of Geisha houses. What a start for a military career!

---

[8]Former Lieutenant in the St. Louis Vice Squad

General McArthur signing the Japanese surrender at the end of the war with Japan, 1945.

The Bomb

A firsthand account of a survivor and affirmed by U.S. officials.

When I moved up from the Philippines as a 2LT to Tokyo we all knew, particularly those of us who were going to be part of the Invasion of Japan starting at "Red Beach" on the southern tip of Kyusho, which is mountainous, the casualties would have been monumental. We were spared this by the surrender of Japan spurred by the casualties in Hiroshima and Nagasaki.

When I arrived in Tokyo in Sept. 1945, Hiroshima was still an open city and was full of radiation the effects of which were not commonly known even to the developers at White Sand Proving Grounds. Shortly after I arrived in Tokyo one of the newspapers there released pictures of the victims in one of the Japanese hospitals near the cities bombed. The victims who were still living suffered from horrible burns and I am sure were mercifully dying of radiation.

In spite of the horror caused by the A-Bomb, one of my Lieutenant friends and I along with an interpreter who was there when the bomb was dropped, to accompany us to Hiroshima which we reached by train from Tokyo and then went by car borrowed from the U.S. 24th Division to Hiroshima.

The scene upon our arrival was one of utter devastation. City Hall which has been shown in thousands of pictures was still standing. The whole area, even though we didn't know it, was radioactive. Here in summary is the account of our guide who was five miles from target at the time.

- Many months before the bomb was dropped, a single plane (B-52) would fly over at great altitude and drop a cylindrical object over City Hall, always by parachute.

- The cylinder was black and contained candy cookies, literature, and all manner of commodities.
- When the people of Hiroshima saw the plane, they would rush as a crowd to it in hopes of getting the contents.
- These droppings occurred many times, always over City Hall.
- Our guide was five miles from target at the time.
- The bomb was dropped in the usual way over target.
- He stated that there was a blinding flash like the sun was coming up and he was thrown into a ditch by the blast.
- When he regained consciousness, he felt prickling sensations all over his body (radiation) and the countryside was filled with people dead or dying.
- The Japanese government was overwhelmed by the magnitude of refugees escaping from Hiroshima and the stories of terror they told. The terror continued because officials couldn't grasp the magnitude and the bomb which caused this horrible event. As a result, they dispatched the Army to surround Hiroshima and didn't allow anyone in or out, thus creating a radioactive killing ground which doomed a city over 100,000 to an agonizing death.

Note

This account closely follows official accounts later on which failed to cover the thousands who died later of radiation poisoning—white corpuscle death. Our boy interpreter died six months later. We stayed in Hiroshima less than an hour. We got past security by virtue of our uniforms and passes.

The Dynamic Demonstration

A true story told by a young Japanese school boy who attended a demonstration of a Kamikaze portable bomb to use against a potential invasion of Japan by the USA.

While I was serving in the 7th U.S. Cavalry in Tokyo, one of our young Japanese interpreters told me this story which certainly has a moral.

"As young students at a boy's academy located outside Kyoto, we were always alerted to the possibility of U.S. Air Raids, but if the U.S. invaded Japan, we should use stones, staffs, sharp instruments, etc. and fight until death.

"Once during a U.S. Air Raid at night, one of the brick buildings on our grounds was hit. To emphasize the need to fight the 'enemy' when the time came, our headmaster marched us to the ruins made the night before, and stood us before the last standing wall which was about thirty feet high and made of brick. In the past we had training that if the enemy invaded, we were to take a satchel charge, run across the line of the vehicle, or other targets, pull the activator, do body roll, and run.

"The headmaster had with him a satchel charge to show its strength, and what it would do to a vehicle, tank, groups of soldiers, etc. To show its strength, it was placed against the standing brick wall of the building, and we students were lined up for the demonstration near the wall. Upon the signal, the activator was pushed, and the wall disappeared with a roar. As the bricks showered down from the sky, we ran for our lives, our Headmaster running with us. We were all impressed, but many of us became pacifists on the spot."

Chicken Kamikaze

Above I wrote of a trip with one of my Army friends and a Japanese houseboy to Hiroshima where he was living when the bomb was dropped.

Recently, I recalled a Kamikaze story which concerned a conversation in late 1946 with a former Japanese fighter pilot *who lived to see the day*. In his own words:

"I was sent to the Japanese Army as a young soldier. One day my group was assembled, and we were 'counted off.' Every third soldier stepped forward and this group was told that they were to be trained to fly in *The Divine Wind Corp* which was a great honor.

"As a group we were treated only to the best food, and while we trained hard, on occasion we were allowed in the neighboring town. We wore red sashes to identify us as Honored Warriors.

"We all knew that as Kamikaze pilots, we were to die for our country as an honor. Nothing was too good for us: food, drink, dancing girls, anything within reason.

"Normal training seemed to be simulated flights, observation, gunnery, photo interpretation."

The day came when his group was called upon to perform its glorious mission over Okinawa. He and his comrades flew in formation to where the U.S. ships were in basic formation in large numbers. Upon command, Kamikaze pilots started their deadly mission.

As our pilot, who was dispatched toward the rear of the flight, saw his comrades go up in flame to a horrible death, he, in effect, said to himself after all the training and visions of death and glory, well, basically said to himself, "Why the hell am I doing this?" as he started to manoeuver for his faithful dive.

Instead of diving into his target destroyer, he pulled up and splashed in the ocean, from which he was rescued by our Navy. The story was told to me by the pilot in Tokyo where I was stationed in 1945.

Getting to the Bottom of the Situation

In preparing to visit a foreign country where English is not spoken, there are the normal details such as inoculations, visas, airline tickets, and so forth. Additionally, one must be able to communicate in the language of the host country about some of the very basic necessities such as: "How are you?"; "What is your name?"; "Can you tell me how to get to Hotel —?"

However, the first and most urgent phrase to learn is, "Where is the toilet?" This phrase must be learned thoroughly by you, and clearly understood by the various indigenous personnel, for sometimes, time is of the essence. Any undue delay may result in total catastrophe. This is particularly true in areas where amoebic dysentery, or other insidious diseases, attack the lower intestines. A visit by any number of these sly intruders makes respond time critical. Some of my old British Colonial friends have commented, "...that a true gentleman can poop in his pants without ever changing expression..." and that has happened, not infrequently, to one not warned about the pitfalls of foreign travel.

After having learned how to communicate about Nature's call, and having found a safe haven in the bathroom, the next challenge is how to work the damn thing. It seems to me that designing the flushing mechanism is done by the minions of Satan himself. Each country seems to have its own carefully guarded design, developed with the express purpose of dumbfounding the visitor.

The old English design was activated by a long chain which dangled down from overhead with a handle which remained tantalizing out of reach; this required a contortions to grapple for the handle, while sitting down, which invariably resulted in a violent Charley Horse between one's shoulder blades, if one had short arms, or was a small child. A precarious balancing act was required while standing up with one's pants down perched on the toilet bowl. One false move and it's into water up to your belly button!

Other versions, seen in Germany, had a mighty foot pedal to perform this function, a simple enough mechanism, except one had to have leg muscles like a beer wagon horse to depress the pedal—certainly not a mechanism for sissy boys. Other versions have small buttons artfully concealed so that one needs inside information held probably only by the *concierge* who reveals the location only under duress.

The most insidious of these which I experienced was one of Spanish design which was built into the floor approximately six feet from the toilet itself, thus putting itself just out of reach with your foot. To flush, one had to make a mad dash with pants at half mast before the water tank was emptied. Obviously this was not a game for the slow afoot. All of these are child's play when compared to those used by the Japanese.

My first introduction to their means of disposal was in 1945 when I was invited to a very posh dinner at the home of a very prominent Japanese in the former government. After participating in many a toast to just about every living thing, I wove uncertainly towards the *benjo* (toilet), situated in a room down the hall. Much to my amazement, it was a tiled hole in the floor with two porcelain slippers in front of it. As I stood staring, uncertainly at this apparatus wondering how to approach the matter of relieving myself, I clearly, saw for the first time why my courses at West Point dealing with any engineering matter had ended almost always disastrously.

I finally saw, since all of us entering the house entered in our stocking feet, that one stood in the slippers and tried to hit the hole in the floor. "Fair enough," I thought, but in order to completely execute all maneuvers to fulfill all of Nature's demands, one had to place himself strategically above the target area, as close as possible, to prevent any target location problems. I finally ended up in the approved position in a state of exhaustion, and being slightly under the influence of numerous cups of Saki, I ran into the matter of target location. I am sure that the conditions undergone by various B-17 bombardiers in bad weather and flack never had it any rougher than I did at that time.

Achieving the approved position, I was suddenly seized with leg cramps, which prevented me from straightening up. My screams of agony reached the ears of the host and guests who were convinced that I was being murdered. As the cramps crept up ever higher, I could hear the pounding of feet down the hall, and to my acute embarrassment, the thundering herd burst through the door, catching me in my full glory, bare assed, squatting in porcelain shoes, screaming in pain. I like to think that I managed to maintain some degree of dignity as I limped back to our table furtively trying to adjust my trousers.

I am sure that a psychologist could easily analyze the psyche of a country by observing its toilet habits. For example, the French happily discuss the affairs of state while standing side by side in the public toilets on the boulevard whose sides only rise to their shoulders for all to see. The Germans, on the other hand, use two tier toilets, the first tier holds your precious offerings while the second tier holds the water. Maybe the psychologist would say that Germans are so arrogant that they have to admire their own shit. The Japanese, on the other hand, are their usual efficient selves, "Do It! Drop It!" No water, no gurgles, no trick buttons or devices to solve, just let all disappear and walk away.

In analyzing the pre-WWII United States, the observer would see the old gracious way of dealing with Nature. My aunt had an old fashioned outdoor "privy," a two holer, which was situated in a wooden shed ten yards from a fifty foot long grape arbor. I'll always remember the leisurely stroll towards the privy plucking grapes along the way, mounting my throne, and settling in with a contented sigh as I improved my sex education by thumbing through the corset section in an old Sears Roebuck catalog, the pages of which, usually the hardware section, were used for the completion of Nature's call. Ah, that was complete satisfaction! Those gracious days are gone forever a victim of mechanization.

You First, Sir!

The reader may envision that I, a twenty-two year old 2LT in whose territory and area of responsibility lay the Suntory Whiskey Works and Cherry Blossom Lane which featured five square city blocks of Geisha houses, had ascended to the Nirvana of all young men. Well, we all know the truth of the saying, "There ain't no such thing as a free lunch," and it certainly applied to me.

Not only did I have to maintain peace and order in Cherry Blossom Lane so as not to attract the interference of various chaplains at GHQ (General Headquarters) and the 8th Army, but I also had to listen to the complaints of the Mamasans who ran specific Geisha houses, and the Japanese girls who would run tearfully after me in the street asking the whereabouts of "Johnny" who had promised to marry them. I became the Ann Landers of Japan. If one thinks that keeping law and order among soldiers who had fought through the jungles of the Admiralty Islands, New Guinea, and the Philippines, and were full of bad Japanese whiskey was easy, please be my guest for the next war.

From the very beginning, my rule was that no one could enter the gates to Cherry Blossom Lane unless he wore the 1st Cavalry Division patch on his arm. As time went on, other less desirable people from other units drifted in so we put guard posts on the border around the area and despite the usual fights and normal incidents, we maintained a low profile.

The spell was broken around 2 P.M. one afternoon when I was summoned by our Officer of the Day detail to go to Cherry Blossom Lane to investigate a murder. To put it mildly, I wasn't exactly thrilled to receive this call, but dutifully I called for my jeep and driver and set off for the scene of the crime. On the way I was picturing all of the gangster films I had seen when the villain are gunned down by the heroes. Going down my list of assets to deal with this, there were my weapons: a .45 caliber pistol; and a .30 caliber carbine. Traditionally, the .45 is about as useless as "tits on a boar hog." You could throw it further than you could shoot it. The carbine was some better, but it had no automatic feature so one had better not miss his first shot if the other party was armed. The last was my driver, who was a hook wormy, scrawny looking soldier who had been with the division since they left Australia three years before; but, had eyes that looked like steel ball bearings, kind of like a shark just before he bit your leg off. But three years as a private? What a screw up he must have been!

Brimming with doubts, I left the jeep and looked for the guards. No guards? Then where were the witnesses? None? OK, then where had the people gone? While trying to get oriented, the punch line to an old joke from the TV show, *F Troop* kept crossing my mind about the "Fugawi" Indian tribe whose name was changed by the sponsors to the Hekawi, *Where the heck are we?* In the joke, General Custer who when he arrived at Little Bighorn cried out, "Where are the Fugawi?" not realizing the enormous numbers of Ogala Sioux he would shortly face. Finally the spell, was broken by a hysterical Mamasan who ran to me crying in broken English, "Dead man here, dead man here!" Dragging me, followed by my driver, to nearby railroad tracks there lay three dead black soldiers who apparently had been run over by a passing train whose engineer hadn't bothered to stop, or was unaware that he had hit the three bodies. Examination of the bodies revealed that they had been riddled with some rather large bullets.

Mamasan then started pulling me to a nearby Geisha house, which I surmised, was her place of employment, and said, "Soldier there. He kill, he kill." Swallowing hard, I advanced to the house and entered with the driver behind me. Mamasan pointed to a very narrow stairway, and whispered, "There, there." In my mind's eye I could see the soldier with a machine gun crouched down around the corner where the stairway met the landing, and as we would come up the stairs, he would step out and cut me down with a short burst.

While contemplating this state of events, the driver, all one hundred ten pounds of him, pushed past me and walked towards the steps saying, "Well, Lieutenant, what the hell are you waiting for?"

Galvanized by the spectacle of a private leading an officer in a dangerous situation, I thundered up the stairs like a crazed water buffalo with the driver in hot pursuit. There, sure enough, was a black soldier apparently sleeping soundly on a Tatami mat.

With my carbine in his ear, we rudely awakened him—he was pretending to sleep. What followed was a masterful explanation of what he was doing there, the essence of which was:

1. He didn't know nothing about no damn soldiers on the railroad track.

2. He just came there to have his laundry done

3. No, he didn't have the laundry; one of them soldiers on the truck done stole it

4. He didn't have the F**ing weapon, so how could he have shot somebody?

5. We were picking on him because he was black.

His defense was bullshit and I am sure that some left wing liberal college professor would have sprung to his defense and we would have ended up as the accused instead of him. At any rate, when we rolled back the Tatami mat upon which he was sleeping, there was the "grease gun," multi-shot .45 machine gun with the shells expended.

Since, no real reporters existed in Tokyo in 1946, we remanded the soldier over to the guards who had mysteriously reappeared and went home unheralded. When I got upstairs the driver and I shared several large dollops of Suntory whiskey to celebrate the moment.

The Great Easter Egg Hunt

When I landed in Japan, early after the Japanese surrendered to General McArthur, late in August 1945, I was greeted by the most unbelievable sight one can imagine. The U.S. Army Air Force had firebombed Tokyo and Yokohama to cinders. Very few buildings had been left standing and even some of those were badly damaged.

Cement sidewalks and roads didn't burn, but everything around them was a void with the exception of hundreds of fireproof safes, which had formerly been part of the business enterprises which lined the streets.

There were almost no young people, only old men and women and a few dogs, which led us rightfully to conclude that all the people who were capable of offering resistance were hiding in the hills waiting to see what the U.S. troops were going to do. The U.S. Armed Forces had been depicted as bloodthirsty barbarians who would kill them given any opportunity; however, after a few weeks of contact with the GIs, the Japanese could see their fears were unfounded.

In one of my former stories, I told of how I fulfilled every twenty-two year old 2LT's dream of running a Suntory Whiskey Works and Cherry Blossom Lane—the world's largest Geisha area. In addition to these onerous duties, I commanded an Infantry Rifle Company whose duty it was to guard the Emperor's moat around his castle and to man guard posts at the Bank of Japan. This bank was not just an ordinary bank, but more like the Bank of England and featured multiple levels—five if I remember correctly—underground, each level having a number of vaults. It was there that the loot stolen from the various countries in the path of the Japanese Army as it passed through Southeast Asia was stored. This bank was under the operational management by a really bad ass Colonel appointed out of MacArthur Headquarters. My first experience with the Colonel came before I knew what was stored in the bank vaults and my guards became stationed at the bank.

Early on General McArthur issued a public proclamation which stated that any found property not belonging to the property owners must be turned into the nearest U.S. Army Unit. No sooner had this proclamation been made than our Squadron—Cavalry Units had Squadrons, not Battalions—HQ received a message, that a farmer about thirty miles out of Tokyo had found "something."

As Officer of the Day, off I went with interpreter and driver in my M-8 armored vehicle to be one of the first to implement the new proclamation. When we arrived on the scene we found an old Japanese farmer standing by the road waving his arms wildly. Excitedly, he led us to a cave in which he stored his vegetables. Apparently he had just returned to his farm after having taken refuge in the hills just before surrender by the Japanese, and had found "something" which did not belong to him. The farmer entered his cave and with a degree of difficulty dragged out an enormous canvas bag, which resembled an old time mail sack. I reached down to feel the contents of the sack because in the very early days of occupation some of the young people were still hiding in the hills and there was always concerns of booby traps and other forms of possible guerrilla warfare. I was puzzled that the contents felt like coarse grained rock salt, the kind we used to make homemade ice cream.

Since I had to make a written report, I had visions of being the first officer to turn in the war booty and having it turn out to be rock salt. With gritted teeth, I opened the sack and peered at its contents and was dazzled. What I saw were thousands of glittering stones. Closer examination revealed they were diamonds of varying sizes, ranging from one half carat to ten carats. Not knowing how to classify my find and not being a gemologist, I made out a receipt for, "One bag of precious stones, obtained from Farmer Oboyashi." The bag and its contents were then transported back to the Bank of Japan for safe keeping. Bad Ass Colonel[9] gave me a receipt for one bag of precious stones, not stating the size of the bag, or the number of precious stones. This I thought was fraught with temptation for Bad Ass, but, that is another story which I will tell later.

This find opened the greatest treasure hunt of all time. Similar bags of jewels, some rubies, some emeralds; bags and bags of jewels of all types were found and turned into the bank. Caches of gold and silver bars were found stored in run down shacks; under fake floors; and even in rivers. No doubt some finds were not reported, the worth of which staggers the imagination! Typical examples of this happened to me on two other occasions: the first being the discovery of $1.5 million worth

[9]Bad Ass Colonel was Senior Officer in charge of the affairs at the Bank of Japan. He appears later on under questionable circumstances as Colonel M.

of silver ingots which had been painted gray and dumped off a boat dock which was part of our squadron area. These ingots had been hidden under a pile of metal pipe and other debris which I continually ran over in my Higgins boat—courtesy of a trade with the U.S. Navy at low tide. Imagine my surprise, when upon trying to remove the debris, I discovered the ingots.

The second instance discovering a cache of two tons of sterling silver tableware, plus thousands of Chinese "trade" dollars underneath the floor of one of my guard shacks in Tokyo.

The treasure hunt was created by the Japanese General Staff, which after the atom bombing of Hiroshima, looted the Bank of Japan and it was every man for himself. They took as much as they could carry in their charcoal burning vehicles, oxen bicycles, etc., and went as far as they could, and hid their loot as best they could They were still uncovering these caches worth millions when I left Japan. I wonder how much was never turned in.

Diamonds Are a Girl's Best Friends

A find of millions in precious stones and gold, plus a crooked officer.

Colonel M was sent by GHQ (MacArthur headquarters) to assume administrative control of the Bank of Japan which acted as the Central Bank for the Japanese Empire. To say that Colonel M was a chickenshit SOB was a gross understatement. My cavalry troop was assigned as permanent guard at the bank, and even though Colonel M was in charge of the bank, my men reported to me. This is the same Colonel M mentioned before when I described turning in my first sack of diamonds discovered outside Tokyo and for which I received a receipt noting, "Received from 2LT. James L. Malony, one bag of precious stones." Please note, again, that the size of the bag was not described.

As time went on my men began to tell me about the nitpicky, little things to which Colonel M was subjecting them. Later he accused the men of stealing a ninety-five cent Big Ben alarm clock. He invaded their squad room, turned over their beds and footlockers in a fruitless search for the missing article. In addition, he started to offer such items as cameras and jewelry to the non-commissioned officers in the guard detail. When I confronted him—very diplomatically of course—I received a world class dressing down for even questioning anything that happened at his bank. As Colonel M's voice grew louder my suspicions deepened, but twenty-two year old 2LT's don't accuse twenty years in service Colonels, unless damning evidence is found.

Even then, one's career is endangered by senior officer backlash. However, irrefutable evidence that Colonel M had been systematically helping himself to the contents of the vaults was shortly forthcoming.

One day, in a San Francisco jewelry store, a well attired lady walked in and inquired as to whether or not this particular jeweler bought and sold finished diamonds. Upon receiving a "Yes, indeed," she emptied the contents of her purse on the counter and asked, "How much are these worth?"

Before the startled eyes of the jeweler was over one and a half million dollars worth of diamonds; among them was a ten carat, bright yellow diamond, which because of its brilliant hue, was extremely rare and valuable. Noting that these diamonds were of a European cut, not commonly used in America, he became convinced that these diamonds had been stolen. Since the informant's fee ranged between twenty and thirty percent, after a fast bit of mathematics, the jeweler turned her into the FBI. Further investigation revealed her to be Mrs. Colonel M who, upon learning that the Colonel was happily involved with a Japanese girl while she was languishing in San Francisco, decided to cash in the diamonds which she had in her possession.

It seems that Colonel M was taking leaves for vacation from Tokyo to San Francisco with the diamonds in his pocket. In those days the Army had their own customs for military embarkation/debarkation, and who is going to challenge a full-blown Colonel? Thus, he passed through customs unimpeded. On Colonel M's next trip to San Francisco, the FBI was waiting to greet him. Searching him they found another five hundred thousand dollars worth of diamonds in his pockets.

He was caught red handed, guilty as hell! After a big stink in the papers Colonel M came to trial where all the damning evidence was presented, including his avenging wife's testimony. When he took the stand to testify, he freely admitted bringing the diamonds through customs and giving them to his wife for safe keeping. He further claimed that in his travels around Japan grateful people gave him the diamonds as presents. The capstone of his defense was based on the position that as there were no records of these particular diamonds as missing, how can anyone prove that he stole them? Since there were no records at the bank noting inventory, it appeared that Colonel M would go free. At the last minute someone came up with the bright idea of, trying to trace the ten carat canary colored diamond which had been confiscated in San Francisco. If the U.S. Government could prove that it had indeed been given to the bank, and Colonel M in turn stole it from the bank, he would be proven guilty. Through a compendium, which listed worldwide rare jewels, the investigators found the canary colored diamond listed as well, as the name of the owner who turned out to an elderly Japanese woman who had submitted the diamond to the government in answer to a call to the people to turn in their diamonds for use in constructing machine tools. With this evidence in hand Colonel M was sent to Fort Leavenworth Federal Prison for ten years.

I trust he has his Big Ben alarm clock with him to make sure he makes Reveille every morning.

Pork À La King

I score well with the Chinese Army.

Unlike my classmate George Benson who became a diplomat star by virtue of creating the Jakarta Giants baseball team, my one swipe at diplomatic fame did not work out well. The problem with me was my inability to keep from breaking out in uproarious laughter at the most inappropriate times. In 1947 my mirth was prompted by one of the funniest sights I have seen while in uniform, but it could have created a real diplomatic melee.

All of us in the 7th Cavalry Regiment had been stationed in Tokyo, Japan for about eighteen months or so without too much discipline, but with female companionship, good whiskey, etc. In this environment many of us got to be pretty "wild and woolly" from our Regimental Commander on down.

One morning, after several rounds of refreshments at Officers Call, our Colonel informed us that he was hosting the Chief of Staff of Chiang Kai-Shek's Chinese National Army which was still on the Chinese mainland fighting Mao Tse Tung, the Red Army Commander. Obviously, the second most powerful military man in China was the Chief of Staff, and it goes without saying that our Commander was anxious that all went well during the reception. As the S-4, Supply Officer, I was tasked to find sufficient refreshments for the occasion, plus appropriate foods. In 1947 there were no U.S. or Scotch whiskeys, gin, brandy or anything else for that matter in Tokyo. The Colonel flew into his customary rage at the news I carried about the refreshment situation, but I did manage to wheedle one bottle of "B-Squad" Scotch from one of the Junior officers with a promise that I would not "Shanghai" him to Korea if he would donate it to the Colonel. Somewhat mollified, the Colonel agreed to share it with the Chinese General, and approved my plan to serve some sort of punch and barbecue a pig on an open large hibachi, a charcoal brazier. Happily, I set to create a punch to end all punches. For the base of the punch, I took a few Japanese swords and traded them to the 42nd General Hospital for ten gallons of pure grain alcohol, one hundred ninety proof. Tom Lombardo, my classmate who ran the Nikka Distillery near Mount Fujiama, sent two cases of cherry brandy. Sadly, Tom was later killed in Korea.

I then gathered cartons of fruit juice of all kinds and started mixing. The result was a rich pale yellow punch which resembled a very bad specimen from the barn yard and which I estimate was about one hundred proof after the dilution of fruit juices. We sampled the punch from time to time, and it wasn't that bad, in fact after the initial shock to the system it seemed pretty damn good. I was in charge of protocol for the Colonel since the Adjutant who usually handled those things was on leave. I set aside some time to learn more about our guest of honor.

The Colonel announced that our guest's name was General Sow and he wanted no smart remarks from either me or the rest of the officers. He then lectured me on General Sow's connections and showed me a picture of General Sow posing with General McArthur. My eyes popped. "My God," I said, "he certainly lives up to his name." Here was a Chinese man built like a mound of Jell-O, weighing, I estimated, about three hundred pounds. I wondered out loud, since we were barbecuing a pig for his reception, if it was one of his relatives. The Colonel was not amused. The confusion of my duties did not obscure the fact that I was to meet my bride that day in Yokohama on one of the first "Bride Ships" from the U.S. No families were allowed to come to Japan for the first eighteen months of the occupation. If my schedule ran right, I could pick up my wife, Patricia, have a few hours of bliss, and still get to the reception with a few minutes to spare.

As all of us who have been overcome with "raging hormones" know that when this phenomenon strikes, time does fly and such was the case with me. Unfortunately, I didn't become aware that I had better get Patricia and myself in good shape to get into the reception line and do the honors for General Sow until I saw by the clock that time had indeed flown and we were going to be late short of a miracle.

Suffice it to say I broke about every speed limit on my way to the house of the Colonel. I arrived screeching into his driveway, scattering a shower of stones. I dismounted smartly, Patricia in hand, and strode into the garden on time and ready to do my duty. As I was vainly looking for people to form up the receiving line, I heard this voice, shrill with anger saying, "Malony, you little son of a bitch, you're late!" Horrified I turned and looked through the foliage around the garden and saw the Colonel, punch glass in hand, sitting on a chair right in the middle of the fountain with water descending like a river on his head and shoulders.

Seeking to try to control the situation, the first step would be to get the Colonel out of the fountain without further fuss. I had burst onto a scene straight from Dante's *Inferno* for here was a group of Chinese officers gathered around a fallen comrade. Knowing the penchant for 7th Cavalry officers for fighting all comers, I started to walk over and continue my damage assessment. All I needed, I thought to myself as I was approaching the crowd of Chinese officers, was to have one of our officers strike a member of General Sow's staff. As I approached the group I noted four of the largest Chinese stoop down and bring up a body which was stiff as a board. It didn't bend one iota in the middle. Closer inspection showed that the body belonged to General Sow and he was the fattest man I had ever seen. The seams of his uniform were straining, and shuddered to think of the physical damage that amount of fat could do to a bystander if the dam should break.

I asked one of the aides, with my heart in my mouth, if the General was sick or hurt. "Ah, no General glunk[10]... he good," said the aide with a gap toothed smile. Further inspection revealed a very happy General, smiling blissfully, with his arms around his chest with four sweaty aides manfully trying to carry the load.

One of our officers had tried to add a nice touch by unbuttoning the General's shirt at the waist; he parted the rolls of fat and stuck one of the Colonel's prize roses into his bellybutton. "A nice diplomatic touch don't you think?" The pig to be barbecued hung limply uncooked!

It turned out that General Sow had gotten the times mixed up and had arrived at the reception two hours early. While the Colonel was having the officers mobilize for the reception, he and General Sow did away with the Scotch and turned to the punch with predictable results. Well, from an Irishman's point of view, the evening was a success!

After all, Patricia was the first bride in the Regiment; the guest of honor had passed out and was being loaded unceremoniously into his staff car and bundled off; and the Senior Officers were busily engaged in throwing newly arrived Second Lieutenants out of the Colonel's first floor windows into the garden. The scene was completed with the usual three minute

---

[10]the General is drunk

fights, interspersed with the opponents pouring each other drinks and getting gloriously drunk.

Since one of our officers had taken pictures of the Colonel in the fountain nothing was ever said about the whole incident. However, there were certain references about officers carelessly making deadly drinks, which compromised the whole regiment and the Colonel's career. Shortly afterward the Colonel received an enthusiastic thank you note from General Sow suggesting that we all do it again at an early date. Two hundred livers owned by the imbibers of the fruit punch cringed in terror!

The Major's Toilette

Malony strikes again in Mechanical Design.

Everyone in his life has a *bete noire*; someone who is in authority and always seems to pop up at the most inopportune moments; and haunts you even in your dreams.

While at West Point, I fought a losing battle with the Tactical Department in the persons of our Tactical Officers. They rained demerits on me for every offense imaginable, resulting in most of my time being spent serving punishment tours on the area. I remained bloody, but unbowed, and I carried my lessons learned in trench warfare with me after I was graduated. I might add, at this point that not only did I lead my class in demerits, but also I was well known as an academic bottom feeder in our class rankings. My independent conclusion was that I was better suited to leading my Infantry platoon up a fortified hill defended by Kamikaze, or fanatical Nazis, than wading my way through a field manual.

With this attitude, I acquired an aversion which is still with me to do this day—I avoid anything to do with engineering. In one of my accounts, I mention our Squadron Commander, who among his other credentials was a South Boston Irishman whose breed was called "Southie." A Southie Irishman is from the docks and waterfront of South Boston, and not only are they tough as nails, but have an avocation for drinking, fighting, and singing; not necessarily in that order. The Major seemed to have a special interest in me since my step-mother and her family were from North Boston and I was Protestant.

However, having been seasoned under our Tactical Officers, the Major seemed to be "duck soup." I have described in one of the preceding stories that I was driven to learn how to "use the system" and this experience is a subject of that story. As you may remember, I was ordered to build sixteen duplex officer's quarters out of nonexistent materials. This drove me to an orgy of construction which I doubt has been duplicated by any twenty-three year old 2LT. During this process, the Major beat me like a donkey to get Quarters #1 (his quarters) finished. Everyday I stood at attention while I was berated for my lethargy and constantly reminded about the downward plunge my career would take if I failed him.

With trepidation, I counted the days and even elicited Nitta Gumi, the contractor, and told him that the owner would cut off his finger if he did *not* meet the deadline (no kidding, he would have done it!). Finally, on the day promised, we were ready with Quarters #1. The Major sent his houseboy over with his uniforms and his stack of "beverages" and I was ready, with great ceremony, to present him with the keys to his quarters. First, however, my training said, "Be thorough, pay attention to detail; make one hundred percent sure that Major will be absolutely enthralled by the great job you have done. Nothing is too good for the Major."

Remembering my courses in Electricity, Physics, Chemistry, and Mechanical Engineering, which my system had totally rejected ten minutes after my final exam, I with great detail, checked out wiring, the heat, and the water in Quarters #1. My check of the electricity (to hell with the wiring—did the lights turn on and off? Yes, that is OK. The heat, well, the wiring is OK, so the boiler is working OK. The water? The cold water came out of the faucet when I turned on the cold water tap, so far so good. I then turned on the hot water tap and cold water came out. "Oh, well," I thought, "that's OK, the pipes are cold so the water will heat up once the pipes get warm and the boiler is cranking away." I turned up the boiler several notches to insure the arrival of hot water, secure in the knowledge that I had, true to my engineering training, paid attention to all of the details thus ensuring a fitting climax to ninety days of hectoring by the Major, proudly I turned over the keys to the Major who reassured me that my career had been saved—and that all was well between us.

With visions of a future general's rank, I saluted smartly and marched across the parade ground, getting about halfway before I heard a shrill cry of rage followed by, "Malony, you little son of a bitch, come back here." The old familiar knot formed in my stomach when I turned and saw the Major standing on his porch with his pants at half mast. I saw my career, once again, sinking into its normal place in oblivion.

I rushed up to the Major who was rapidly becoming epileptic with rage, saluted with quaking hand, and asked brightly, "Is something wrong, Sir?"

His reply came out somewhat garbled, but it sounded like, "You dumb

West Point bastard! Look what you did." With that he turned around, and to my utmost horror I saw that his ass had turned a flaming red; blisters the size of a nickel were rapidly forming. Since my infantry training had taught me to observe and make conclusions, it occurred to me that the Major had been christening his new toilet and had in some manner injured himself.

With the Major's curses and cries of pain ringing in my ears, I rushed into his bathroom and was greeted by a steaming cauldron emitting from the toilet. Lo and behold, I had allowed the hot water to be hitched to the toilet instead of the sink. In our efforts to turn the hot water boiler up to its limits so that hot water would come from the tap instead of the cold water I had originally experienced on my check, I had created a mini version of the geyser "Old Faithful."

While the Major carried around the rubber donut issued him by the 42nd General Hospital and yelled Irish curses at me, I immediately set to work to remedy the plumbing disaster and dispatched a Japanese technician to remedy the disconnect. All seemed to be going well with the repair and the Major's commode would soon be deemed worthy of his presence.

While still in disgrace, and my career possibly in ruins, I still held some faint hope that a speedy repair might calm the Major's nerves. I was reassured by the sound of tapping and the hiss of acetylene torches under the Major's quarters when suddenly, I heard the familiar hooting and hollering from his direction, and before my horrified eyes appeared the Major, rubber donut in hand, pants down, screaming imprecations in my direction.

After calming, him down, I learned that in order to repair the plumbing, a trap access door had been installed at the foot of the Major's toilet to give access to that critical junction of plumbing. While the Major was being assured that all problems were solved, he settled comfortably on his throne (the toilet) and was intently reading *Stars and Stripes*, the American Army newspaper, the Japanese plumber became lost amongst the pipes. In a panic, seeking a way out, he sprang up through the trap door beneath the Major's toilet and between the newspaper and the Major, thereby terrifying the Major who once again ran out with his pants down.

After that, the Major transferred back to the U.S. and the last I heard about him was in a medical bulletin from Walter Reed Army Hospital about this Major who had remained constipated for ten years. Our Tactical Officers would have been proud.

A Wise Ass From Brooklyn

Private "Wise-Ass" was absolutely the worst excuse for a human being that I have ever encountered. I can't think of a more appropriate punishment than he received by accident.

Every outfit has a wise guy—this one got what he deserved.

Amongst people from the southern part of the U.S. (circa 1945), the worst thing one could encounter, next to finding a scorpion in your Army boot at Reveille, was a wise-ass from Brooklyn. In the first place the average Southerner couldn't understand the wise-ass when he spoke; secondly if he was a wise-ass, there wasn't a thing he didn't know. They were big city boys who didn't take to well, to discipline, and in many cases were prone to screw-up; in short they ranked just below the Bubonic Plague on the list of things a true Southerner wished to avoid.

As an Infantry Company Commander in Tokyo, Japan, I had the pleasure of commanding a group of "good old boys" basically from the Southwest; we were considered to be the best company in the fabled 7th U.S Cavalry Regiment and jealously guarded our reputation. In 1945–46 large numbers of men were being redeployed back to the U.S. and were being replaced by draftees who were green as grass. Most of my non-commissioned officers had re-enlisted so they stayed with the unit, but we started to receive replacements, most of whom were okay after receiving the gentle ministrations of my "non-coms."

On the day "Wise-Ass" arrived our idyllic existence changed for the worse. Our First Sergeant was summoned by the Military Police to relieve them of a private who had in turn relieved himself on the walls of the Dal Ichi Building, which was General MacArthur Headquarters, and had papers indicating that he was to be assigned to my company in the 7th Cavalry Regiment. The next day my First Sergeant dragged in a bleary eyed, hung over soldier who looked like the last rung on the food chain and who had just returned from the medics where, after having a blood test, it was revealed he had all three kinds of venereal disease. This ruined our record of no VD for two years, and since my efficiency report was affected by the incidence of VD, I was not at all pleased.

Private Wise-Ass, it turned out, in addition to the above charming attributes was not only a "barracks lawyer," but caused an unending series of incidents with our Southern contingent who hated him royally; and because of this I started to hear from our Regimental Commander who was hearing through channels from the Congressman from Brooklyn about mistreatment of his constituent.

As in all things, a day of retribution arrived, and in most cases retribution assumes the punishment that ideally fits the crime. One very hot summer day my company was training close combat street fighting tactics and Private Wise-Ass was a member of a team which was laying wire from my Headquarters. Private Wise-Ass chose to stand on a board stretched across a stone well to string wire from a tree. Passing by, I noticed two things, the first was the board was rotten, and second, the harmless stone wall with innocent looking green moss over its surface was not all that it seemed. People who have been in Japan know that the best fertilizer in the world is human excrement, and the Japanese store this in wells for future use. Knowing this I secretly hoped the board would break, but I felt I should at least warn him off the board for safety sake. My suggestion to get off the board was answered with a dissertation about his merits as a wireman. During this speech, I was looking with fascination at the board bending slowly to the surface of the well, suddenly the board broke sending Private Wise-Ass into and through the moss covered surface. He disappeared beneath the surface with a sickening sound for what seemed to be an inordinate period of time, when suddenly, he emerged uttering probably the most ear splitting cry I have ever heard.

This cry was accompanied by the most gorge raising odor I have ever encountered, as he climbed out of the well. All that could be seen from his brown covered exterior were the whites of his eyes. At the sight of this creature, which could have well emerged from a swamp, my whole infantry company started running away at breakneck speed with me in the lead down one of the main thoroughfares adjacent to where we were maneuvering. Private Wise-Ass was in hot pursuit waving his arms and clumping along in his excrement filled combat boots crying out, "Lieutenant, *wait for meeeee*!"

Startled Japanese pedestrians when seeing the leading contingent pass by and what was pursuing us soon joined up running pell mell down the street. Finally we had gotten far enough ahead where we could give pertinent instructions. So from a block away, I said, "Wise-Ass, take off all your clothes and place them on the curb."

I told my First Sergeant to call the fire department, which he did through our interpreter. Upon arrival of the fire department the private was hosed down with high pressure during which time he swallowed enough water to float the Queen Mary. All the while he was calling out, "I'm *freeeezzing!*"

"May your balls drop off," replied the First Sergeant.

Now we had the problem of getting this still smelly, naked man back to our Regiment. So we made him stay put, put his trolley fare on the curb, flagged the next trolley, had him pick up his fare and get on the trolley naked. Well, although the Fire Department had done the best job they knew how under the circumstances, they were not able to overcome the odor from the well. As soon as he entered the trolley the Japanese inside streamed out of both ends like rats leaving a sinking ship with only the poor conductor and Private Wise-Ass remaining.

The next day he asked for a transfer to some Port and was never seen or heard from again. Probably to this day people may not want to sit next to him when the temperature is above eighty degrees Fahrenheit.

Using the System (Having One on the House)

A case study on how to move mountains using the ruler.

Personally, I detest bureaucracy and bureaucrats, but I recognize that in orderly society, they are a necessary evil as long as it's not overdone. The trick in dealing with layers of rules, regulations, and levels of management is to know who the real decision makers are; and how to get to them, and to know their rules better than they do.

My own experience with the rewards for adhering to the above came to me at the tender age of twenty three when I was assigned to the job of S-4, which is Squadron (Battalion) Supply Officer with the 7th U.S. Cavalry Regiment. My original concept of the job, as taught at West Point, was mundane record keeping and administration of supplies and equipment. Even though to this day I hate all forms of administration, I nevertheless, plunged bravely into a sea of paperwork when my comfortable, but boring existence was shattered by a summons from our Squadron Commander, to report to his office.

Seeing that he was in his usual throes of severe hangover from the night before, I assumed my most mouse like demeanor to await his words of wisdom. What did emerge changed my life forever. Rolling his bloodshot eyes at me (the Major drank more than just a little) he said, "Malony, I want sixteen duplex quarters built for the officers within the next ninety days."

Now to show the impossibility of fulfilling that outrageous request, one has to picture Tokyo/Yokohama after the fire bombings of 1944–45; the entire area was burned to the ground with a few exceptions such as the Dai-Ichi Building, Imperial Hotel, and the Emperor's palace which were left standing.

There just wasn't a piece of wood, a pane of glass, a brick or a bag of cement to be had; there was not even enough material to build an outhouse.

"But Major, Sir," I replied in my best mouse like manner, "look around you. There just isn't enough material left to build anything."

I cringed inwardly when I saw blood rushing to his head, making his red eyes even redder. He opened his mouth to roar at me, but he only made gargling sounds; after a period he regained his composure long enough to inform me in a voice slightly louder than an on-rushing locomotive, that not having any building materials was a "pee poor" excuse for not building houses and that was not an acceptable excuse for failure to perform my duties.

Duly chastised, I slunk off to my S-4 office to mull over ways and means to create building materials when there weren't any. My Supply Sergeant and I felt at least we had to try to satisfy the Major's preposterous demand, so we sat down, drew up a proposed bill of materials, and duly made out requisitions for every item. Knowing the bureaucratic penchant for shelving any paperwork which might entail extra effort, we decided to hand carry the paperwork through Squadron, Regiment, Brigade, and Division—and to explore the unknown bureaucratic world beyond those organizations. At each stop, we were met with, at first, disbelief, and later, derision.

Didn't we know that the Army didn't have one stick of wood or bag of cement? Well, yes, we did, but the fury of the Squadron Commander drove us forward. Armed with signed requisitions at Squadron, Regimental, Brigade and Division level, we were sent to 8th Army Headquarters (HQ) in Yokohama, then to local Military Government, and finally to General Headquarters (GHQ) in Tokyo—that's seven layers of command to go through, each layer signing the requisitions with amusement and curiosity as to how far we could get in this fruitless chase after building materials which didn't exist, but which, if we found the mother lode, they could move in and take the materials for themselves. As the Sergeant and I moved along the levels of command, we gained an inside knowledge of how to work the system, so by the time we got to GHQ (General MacArthur HQ) we knew exactly what to look for. So, instead of looking up the G-4 who was a two star general, we located a corporal sitting over in a corner who kept the approval stamp. With the persuasion of several bottles of Suntory Whiskey (please refer to my story: *Young Man's Dream*) we gained access to the stamp any time we needed it.

Thus, we decided that approval of the other six layers were not needed as long as the seventh level stamped it "approved."

Alas, the whole exercise was fruitless if there were no materials to be had. Another bottle of Suntory elicited from the corporal that our requisition had to make one more stop and that was the critical one—this was a Japanese Bureau called the Japanese Liaison Office where they approved and released materials belonging to the Japanese Government for approved Japanese construction projects for U.S. and Japanese needs. Further discussions revealed that costs of U.S. projects would be borne by the Japanese and placed in a war reparations account.

Suddenly, it dawned on me that here was what amounted to a blank check to do anything—*anything at all and it was all free because the* U.S. *never would be involved in payment of any kind, nor really have any knowledge of the transaction at all and besides, nobody ever paid war reparations. What an absolutely startling discovery!*

This situation meant that to get things done, no requisitions had to be signed: it would merely be a transaction between a U.S. User; a Japanese contractor; and the Japanese Liaison Office—and it would all be honest as long as I stayed strictly within existing regulations—and where there were no regulations governing the situation to remain pure as the driven snow.

Now all I had to do was find a suitable Japanese contractor, and a way to get approval for the projects from the proper person in the Japanese Liaison Office. After a little preliminary exploration, I located a smallish contractor run by a former officer in the Japanese Army Corps of Engineers who looked like to me a tough little guy who could get the job done. His company was named Nitta Gumi. I visited him in his office and explained to him that if he could comply with my approach to the Liaison Office, I would make him a millionaire.

I got his immediate attention. I pointed out that I could give him construction projects, but that he had to figure out how to get paid at the Liaison Office. I further stated I would give him a request for quotation in general terms and we would then draw in the plans. I would approve them, and he would go to work. This whole scheme, while too good to be true, still had the major obstacle of getting paid.

Three days later, the head of Nitta Gumi appeared with a distinguished looking gentlemen in tow named Mr. Yama. Mr. Yama was heavy set, lots of white hair, and was resplendent in a genuine cashmere overcoat, a Homburg hat, a gold headed cane, a full set of gold teeth which he displayed at every opportunity and had a perfect Oxford accent. He was certainly an incongruous sight among the raggedy clothed, underfed, defeated Japanese which were an everyday sight in Tokyo.

As background to what I am about to say, while the Japanese armies in Burma, Malaysia, New Guinea, etc. were thoroughly decimated and crushed by the Allies, this was not true of their army in China which in, the eyes of the Japanese, won their war. Thus the soldiers redeployed back from China were in their eyes, returning to Japan as victors. It was easy to pick these people out of a crowd as their arrogance and disdain for U.S. troops stood out like a sore thumb. I always avoided dealing with the China veterans as I didn't trust them under any circumstances.

With this in mind, I questioned Mr. Yama as to his whereabouts during the war and got a series of evasive answers, which included a vague reference about being in Hokkaido which is not only a rugged, cold, forbidding part of Japan, but it was there that many captured Americans from Bataan and other areas were sent to work in the copper mines. Their subsistence was a hand full of rice daily, many were starved to death under appalling conditions. When Mr. Yama referred to Hokkaido, my hackles rose and I became more insistent as to the nature of his activities. Finally, in exasperation, I ordered him off the premises and to take the Nitta Gumi CEO along with him. A hurried conference ensued, and he finally confessed that he had spent the war years in jail.

He then explained that he was in jail due to a "misunderstanding;" the "misunderstanding" turned out to be that he was selling spurious gold mine stocks which, of course, he didn't know were spurious. When I asked the head of Nitta Gumi, "Why in the hell, are you introducing me to a man like this?" he replied, with a Mona Lisa smile, "Mr. Yama is the new administrator in the Japanese Liaison Office." After recovering from my astonishment, I gave them both my "straight arrow" lecture and left feeling sure the Nitta Gumi had found a solution to the approval problem.

In the following year we easily met the Major's deadline for the duplex quarters, built an Enlisted Men's Club which was a replica of a cowboy bar only larger, complete with knotty pine paneling, hangman's noose, etc. We constructed a non-commissioned officers night club laid out in a Busby Berkeley 1930's style, complete with sliding roof, and the longest bar in the Far East; constructed an Officer's Club on the Sumida River; laid out as a gentleman's club with pool tables, mahogany bar, full kitchen all with dark oak paneling, etc.; and staffed with the elite cooks from the

NYK Steamship Lines (the bulk of which rested on the bottom of the Pacific).

Flushed with success, I took over an entire city block in the center of Tokyo, built an Olympic size swimming pool and a large bathhouse with roof garden and bar. While we were at it, we renovated the entire block making a park with all the appropriate blooming trees, bushes, and fountains with the beautiful Japanese perch (goldfish). We added finishing touches with a tennis court, and a baseball diamond for Nitta Gumi's team. In short, I was on a roll, the magnitude of which knew no boundaries.

The Japanese have a squatters law which states that if a property owner leaves his land fallow, or unimproved in an urban area a squatter can occupy that land and the owner loses his right to evict him. Once the land owners saw what I did with developing the park, I was besieged with offers of priceless land which today would be worth millions for even a small plot. Many of the offers came with suitcases full of money if I would just build a modest anything on their land. For obvious reasons, I did not accept their money or their land, but in fact I could have owned half of Tokyo if I had enough things to build. Fortunately for all concerned, my tour of duty was up and we folded up shop.

I always look back on that episode of my life as one of the most amazing set of circumstances. Imagine having *carte blanche* to build anything I wanted, and since all of our construction was for our officers and enlisted men, it all to the good. And it all came about by learning how to use the system.

Post Mortem

Before returning to the U.S. upon completion of my tour of duty, I was required to turn over all squadron property to my successor. Days were spent performing inventory on picks, shovels, capital equipment, and he was as busy as a one armed paper hanger signing off on various items. Finally, we got to the various buildings I had constructed, including the city park. His eyes got bigger while I explained only in general terms the lack of paperwork to cover the acquisition of millions of dollars worth of property. I finally quieted his astonishment by explaining that the Japanese lost the war so this one was on the house. I still expect a knock on the door one of these days from an old Colonel with a bill for one million dollars in his hand.

Pedestrian Polo

This was a game invented by myself and my jeep driver in Tokyo (not recommended for play in the U.S.)

The traffic in Tokyo in 1945–48 was absolutely impossible!

All possible roads were filled with people walking in the middle and on all sides, interspersed among them were people on bicycles and decrepit vehicles propelled by steam generated by charcoal furnaces embedded in the rear of the vehicles—what you have is a picture of complete chaos.

While all of this was frustrating enough for people like us who always seemed to be in a hurry, there existed the most fearsome presence of all, the Honeybucket Carrier! To fully appreciate the menace the "Carrier" created, it is necessary to understand that the term "Honey" refers to human excrement which the Japanese used as fertilizer on their vegetables and fruit and boy did it make things grow! I've seen strawberries half as big as tennis balls, oranges the size of grapefruit, etc., all of which we were forbidden to eat.

Obviously a bucket of "honey" announced itself at a range of two hundred yards depending upon the strength and direction of the wind, and it goes without saying that being down wind was an unforgettable experience. Although the bulk of the fertilizer was carried in liquid form in wagons drawn by oxen, some "carriers" were men on bicycles carrying two buckets, one on each end of a pole which they balanced on their shoulders as they pedaled unconcernedly in the road. A "carrier" on a bicycle was one to avoid at almost all costs.

To cope with the scene described above, and to prevent from being run over, my driver and I invented a game which we called Pedestrian Polo. To play the game we devised two long poles with boxing gloves attached to one end; the driver had one fastened to his side of our Jeep and the front seat passenger had the other which in turn was fastened to his side. Both poles were held by clips for quick removal. As the vehicle would move along the crowded streets in Tokyo, our headquarters for the 7th Cavalry Regiment, we would poke people who were in our way with the boxing gloves fastened to the poles. There were points given for various types of people.

For example a young boy was worth one point; if he was poked, a fat man was worth two points, etc. More points were added for various areas of the anatomy and whether the victim ran, walked faster, fell, and so on. The highest score on the list was twenty five points for a "carrier" on a bicycle with two honey buckets balanced on his shoulders. Suffice it to say, we studiously avoided that particular challenge. If a player accumulated fifty points during a particular trip he was the winner and the possessor of six cans of beer. I must admit that poking Japanese with long poles is not conduct becoming an officer, but it did have its therapeutic effects in that it kept the pedestrians from walking in front of our Jeep; and it relieved the boredom and the strain on our nerves in dealing with the chaos and bedlam which seemed to perpetually surround us.

I sometimes let my driver use the Jeep on Sundays to do as he pleased and on these occasions he took great pains to have the Jeep washed, waxed, and shining when he showed up for duty on Monday mornings.

On this particular Monday there was no driver and no bright shiny Jeep. Repeated calls to the motor pool failed to find my driver. I marched grimly to the motor pool to locate the driver who was now one hour late. Upon looking around, I observed a huge geyser of steam on the outer edges of the area. Closer inspection revealed my driver stripped to the waist cauterizing my Jeep as if he were trying to remove the paint. As I grew closer I detected the old familiar smell of "honey" and I could understand the reason for the banishment of my Jeep to the remotest point of the area.

After venting my wrath (up wind from the Jeep) I finally got the complete story.

My driver took his buddy on a Sunday drive and was teaching him the elements of Pedestrian Polo. As he explained what happened, I could see in my mind's eye, the Jeep approaching the Honeybucket Carrier pedaling along on his bicycle, minding his own business, when my driver, sensing a twenty point opportunity, bore down on the poor Carrier and, like an ancient knight riding from his jousting post, poked the Carrier with his lance. Apparently, the poke caused the Carrier to lose control of his bicycle, and as he veered towards the Jeep, my terrified driver also lost control. One of the buckets, the leading one, dumped its contents in the front seat of the Jeep. As the carrier swung to avoid the Jeep, the second bucket followed the first, depositing the contents in the back seat of my Jeep.

My Jeep stood there for months isolated from all other motor pool activities, and a year later one could walk down the inspection line of vehicles lined up hub to hub to my Jeep with a handkerchief in his face and say, "There's the Jeep that hit the Honeybucket Carrier." Pedestrian Polo was outlawed by the Regimental Commander and a once great street sport slid slowly into oblivion.

A Midnight Dip

As I have previously mentioned, the 7th Cavalry Regiment of the 1st Cavalry Division of the U.S. Army took great pride in the tradition of having been massacred in total by Chief Sitting Bull and his warriors at Little Big Horn. Frankly, I could never see much glory in all of this, but I dutifully sang all of their regimental songs and kept my peace because some of our officers were with the 7th Cavalry before WWII and brooked no smart ass remarks from 2LT's.

Our regimental commander was Colonel F, and as replacements were needed he filled the vacancies with Irish officers, most of them "Southies" from South Boston and a wild bunch they were. They loved to drink, sing, and fight and I don't mean just pushing and shoving. I mean brawling, but there was a sense of honor evident for after beating the hell out of you, they pick you up, dust you off and buy you a drink just to show there were no hard feelings. Our Squadron Commander, in spite of his choir boy appearance seemed to be a magnet for such activities and although he was never the winner, losing always seemed to whet his appetite for more. The main prime contender in these altercations was the Executive Officer for the regiment who also was a "Southie."

One day we were requested to hold Officer Call at the Colonel's house instead of the usual Conference Room at Regimental HQ. Upon arriving we noted that a boxing ring had been set up on the lawn and chairs were placed around the ring. The Colonel announced that he was damned tired of all of this fighting at the Officers' Club and that he was going to put a stop to this *right* now! Whereupon he ordered our Squadron Commander and the Regimental Executive to strip to the waist, put on the boxing gloves and fight to the finish—there was to be no respite, no rest until there was only one man standing.

Now these were not young officers and years of hard drinking had taken their toll; their faces had that red liquor flush, and their skin had the pallor of a frozen chicken. All of this was set off by a layer of flab flowing over their belt lines. I'll have to say that for about two minutes they really had at it and were bleeding from punches to the nose; however, they gradually slowed down wheezing like an old-fashioned steam calliope. The fight dragged on with the Executive Officer throwing up on the lawn and both fighters hanging onto the ropes unable even to move their arms. Their exhibition slowed down but didn't stop the fighting entirely. Our Squadron Commander did give lip service to the Colonel's order about fighting by installing Bob Hayes, who was a starting tackle on Army's great 1944 football team, to maintain order at significant social gatherings.

Part III

The Edsel Odyssey

Overview: The Edsel 1953–58

My first experience with large corporations was with Ford Motor Company and what an experience it was! Quite by accident, I was hired by Ford to be a Product Planner for the Special Products Division, later to become the Edsel Division which incurred the largest industrial loss in U.S. history up until that time—$450 million. Some of the details are in the stories which follow. I received incalculable business experience as a result of my association with this program.

The Edsel Program was a major example of drinking your own bath water, resulting in a corporate loss of epic proportions. The amount was over *$450 million in 1957 dollars*, which in today's economy would be well over three billion. Having been an eyewitness to the inception of the program I shall accurately describe the problems which old-line corporate thinking failed to appreciate and solve.

To Plan a Failure

To follow is a series of stories which chart the progress of a major automobile to be developed and sold by the Ford Motor Company. It highlights some of the characters which used to abound in the automobile industry and an account of the $450 million debacle which was the largest loss in the automotive sector up to that time.

The Edsel Division of the Ford Motor Company was funded by the parent company, Ford Motor Company, for its start up costs. This included all direct labor, general and administrative costs, overhead, and of course research and development. The total budget for just the development and field sales costs for two years was four hundred fifty million. In total dollars in the year 2011 this would be equivalent to well over three billion dollars; so as you can see this was a major corporate commitment and the eyes of the corporate world were upon it.

As it turned out, the project was doomed from the start by one miscalculation after another, and as a result it is a case study at Harvard Business School. I was there at the beginning, and almost at the end. I was present when the Director of Product Planning and the Manager of Division Marketing made one of the best presentations I have ever seen to Henry Ford II and Ernest Breech the Chairman and CEO respectively of the company.

The theme of the presentation was that there were two major gaps in the Ford product line in which the major competitor, General Motors, had no competition and as a result many Ford owners who wanted to "buy up" migrated through these gaps into the General Motor family of cars. In fact, it was irrevocably shown that as many Ford owners buying up purchased the General Motors medium priced lines of Oldsmobile, Pontiac, and Buick as Chevrolet owners buying up (obviously in the GM family).

This brought down the house and Mr. K, the Edsel Division General Manager, got his four hundred fifty million dollars and we were off and running out of the starting gate, but we should have known that it was to be a long and arduous road.

As a first step, Mr. K set up a product-planning group, which was to coordinate and develop the product. Each major part of the car was assigned to a corresponding section. Mine was the planning for the electrical systems and the options and accessories for the car. Those of you who know me know that I have always boasted I never believe in anything I can't see, and since I can't see electricity, I have a problem with it especially in the engineering sense. I am sure that electricity is generated by tiny leprechauns who secretly work by night to make electricity; this is a secret shared by myself and Ben Franklin—and we'll never tell.

While all of us were planning away energetically, we were starting to look at the industry sales reports which came out every ten days. In those days there were American Motors, General Motors, Ford, Chrysler, and a smattering of imports.

American Motors was offering the Nash Rambler which was comprised of parts left over from models made by Nash Motor Car Company prior to WWII. Actually the Rambler wasn't bad at all; in fact it was a fore-runner to the modern compact car. However, as we watched Rambler creep up in market share, we were also aware that the European small cars were being introduced into the U.S. to include Fiat, MG, Volkswagen, and Renault.

At first sales of these cars and Rambler were only two percent or so of the total market, and were viewed as fads only; fads which would soon die out. As weeks went by, the market share of these cars was growing steadily and the question among ourselves as to whether we were observing a trend or a fad became a matter of great concern. If it was a trend, it would adversely effect the market plans for our product, but if it was a fad no big problem. As our deadline for ordering the tooling for our product was fast approaching, and our first tool was for the roof at a cost of fifty million dollars, it became mandatory to pinpoint the matter of fad versus trend.

When this phenomenon was presented to the corporate people, their derision was heard clear across Lake Michigan:

Didn't we know that it cost almost as much to make a little car as a full sized one? All those chickenshit little cars come apart at the seams; there are no dealers to service them; and only college radicals will buy them!

Thus, the decision that was to haunt Ford Motor Company for decades to come was made at a penalty of four hundred fifty million dollars. From that moment on, the medium priced car market started to shrink as the glory days of Buick, Pontiac, and Oldsmobile went into decline for the next two decades, and the compact car market was born.

Once our tooling for our new product was created, there was no turning back—we were irrevocably committed. Life went on for a year with corporate "suits" clinging to the myth that the medium priced car market would soon recover and profit as never before.

Then came the biggest "boner" of them all! One day, about a year before product introduction, the Corporate "suits" started discussions with our division sales people about how they were going to set up the national Edsel dealership. Did I say Edsel? Well, the secret is out!

We spent days and weeks thinking up appropriate names for our new car, but with the express orders that under no circumstance would the "suits" consider the use of the name Edsel, Henry Ford I's only son. (Henry Ford II was Edsel's son). After several months of wracking our brains, we were told that the product line name was Edsel: *So get used to it.*

I can't think of a more unattractive name, but some of the GM names weren't so hot either.

Well, back to the dealer question.

In answer to the question of the corporate "suits," our VP of Marketing brightly said, "Well, of course, we will use the Ford Dealers nationwide."

The "suits" roared out their disapproval based on the fact that given a medium priced product, they would run the Lincoln-Mercury dealers out of town.

The VP of Marketing then fell back to his alternate suggestion: "We will place the Edsel franchise in the Lincoln-Mercury dealerships, and they will strengthen the market position of these dealerships."

Reportedly from eye witnesses, the response roared again louder than ever:

Where had he been for the last thirty years? Anyone with an ounce of sense knows that Lincoln-Mercury dealers were all borderline and that there was no way they could handle the additional burden of another product line.

Not to be denied, the VP then volunteered that Edsel would steal the major GM dealers in key market areas and thus, set up a killer dealer organization.

Absolutely wrong again!! With less than a year, Edsel would build a dealer organization from scratch made up of successful GM dealers? This was the straw that broke the camel's back! First the market for the product had been invaded by low priced compact cars, and the product name and styling was really ugly; but now the "suits" failed to plan how their product was to be sold. They were planning to staff the national dealer organization with successful GM dealers who would gladly give up their profitable GM franchise for a Ford Company product, the design of which could not be shown due to company policy.

How practical was that?

These guys must have been inhaling too many gasoline fumes; the whole project was a disaster. Soon I was getting verbally beaten up by successful GM dealers when I explained to them that for only two hundred fifty thousand dollars, they could be the lucky recipient of an Edsel franchise; and they would have to give up their GM franchise for the privilege; *and* no they couldn't see a real Edsel unless they put up the two hundred fifty thousand dollars first. Many of the dealers I contacted in my new assignment as Business Management Manager of the Washington D.C. region felt sorry for me, as you would the Village Idiot, and the others thought that I must have been drinking to seriously offer such a proposition.

Once the Edsel was introduced our troubles started. Our dealers were ex used car salesmen, dealers of now defunct car companies such as Studebaker, Kaiser, Nash, etc.; or just plain crooks. My adventure with these bad boys would fill a book. As our sales started to sink slowly into the mud, I met one of our ex field people who had gone to American Motors, and over several cocktails we both agreed that if our dealers just had a second car line they could probably make it. We agreed that if I could get the American Motors Rambler in my showrooms, and if he could get a decent medium priced car (i.e. the Edsel) in his showroom, maybe we could turn a profit in our region.

However, we were both limited by the fact that both of our companies had positions against dual dealerships; that is a Ford dealer couldn't sell anyone else's cars from his dealership and vice-versa.

Our sense of complicity, shared by additional "refreshments" developed a way to get our car-sales *up* and our dealerships profitable. The bottom line to all of this was, I put Edsels in his showroom which was located away from Washington, and my dealers got the Rambler. Ramblers would show on the books as used cars; and technicality it is true that once a car is driven out of a dealership (under certain conditions) it is a used car. The long and short of it was our Edsel, which we billed as new cars sold on my dealers books, ended up as used cars in my friend's dealership and vice-versa.

Our region led the national Edsel organization in used car sales and we came very close to meeting a very unrealistic quota for new car sales. The Edsel people wanted me to move back to Detroit to show them how I achieved these fantastic sales. I declined, with thanks, took over as Regional Manager for Litton Industries at the magnificent salary of twelve thousand dollars per year selling defense systems; in 1958 money of this kind wasn't bad! I departed hastily as the king of used car sales out of the wreckage of a four-hundred fifty million dollar investment.

The Best Sales Job I Have Ever Seen

As if most of you have never guessed, the automobile business is one of the rottenest businesses in the whole world, staffed by a breed of bandits that would put Jesse James to shame. I had the privilege of being the fifth person hired by the Special Products Division of Ford Motor Company, (my adventures there are covered in other stories).

After a period of middle management experience, I was dispatched to the field as Administrative Manager and Business Management Manager of the Edsel Division Eastern Region (that's what we were named by the Special Products Division of Ford), where I was exposed to the real car salesmen whose assets were greed, resourcefulness, cunning, duplicity, plus other attributes too numerous to mention.

My friend, Harvey, who came over to us from Chrysler Corporation, had as a car salesman been king of them all. Placed in a staff position as Assistant District Manager, he exposed us all to the principles of what he termed salesmanship—although dwelling on his every word, I was somewhat reluctant to follow his pronouncements with my actions. Our Regional Manager was Mr. John C, a real Irish SOB from New York City, whose motto was: *I may not be very smart, but I sure know how to put on the pressure.*

How right he was! Genghis Khan inspired as much terror as John C. He would sweep into a district, fire a few people, reduce the secretaries to tears, and tramp out to descend upon another unsuspecting district. Obviously, not a person to take lightly.

Three years of planning came to a climax at the Sheraton Hotel in New York in 1956 when the Edsel Automobile was introduced to an unsuspecting public. Harvey and I had spent at least ten hours handshaking prospective dealers, writers, etc. To ease our fatigue, we retired to our hotel bar where we made a determined effort to lower its liquor inventory, and we were making some headway when the bar was closed leaving us dry, but in control of our senses.

As we were entering a crowded elevator in the lobby, I asked Harvey, "Have you seen Mr. C today?" Harvey answered in a resounding voice which bounced off the walls of the elevator, "Hell no, and I don't care if I ever see that son of a bitch again!"

As Harvey's words ceased their bouncing off the walls, the elevator became as silent as a tomb, and a voice came back from the rear of the elevator saying, "Harvey! What did you call me?" I am sure that Harvey's socks turned yellow from urine—I know mine did. When he turned around, there was Mr. C smiling much like cobra eying its next victim. Harvey, without hesitation at all, walked over to Mr. C and said, "Mr. C, I called you a son of a bitch," and putting his arm around him said, "but, you're a nice son of a bitch" and he got away with it.

The next night Harvey, succumbing to the temptation of the flesh, found a particularly attractive *femme de joie* and was escorting her to his room to show her his stamp collection (Harvey's room was on the thirtieth floor). Mr. C entered the same elevator on the second floor and was eying him and his nymphet with a suspicious Catholic eye. Harvey sensing impending doom proudly said, "Mr. C, please meet my dearly beloved sister, she is going to be a nun." He got away with it again. I don't know where Harvey is as I write this, but if there is a salesman's heaven, he is sitting on the right hand side of the boss.

Santa Claus Done Come and Went (to the Hospital)

This is a one of the funniest adventures which I have ever had.

The Edsel Division of Ford Motor Company of which I was a member (developer of the famous Edsel automobile—now a collector's item), decided in its first year of existence to hold a Christmas dance, complete with orchestra, drinks, and a real live Santa Claus. One of my friends, a young aspiring executive (like myself), duly volunteered to act as Santa much to his eventual regret.

The site of the party was to be at the Union Headquarters of the United Autoworkers Union, Local 800, located on Ford Motor Company property at the River Rouge Plant, which was at that time the world's largest integrated auto manufacturing plant. Iron ore would go in one side, and a finished car would come out the end. In back of this plant flowed the River Rouge which was polluted enough even in those days (1952) to walk across without getting your feet wet.

In anticipation of a glorious Christmas dance, we bought new suits for ourselves, and dresses for our wives, and set out for the Union Hall with roses in our cheeks and eyes gleaming in anticipation of free drinks for all, right in the midst of a Michigan snow storm. Once in the Union Hall, there was the band playing 50's music, a very busy bar, and at some distance down the hall was, of all things, a shooting gallery with several .22 rifles and a large supply of .22 "short" cartridges.

I could see immediately some very interesting possibilities occurring. Clustered around the gallery were a number of machinists who obviously had gotten a head start in the drinking department. The bulk of this particular group had come from the Hamtramck area in Detroit which is almost 100% Polish; and anyone who has ever been to the Polish-American Social Club on a Saturday night will attest that it is easier to tame a herd of water buffalo than an equal number of drunken machinists. No sooner had I made it to a refuge at the bar, than the crowd at the shooting gallery loaded up the .22 rifles and started shooting. Some of the more argumentative fellows started to fight over who got to shoot next, and the ensuing scramble resembled a shoot out at the OK Corral. .22 shorts were peppering the ceiling and walls of good old Union Hall #800. We, at the far position, kept our junior executive cool and the band played on!

Our division manager finally quelled the shooting and left the machinists to sort things out in the snow outside. After all concerned had calmed their nerves with several libations, the real show started.

Santa, seeing that vast quantities of various spirituous liquids were being consumed, decided to single handedly reduce the chances of all of us being tipsy on his holiday by drinking up the inventory himself; and although he made admirable inroads he was failing fast. On the other hand, having gotten our second wind, we enthusiastically lent our aid to this arduous task. The results were most predictable; my friend John, emboldened by a close acquaintance that night with John Barleycorn, was deemed by his wife to be dancing too close to one of the more nubile ladies and all hell broke loose—tears, recriminations, accusations, and every other "ation" known to man. All of this ended in a demand by his wife:

You're drunk and we're going home.

All of you men are familiar with this. John, of course, refused, but the overly solicitous wife of Henry, one of our other friends, offered to take her home alone. Henry was dragged off by his wife to the car along with John's wife in the snow storm, which had increased in intensity, with the roads all but impassable. Half way home "Mrs. John" became so maudlin about John being drunk and alone that Henry was made to turn around and trek back to the dance.

As Henry turned onto the road to the dance, a naked figure waving its arms and shouting obscenities emerged from behind a bush in the driving snow. It was John, naked as a jay bird. Henry stopped the car, stepped out, and grappled with John to try to get him into the car which was about as easy as trying to inject a piece of wet spaghetti in a wildcat's behind.

John broke away and ran headlong back into #800; sprinted the length of the dance floor naked; disappeared out the back door; and dove into the River Rouge with Henry in hot pursuit followed by two screaming wives. Well, after being shot up by the machinists, and putting up with a drunken Santa, we were pretty callused about seeing a nude man running around the dance floor in a snow storm—so the band played on.

Some of us, leaving our wives aghast, followed Henry out to help rescue John who was floundering around trying to reach the opposite bank. Santa was staggering along shedding his Santa clothes, as he made his way to the river. Henry had jumped in to *pull* a thrashing John to safety, new suit and all. I arrived in time to see Henry's new suit coat serenely sail away from the bank where he thought he had put it and sink under the oily waves like the good ship *Titanic*.

Some genius on the bank found a coal shovel and decided that vigorous application on John's head might help Henry and Santa in their efforts. In the darkness I heard the genius say, "Hold him still!" The next sounds of *clang, clang, clang* were punctuated by outraged shouts from Santa and Henry saying, "You son of a bitch, you're hitting us."

The clanging and shouting finally alerted the Ford security guards that something was amiss and they started to give the alarm. The reaction to this was a Le Mans Road Race rush to cars, followed by a watered down version of a demolition derby. I was first out, followed by the thundering herd, leaving Santa, Henry, and John plus wives to face the music. I was told by Santa later, that they were accosted by the security people who placed them under detention and marched them back through the dance area. By then machinists had retreated back to the safety of Hamtramck, the bartender was hastily hiding the booze (no drinking on company property)—and the band was still playing on.

What a country!

Santa, John, and Henry were confined overnight to the Henry Ford hospital for observation because of their immersion in the River Rouge. The next day John and Henry were mournfully plodding around the hospital halls in their pajamas wondering when they could go home. They ran across an intern who informed them that, "No they couldn't go home. They were quarantined because their companion had contracted some very strange and probably exotic disease."

Panic stricken, they asked the intern what were Santa's symptoms. The intern replied, "He is extraordinarily flushed in the face and neck areas, and gives evidence of a high fever; he complains of severe head pains and nausea; but when we take his temperature it records normal. We have our top people trying to determine what he may have caught in the river and we have alerted Mayo Clinic that we may evacuate him there." John and Henry, seeing as how they were going to be quarantined anyhow, got permission to go see Santa in his room accompanied by the intern. After one look at Santa, they both collapsed in a heap, convulsed with laughter for here lay poor Santa with a paralyzing hangover, red eyeballs and all with a bright red blotchy face and neck, no doubt a frightening sight to someone who didn't realize that Santa in his drunken plunge into River Rouge had given his Santa Clause make-up enough moisture to make it run and spread itself liberally on his face and neck. All culprits were released that morning, sent home, and no doubt received severe punishment from their wives.

The company admonished Santa and Henry. John was transferred to some Ford operation at the end of the world (probably Tierra del Fuego).

The Fickle Finger of Fright

This account involves the long-standing enmity between Local 800 of the United Auto Workers Union, Ford Motor Company strike breakers, and the "College Boys" who typified "management." It had been a bloody time, and we "College Boys" were reminded everyday to not "tease the animals," and to stay away from the assembly lines. This story starts with a planning meeting between the union and management, supported by two of us "College Boys." The fireworks this meeting ended with were more explosive than the 4th of July. It is one of my fondest memories.

In the 1950's the automotive business in Detroit was still pretty much rough and tumble and many of the people in the manufacturing and sales sectors were sons of the workers who came off the assembly lines and spent Friday and Saturday night brawling in the bars along Michigan Avenue and the Polish enclave of Hamtramck.

The rough edges of the upper echelons of corporate management had received some degree of smoothness by virtue of education, the higher levels afforded by various colleges. Once out of the comfort of staff activities, things could still be pretty raw. We fledgling junior executives were emphatically instructed to never wear a coat and tie when visiting the assembly lines manned by Local 800 of the United Auto Workers Union.

These were the guys that fought the fabled Battle of The Overpass which pitted Walter Reuther's union organizers and Ford Company strikebreakers over access to the River Rouge assembly plant, the largest in the world at that time. There were fatalities and scores of people sent to the hospital after the battle. Although that Donnybrook had occurred over fifteen years earlier, and despite the fact the Union won, the rancor left on both sides was palpable when "College Boys" went into any Local 800 plant. The least one could hope for would be rude references to the ancestry of the intruders, and the norm would be some form of physical abuse to which, of course, there would be no witness.

In our duties as product planners for our new product (the Edsel) we held coordination meetings with the machinists to cost out certain configurations of sheet metal, engine blocks, and other assorted parts and pieces while the product was still under design. The machinists were members of Local 800, and as such were hostile to the maximum and with whom generally it was very hard to hold a decent meeting.

I ordinarily enjoyed these meetings as it gave me a chance to bait the machinists, and to take great joy in their threats to separate various body parts from my anatomy much to the discomfiture of the various management types who sometimes intruded into our coordination meetings. A fellow agitator was my sidekick, Charley, a burly Boston Irishman, who had previously served in the FBI in Detroit. Charley was just as rough and tough as the meanest machinist and consequently was left alone by the Local 800 boys.

At each major discussion point in the development of the Edsel, we would have to present the facts and figures to our Division Manager, and the estimates in cost were submitted by the machinists, who would very reluctantly sign off after referring to the Junior executives as "Dumsonovabitches" who didn't have sense enough to "pour piss out of a boot!"

At the particular meeting that I'm going to talk about, we were to give a full blown presentation to Mr. K to secure approval for a very major item for our product. The attendees were decked out in their new pressed corporate plumage; we junior executives in our forty dollar suits; Mr. K dressed in his two hundred dollar suit; plus all of his staff dressed in suits. The machinists sat all on one side of the table looking extremely uncomfortable in suits which looked to be several sizes too small; with collars much too tight giving their eyes a bulgy, fishy look. All in all they looked ready to explode into a rain of buttons, elastic and torn fabric at the slightest disturbance.

The machinists were fresh off a long weekend and they seemed to have had a number of cocktails during that period. I'm sure that General Custer at Little Bighorn didn't face as many mean tempered adversaries. Mr. K called the meeting to order, and I reviewed the action items to be accomplished by all before the deadline of the present meeting.

Mr. K beamed his approval as I went down the list praising the junior executives for meeting their commitments. When I started on the list of machinist action items, it became apparent to all that they hadn't paid the slightest attention to their commitments on the action item list. As I read off each action item and the non-compliance by the machinists, I grew more sarcastic and, I thought, extremely funny. As I reveled in my own humorous (so I thought) comments, I could see the thunderclouds gathering on the machinists' side of the table. Upon the conclusion of my report, I recommended that we hold the next meeting at the Little Poland Bar in Hamtramck where the machinists might make more sense, drunk than sober.

With that, the largest of the machinists stood over me and poked my chest with a finger the size of a Coney Island Frankfurter saying and I quote:

Look here you little college boy piss ant, one more word out of you and I'll pound your ass into dirt!!

Whereupon, Charley said in a very quiet voice, "Don't you point your finger again at Malony because if you do, I'll break it off." The management types collectively sucked in their breath so rapidly you could have had vapor lock in the room, Mr. K blanched a little, but manfully restored order and we all were warned that there will be no more of *that* and to act like executives should. The meeting settled down to normality.

After the business part of the meeting was drawing to a close, Mr. K launched into a lecture about staying fit both mentally as well as physically and I, still seething from being called a "little piss ant" commented in the direction of the machinists, who sported a number of beer bellies, that most of them had more chins than a Hong Kong telephone directory. At that the dam burst and my previous tormentor who had said that he was going to pound me, arose (his demeanor was stage one apoplectic) and pointed his finger at me in preparation to follow up on his threat.

Before he could utter a word, Charley reached up grabbed the offending finger; the ensuing crack sounded like a pistol shot in the conference room, and the machinist's scream could be heard throughout our floor. The scene was utter chaos as the machinist stared down at his forefinger which was pointing straight up in the air and at right angles to his hand. Management, at the first bellow of pain, quickly evacuated the premises and declared the meeting adjourned leaving Charley, me, and the junior executives to face the machinists.

There was an absolute silence in the room except for the moans of the machinist. Before anyone could react, I addressed the other side of the conference table and said, "Now look what you've done. You have gotten Charley angry. I'll try to control him, but you had best leave now!" Charley put on his meanest face as they all filed out muttering to themselves. The next day we sent a bottle of Polish Vodka to the head machinist and one to the injured man suggesting that we meet at the Little Poland in Hamtramck.

We arrived in fine form the next day at the bar and got gloriously drunk. We even used the aggrieved man's injured finger in its cast to stir our drinks—I loved it! So did the mechanics. We never had any trouble after that. That incident occurred very early in my business career, but many are the times, in other situations, when I wished I had a Charley type person to apply a little pain to objectionable bullies who trod the corporate halls.

The Big Rip Off

In the 1950's the ranks of the upper echelons of management in the companies who made automobiles, (i.e. Ford, General Motors, Chrysler, etc.) were generally filled by two types of executives. The first group were the hell for leather, hard drinking, ass kicking old timers who had gasoline for blood. They were the group for which I had an affinity. The second group were the new comers who were not automobile guys at all, but were real "smoothies" such as the "whiz" kids who included Robert McNamara who later became Secretary of Defense under both the Kennedy and Johnson administrations. These people were hired by Henry Ford II to rescue the company, which they did and became millionaires for their trouble. The "whiz" kids brought with them "Junior Smoothies" and a sharp line was drawn between them and the old guard. Some memorable battles were waged in Executive Meetings over which Henry Ford II and Ernest Breech, who was formerly a top man at General Motors, presided. Both men enjoyed these battles and poured liberal amounts of fuel on the fires which resulted between the contestants.

The stakes were high in these battles. If the VP of Manufacturing accepted a very stylish curve on a section of the car model presented by a division manager, and if it turned out that he would have to introduce an extra operation that could have added several dollars of cost to achieve this styling feature, it was the VP of Manufacturing who had to pick up the cost which could be several millions of dollars over his budget. Each person had his own agenda and the cost controls were merciless!

To design a new model required three years from inception to final acceptance. Literally each model started out as a shapeless mound of clay which would be put on a wooden frame. A team of technicians would lovingly place clay on the frame and shape it into a final design thirty months later. The first phase was merely a series of toy sized models. The shape and features of the car would evolve through hundreds of changes into a half size model, and from there into a full sized model. Every inch of this model had to be accurate to the smallest detail since this model would dictate the finished products exact measurements and the tools to produce the vehicle would cost hundreds of millions of dollars. Obviously, during the last phase of the development of the model, the technicians put in hours of overtime on weekends and vacations. When one went into the styling studio the tension among all concerned including the stylists, designers, and production engineers was palpable—it was so thick you could cut it with a knife.

Well, the final day came when the completed clay model was to be unveiled for final review. Representatives from manufacturing, marketing, and engineering, along with Mr. K, our Edsel Division Manager, and the product planners were present to see the fruits of our labor. With a flourish our Chief Stylist whipped off the canvas covering the 1957 Edsel. It looked absolutely beautiful! It was painted emerald green, the chrome shone like silver and altogether it made the three years of exacting labor well worthwhile. The Technician and Chief Stylist beamed with pride. Mr. K made a little welcoming speech, and the acceptance procedure started. The clay model Edsel looked exactly like a complete new car, perfect in every detail. It was difficult to imagine that it was really only clay painted emerald and placed on a wooden frame.

All the prestigious attendees said nice things about the final model, until the Corporate Director of Manufacturing stood up and assuming the pose of Zeus hurling thunderbolts from the top of Mount Olympus, ranted and raved like a maniac about every single feature of the car. The lights weren't placed right; the bumpers looked like shit; the styling stunk; the roof looked like it had been jammed on; etc., etc. Now it didn't take a genius to quickly realize that this was a genuine white socks wearing, greasy fingered, and gasoline as blood, old time automobile man who had worked his way through the ranks to the top of his profession. It further didn't take much to realize that he hated the Edsel with a passion. As his rage mounted, his language grew stronger; one could almost smell sulfur burning. The company officers stared at the floor in stunned silence. The technicians, who had spent almost three years working on the model making thousands of changes to achieve perfection, were at first appalled.

When the shock wore off, I could see their anger rising, but after all, one did not talk back to a Corporate Vice President. The company officers who had committed four hundred and fifty million dollars to the project were inwardly shuddering at each criticism which had started to assume the character of an accusation.

As his accusations rose to a crescendo, the Vice President snatched at the door handle forgetting that he was dealing with a clay model and shouted, "Now let's see what this piece of shit looks like on the inside." He gave the handle a violent jerk, and not only did it come off in his hand, but the whole side of the model slowly broke into pieces and slid to the floor.

It seemed that a vacuum had suddenly sucked the air from the studio. There stood the VP with the door handle in his hand, looking at the pieces of the model on the floor. The corporate people were frozen with their mouths gasping in horror. If the event hadn't been so serious the rest of us might have suppressed a giggle or two; however to be truthful, we were as horrified as the rest. It seemed like an hour elapsed before anyone uttered a sound. Suddenly the whispers among the technicians grew to a mournful rumble which was brought to a crescendo by the Chief Technician screeching, "*You Dumb Son of a Bitch!*"

The main body of technicians joined the hue and cry, and heaped abuse on the culprit as he approached the corporate attendees, I guess to try to "circle the wagons." The corporate people retreated in confusion towards the studio exit in an attempt to disassociate themselves from the perpetrator, and the nightmare they had just witnessed.

I am sure that the technician would have gladly torn him to bits if unbridled. After the studio had been evacuated, we stood mournfully among the shattered model of our clay model of the Edsel, brightened only by the thought that the VP of Manufacturing just lost face with the corporate folks and his execution was just around the corner.

The pieces of the Edsel laying scattered on the studio floor were symbolic of the fate of the car thirty months later. It was the largest industrial loss in U.S. history (four hundred fifty million dollars) and I was there! Ford covered up the four hundred fifty million dollar loss by floating a bond issue. I later left Ford for the Defense Sector and we all lived happily ever after!

The Greening of Walter B

Walter B. gets his just deserts.

In all large corporations, and, I guess, small ones too, there are constant power struggles over "who is who in the zoo" namely the place in the pecking order one is struggling to achieve. Sometimes the struggle is over money allocations; sometimes over who gets the corner office; and sometimes over which activity gets what charter to do business in a certain sector. The outcome of the latter type of struggle is usually more intense than the others as it involves jobs, careers, and money.

This was particularly true in McDonnell Douglas Aircraft. I had been hired by one of my West Point classmates to be Director of Marketing of the Electronics Divisions, and our charter was basically Airborne Communications which included just about every type of gear imaginable, including systems for space vehicles. But it was not clear where one charter stopped and that of the division that produced space vehicles started. My classmate had created a sterling reputation as a test pilot and also as Program Manager for the most successful aircraft program that McDonnell Douglas ever had up until that time, but the space vehicle boys had Walter B who had successfully fielded the Mercury and Gemini space vehicle programs. Walter B had cast envious eyes on our division and was apparently trying to convince J.S. McDonnell to cede our activities to his domain. My classmate was hard pressed to defend us due to some depressing news about losses on a few programs that kept emanating from our division.

Walter B himself was a disagreeable old fart—he never had good thing to say about us, and fought like a tiger against any allocations of money for business development for our endeavors. We both feared and detested him, and dreaded the day be might take us over.

One of the critical programs upon which we were working was a trainer for the Boeing 747 which was the largest passenger aircraft built at the time. The trainer itself was a replication of the cockpit of the 747 mounted on a number of hydraulic legs. The up and down action of these legs which were computer controlled emulated pitch and yaw motions in the cockpit by hydraulic action. To be able to do the required four modes of motion which were very difficult and our engineers were under severe pressure to solve the hydraulic problems and to get the project back on track. Walter B was in full hue and cry with J.S. McDonnell claiming that the lack of progress on this critical trainer was proof positive that our division needed his management skills.

Finally the problem was solved and the date set for a dynamic demonstration of the entire system, prior to final acceptance by Boeing, the customer. Members of the top management of the company were in attendance led by Walter B the Program Manager, the trainer was activated and put through its paces. Walter B stood transfixed watching the operation of the trainer with a critical eye, when suddenly I saw a green mist emanating from one of the hydraulic legs directly opposite Walter B. "Well, that's an interesting phenomenon," I thought to myself until I realized that the hydraulic fluids used in the four degree operations were green. It seemed that one of the seals in the leg had parted ever so minutely. Fascinated by this small, very unnoticeable malfunction, I opted to keep my fingers crossed and hoped that the test would be over with no further mistake. Suddenly, as the four degrees of motion were at their climax, the stress placed on the seal caused it to part ever so slightly and much to my horror a tiny stream of green fluid shot out from one of the hydraulic legs onto Walter B's suit.

Walter B was completely unaware of what was happening to his suit, and the stream just kept on coming out soaking his trousers from the waist down. Others had noticed this occurrence and since there were no Walter B lovers, we all kept our silence. As the test neared its grand conclusion and Walter B's pants had changed a nice green color and Walter B, smelling a strange odor looked down at his pants, all of us who were stifling laughter, were suddenly shocked by a shrill cry of rage emanating from Walter B. Wild-eyed, he charged the offending hydraulic leg, gave it a resounding kick, rupturing the seal which responded by releasing a gush of vile green fluid which streamed out on the floor engulfing his shoe tops. While the non-observers watched, thinking that Walter B had had some sort of seizure, we fled the test giggling like a bunch of schoolboys. My last view as I left the area was the non-observers slipping and sliding in the green fluid trying to help the marooned corporate people to safety, leaving Walter B in the lee. It was a scene right out of an old time Keystone Cops movie. We Plebeians laughed until we cried.

Post Mortem

Walter B took over our division and my classmate and I were sent merrily on our way.

Part IV

Jimmy Takes On the Dark Continent

Overview:
Africa the Dark Continent 1976–1984

Dark is right, two assassinations and four coups in my customer areas; that and having my life threatened by a most despicable character highly placed in the inner circled in Nigeria, were enough to put color in anyone's cheeks. The scenes of these stories are in Nigeria, the #2 supplier of oil to the U.S. at the time (now it may be Mexico); and in Liberia, a nation created by U.S. freed slaves transported by a total of thirty ships during President Monroe's time and controlled by descendants of the two leaders of the groups—Tubman, and Talbot.

Both countries have a history of violence and greed. What follows are events both comic and serious which I experienced there during a period of eight years.

Catch 22 in Liberia

Jimmy deals with African diplomacy.

My first trip to West Africa in 1982 was a Swiss Air Flight from London straight to Monrovia, Liberia. Although, I was later to spend over eight years traveling to various places along the West African Coast, I was faced with some tribulation my first excursion into the unknown not having the slightest idea of what I might be getting into.

My traveling companion was a Liberian who was a Director of the Meserado Fishing Company which was in fact a very large trading company owned by the Talbot family who were slaughtered *en masse* by Sergeant Doe some years later. During the flight we availed ourselves of the various cocktails served by Swiss Air and we bathed in the beauty of the stewardesses who seemed very accommodating.

As we approached Roberts Field, our destination, my companion informed me that Roberts Field was at least fifty miles from my hotel in Monrovia, the capital, but that he would drive me there after a few stops after we landed. His invitation was gladly accepted and after being whisked through customs we were met by his driver and started out in the pitch blackness of West Africa.

We wound down a meandering, one lane dirt road leading through the loneliest, most deserted "bush" I had ever seen. My imagination was running wild as we bumped and swerved on and on. *Was my congenial host going to kill me? Why are we out here fifty miles from Monrovia? If I got out and ran would the wild animals eat me?*

Suddenly we stopped in front of a very large thatched hut and my host went into the hut where I could see his silhouette against the light from a kerosene lamp toasting someone. The only encouraging sign I saw was that he poured some of his drink on the ground—this is what the old lineage Irish did to respect the spirits of their ancestors.

My host rejoined me and confirmed my theory about pouring drinks. It turned out that he was visiting his parents—why they chose to live in a thatched hut when he was a director of a very large trading company, I'll never know. Well, off we went to his house which was nearer to Monrovia, so at least we were making forward progress. His home was very spacious and elegant, and he asked me to make myself at home while he attended to a small errand. Although somewhat saturated with Swiss Air wines, brandies, etc., I managed to choke down a liter of beer while awaiting his return; once again being slightly uncomfortable alone in a strange house belonging to a strange man in a really strange country. Suddenly the door burst open with my host leading a bevy of three ladies and one male, obviously his close friends.

Even though I have never been very good with numbers, I could add three and three and this time I didn't like the results at all! My sixth sense told me that I was headed for a spot of trouble as one of the ladies was obviously for me.

But the question was, "Who's Who In The Zoo?" (the title of a popular children's book) since I didn't want any of the three I had a real diplomatic crisis. If I refused I would be insulting my host's hospitality. If I chose the wrong one, I might be choosing somebody's wife, or girlfriend. Either way, I was a long way from Monrovia without a friendly face within miles. Desperately, I looked around for some sort of hint of who belonged to whom. Five sets of unblinking eyes stared at me waiting, just waiting for me to make my move.

Finally one stepped forward to make the drinks. "Ah," I said to myself, "she knows her way about the house, so logically, she is the wife, or girlfriend." That left two candidates with rings on all fingers of both hands. The host's friend had started to fix me with a cold glare which could be a preview of "coming attractions."

Although the whole scene had taken ten seconds at the most each second seemed like an hour. Through the maelstrom of panic I heard the words of my host, saying, "Come now. James, choose your lady. I am sure that John (his friend) won't mind if you pick his wife."

At that one of the ladies piped in and said in broken English, "You like Push, Push? Me like Push, Push."

John would not mind? The hell he wouldn't!

Please God, I thought, *get me out of this.*

Suddenly the solution appeared. With a loud cry, I clutched my stomach and writhed my best writhe on the floor, rolling my eyeballs, and uttering a mix of sobs and moans. This certainly broke up the party and I was dispatched hurriedly to the Ducor Hotel in Monrovia, with a note saying that I seemed to be having the onset of Amoebic Dysentery, a disease "guaranteed" to make you poop your brains out and my host certainly didn't want to have to deal with that.

I made a miraculous recovery as soon as the lights of the house of my host were fading in the rear view mirror, and with a sigh of relief I checked into the Hotel Ducor. But lest you think poorly of me, I really do like "Push-Push."

You Are My Sunshine

To this day I still go to my skin doctor periodically to be treated for disorders received in Liberia while pursuing my favorite proclivities: pretty girls, good wine, spicy foods, and dance.

I recall one day I arose and looked innocently out of the window of my room at the Hotel Ducor in Monrovia, Liberia to inspect the premises close by. My love of nature was rewarded by the sight of a lady of amazing proportions sunning herself by the hotel swimming pool. Her name later turned out to be Jasmine.

I reported post haste to the pool area while tugging on my too tight bathing suit. With lust in my heart, I approached the object of my desire much in the same manner as Bela Lugosi, the vampire in the 1940's movies, who would try to sink his fangs into the neck of his female victims to relieve them of a pint or two of their blood. Upon announcing myself to Jasmine as Lance B. Stunning, *bon vivant*, teller of tall tales, Olympic class martini drinker, etc., she rolled over and affixed me with emerald green eyes set in a Mid-Eastern facial caste with skin the color of very light coffee.

That, coupled with mammaries that stood out like twin Titan Rockets in launch position, stopped me dead in my tracks. In my stunned state I could only babble words like, "Ugga, ugga haystaka boomalaka sis boom ball!"

Well, in time we were chatting away in English interspersed with giggles and protestations of sincerity on my part, and as the old Xmas poem goes, "sugar plums were dancing in my head."

My dreams were rudely shattered when I saw looming on the horizon a very determined Irish lady complete with chicken skin, freckles, green eyes and red hair. Without any ceremony Jasmine's mother plopped herself down between us, thereby drawing a pall over my brilliant dialog which, I had hoped, would lead to better terms with Jasmine.

Suddenly an Iraqi gentleman arrived, my depression deepened when he dutifully kissed his daughter, Jasmine and his wife, the Irish lady. I did notice, however, that he carried under his arm a rather large wineskin from which he offered me a drink. This wineskin had a large tube affixed to one end so that when one squeezed the other end of the skin, wine was forced out of the tube into one's mouth. He artfully diverted my baleful glances at Jasmine's mother to the wineskin by demonstrating the art of holding the wineskin at arm's length and squirting a stream of wine down one's throat. I finally got the hang of it as the sun beat down on my uncovered head. After several hours of discussing Mid-East politics and developing eyestrain from ogling Jasmine, I found myself gloriously tight and sunburned—so sunburned in fact that I couldn't bear the pressure of the sheets of my bed on my skin.

All thoughts of "having it on" with the lovely Jasmine quickly fled, and I concentrated on getting in shape to fly down the coast to Lagos, Nigeria for my first trip to that country. I noticed I was starting to peel large patches of skin from the top of my head as I was on my way to Roberts Field outside of Monrovia. By the time I landed in Lagos I resembled a particularly repulsive species of spotted Hyena.

To any traveler along the west coast of Africa the word "Lagos" arouses many memories, most of them bad, and most of them emanating from the misery of dealing with louts, hustlers, criminals, crooked customs people, plus others who would have cheerfully been paid up members in Dante's Inferno. To the uninitiated, the first view of Nigeria is the airport officials, many of whom bear tribal scars making them even more villainous appearing. Upon landing, I assumed, my place in the nearest line, with the appropriate apprehensions which were fulfilled upon my arrival at the customs desk. The official, when I presented my passport and health certificate, took one look at my peeling head and decided that I had leprosy and informed me that I was to be detained for testing. I asked for more details and tried to make him understand that white skin was different than black skin and peeled when sunburned. He showed me through the window of the customs shed to a spot cornered off by barbed wire (this area contained goats, chickens, and all manner of individuals with hideous skin diseases). This is where I was to spend as long as it took for me to be tested! I hastily pulled out hundred dollars and my health certificate and respectfully asked that he review it in view of my claim to sunburn.

I was waived through with no further problems (except for a small yellow stain in my jockey shorts). *Viva la crime!*

The sunburn received while pursuing my quarry at the Hotel Ducor became a permanent condition requiring several trips to the specialist per year. He doesn't believe me when I tell him that it is a direct result of a glandular condition years ago.

Sergeant Doe

West Africa was and still is one of the bloodiest areas on earth with killings of individuals, tribal, religion (Protestants, Catholics, Muslim) and nations. Sergeant Doe was an enlisted man in the Liberian Army who seized control of Liberia by force and killing the families of the original founding fathers as well as all prominent government and military officials.

In the mid-1800's, a series of ships loaded with slaves freed in both the North and the South of the U.S. were sent back to West Africa from whence they came.

It was the intent of the various religious groups in the U.S. to repatriate the slaves and to form a free utopian government in which a democratic rule would provide them freedom of spirit and freedom from want. Accompanying these ex-slaves were black religious leaders whose word the people accepted as law. Among these leaders were Reverend Tubman and Reverend Talbot, whose families maintained political and commercial leadership throughout the generations up to the 1980's.

They named their country Liberia in the name of Liberty, which they were seeking, and their capital Monrovia in honor of President Monroe.

Liberia itself is rich in minerals especially iron and manganese. Large rubber plantations sprang up and with a successful fishing enterprise created a fairly well balanced economy. The U.S. dollar is the unit of currency and the U.S. Congress consistently supported the various governments with subsidies.

Unfortunately, the concentration of wealth and power gradually shifted to the Tubman and Talbot families who, in accordance with human nature, abused that power, thus creating all kinds of corruption to include higher-ranking officers in the Liberian Army. Even though the government, which was organized along the lines of the British system, the Tubman and Talbot families controlled the way things went.

The only other source of power was the Army, which gradually evolved into a major influence and increasingly became a threat to take over the government; obviously the major families continued to pull the strings.

Finally, as the government was groaning under the weight of its own corruption, a lowly Sergeant named Doe with the aid of elements of the army and members of his tribe mounted a bloody coup and took over the government. His first order was to execute all members of the Tubman and Talbot families including women and children. He next killed all officers of field grade rank and above. Having dispatched the cream of the Liberian Army, he next executed all Ministers and the Permanent Secretaries, thus eliminating any administrative discipline in the government. The only Permanent Secretary that he missed was Sam Butler, who ran the Postal and Telegraph Ministry. He was visiting the U.S. at the time and was my customer for one of my clients for whom I was consulting at the time. I considered him also as a friend.

After the first rash of killings was over, Sam Butler told me that Sergeant Doe had contacted him and asked him to return as he considered him the only honest man in the cabinet, and that he need not worry about his family in Monrovia, the capital.

We begged him not to return, but he honestly believed that he could help his country and left for home in spite of our warnings. We never saw, or heard, from him again. Others who were on the same flight back to Liberia say that when the Pan Am flight landed at Roberts Field, he was met by a squad of soldiers who drove him down to the end of the runway and shot him in plain sight of the horrified passengers.

The insane executions by Doe kicked off a bloody civil war among tribes supported by assorted Army units. Later Sergeant Doe was captured by other units seeking to unseat him and was forced to eat his own body parts before being killed—the war continues to this day.

West African Diamonds

This chance meeting at the bar at the Ducor Hotel in Liberia was the beginning of a rush by the diamond industry to a neighboring country, Sierra Leone. My involvement in the diamond trade occurred later on. The character who I met in the bar in Liberia became a millionaire, I am sure.

In my life I seem to attract treasure troves of precious metals and precious stones, particularly diamonds. In my earlier experiences in Japan I located and turned in to the military authorities, large caches of loot which the Japanese Imperial Staff had taken from the Bank of Japan and hidden with the intention of recovering after the occupation forces had left. A substantial part of this burled loot which passed through my hands was in the form of diamonds. Thus you might say I have an acquired taste for the glittery things in life.

This affinity for diamonds followed me years later to a dingy bar in the Ducor Hotel in Monrovia, Liberia where I was starting on a wild, eight year business trek in West Africa. As I was morosely staring into my beer, wondering what in the hell I was doing in West Africa, another white person strode into the bar, sat down beside me and ordered his drink. The person, who turned out to be a German, came down from Frankfurt every month to do business in Liberia and other countries down the coast. He was a bit vague describing just what kind of business he did, but he looked the part of a character out of a Hemingway novel, complete with ragged shorts, desert boots, and a "bush" hat—all of which was covered with a layer of red dust.

After a bit of perfunctory conversation, he indicated that he was going to have a business meeting at this particular bar, so if he had to abruptly excuse himself, he hoped that I would understand.

As time went by and we had more beers, he became more friendly and indicated that when his customer arrived I could stay, if I wanted. Moments later, a tall, gaunt, black man wearing a dirty white robe and carrying a long pointed staff appeared in the bar and started slowly towards the German who promptly sprang from his bar stool and hugged the man greeting him effusively.

The preliminaries out of the way, the German said, "Well, John, what do you have for me today?" John wordlessly reached into his robes and pulled out one of the dirtiest rags I had ever seen and laid it on the bar. The German in turn reached down under the bar and retrieved a battered and scarred old leather briefcase which he had brought with him, placed it on the bar, and opened it revealing a sparkling new set of optical instruments. While I was still trying to take it all in, he gingerly unfolded the rag revealing to me what looked like a handful of broken glass with rounded edges—yes, they were uncut diamonds.

After painstakingly examination of the stones, the German wrapped them in cotton, placed them in a box, tucked it into his briefcase, and deftly flipped out a Mercedes Benz catalog, placing it before a google-eyed "John." He then leaned over and while talking about the merits of the Mercedes, flipped the pages showing these wonderful cars. "John," with great enthusiasm, ordered a red one, fully equipped with everything but the kitchen sink, and the deal was consummated: the car to be delivered FOB Monrovia in exchange for the diamonds. The black man then gathered his robes around him and strode off with great dignity.

Witnessing this transaction whipped my entrepreneurial instincts to a froth, and I expressed some skepticism about the source of the uncut diamonds—plus the observation that the roads in Monrovia were not fit for travel by a luxury car. *But*, any deal where one could get a handful of diamonds for a car had to be well worth doing. The German indicated that, indeed, the diamonds did come from a diamond field of unknown location, but he suspected that it was located in Sierra Leone, a neighboring country, and, furthermore, he had taken great pains *not* to know anymore about the source other than his monthly meetings with the scroungy looking black man in the Hotel Ducor bar. The only thing he did know was that the black man was an obscure chief on whose lands was a blue clay bank so rich in gem stones that the natives mined them by poking a long sharp pointed stick, such as the chief carried into the bar, into the clay until it met resistance. The natives would then dig with their hands until they uncovered the object. The diamonds themselves were a mixed bag as far as quality went, ranging from industrial to gemstone quality—most, probably, were in the medium and high-end grades. The obscure chief did let the German know in no uncertain terms that his tribesmen would kill any intruders on their land—this certainly got my attention. This chance meeting in a Liberian bar set off a whole series of experiences along the West African coast about which I will recount in chapters to follow.

The Assassination

My good relations with the "Market Woman" undoubtedly saved my life.

One of the most colorful parts of my international experience was the eight years I spent commuting from New York to various spots in West Africa. I traveled mostly, in Nigeria and to a lesser extent in Liberia. During this time I was successful in setting up a number of joint ventures, as well as obtaining contracts with the governments in place at the time.

In Liberia we acted as technical support for the Liberian Postal and Telegraph Ministry; in Nigeria we provided technical and operational support for the Nigerian Army. As a result of my activities, I got to know a great many officials especially in the Nigerian government. Unfortunately, I had a number of obstacles in achieving success. These were characterized by coups (four in number), and assassinations (two in number); one of which I became involved in personally.

The second coup during my stay in Nigeria brought a General Officer and former Minister of Communications to power. His name was Murtala Mohammed.

Although Mohammed, as Minister of Communications, had firmly been on the *sub rosa* payroll of a foreign country, he was a determined and dynamic leader during his reign.

One evening, around midnight, I received a mysterious telephone call and was told by a female voice not to keep any of my appointments the next day. I asked her if she was calling me from the desk at my hotel and she answered affirmatively. Thinking that it was someone, a competitor perhaps, who was sending the woman to frighten me off, I rushed down to the desk to talk with her. When I arrived the clerk assured me that no one had called me from there. Puzzled, I went back to bed and arose the next morning ready to keep my appointments for that day.

One of my Nigerian partners joined me and by taxi we merged with the daily traffic jam to reach our first appointment in the middle of the capital city of Lagos. Our route took us past Dodan Barracks, which were the offices of the Ruler of Nigeria (Mohammed), his Ministries, and the Honor Guard Division. As we joined the line of traffic behind a native bus, I noticed three men in French suits (white/cream color jackets and matching pants) run after the bus and catch on by hanging onto the outside. Since this was nothing new, none of us paid much attention, but we did notice an army sedan which forced its way in front of us.

The occupants were General Murtala Mohammed, the ruler, his aide, Lieutenant Akintunde, and a driver. As we neared the gates of Dodan Barracks, the three men on the bus jumped from it and ran down to a group of three men standing opposite the gate. As General Mohammed's car came abreast of the gate, all six men reached under their coats to reveal Kalashnikov automatic weapons. They ran up to the car, fired into it and fled to the golf course which surrounds the barracks.

As we were right behind Mohammed's car, when the smoke cleared we saw Mohammed slumped in the back; Lieutenant Akintunde dead and halfway out of the car; and the driver severely wounded.

We sat there paralyzed with shock when a multitude of market women from the market nearby started to run toward the scene screaming at the top of their lungs. Realizing the viciousness of market women in general, I requested of my partner that we get the hell out of there. My partner, who was in terror, firmly declined, pointing out that running is an admission of guilt and these women would literally tear us to shreds when they caught us, which they would!

One thing I learned about Africans is that when they get a glazed look in their eyes, they are going to do something violent and if you are standing nearby, it may be to you. While we were trying to decide how to deal with the dead bodies and screaming women, a soldier came running up to our taxi screaming, "Get Out!" He had that look in his eyes. Did he mean, "Get out of the taxi," or did he mean, "Get the taxi out"?

If we tried to leave in the taxi, would he have shot us because we ran?

In the meanwhile (I was white in a black African mob with a coup going on), with as much calm as I could muster, I had the driver fall out of the line of traffic behind us and go back the wrong way.

With my heart in my mouth we started back, and had only gone about one hundred yards from the gate when we were passed by another staff car going to guard the gate with the Chief of Staff in the rear seat. His arrival was greeted by a burst or fire from the assassins who had circled back from the golf course and he too was killed along with his driver.

Fairly shaken, I finally got back to the hotel where I was met by a Technical Representative (Tech. Rep.) from Ford Aerospace, one of my clients. I have always had a soft spot in my heart for Tech. Reps who support projects all over the world under sometimes very primitive conditions. As a breed of cat they are usually unstoppable.

Ralph was no exception.

As I entered the lobby there was Ralph who complained that all he could get on the radio was martial music, and reckoned, thus, that there might be a coup on. When I babbled out what had happened, he put his arm around my shoulders and said, "Jim, I was in Viet Nam when they killed General Diem, the ruler, so I am experienced in these matters. I noticed that you had a bottle of Boodles gin in your cooler, I have the ice. Let's go up to my balcony on the tenth floor and drink your gin cooled by my ice and observe the coup in style."

From the tenth floor we could look down into Dodan Barracks where the elite guards division was quartered and throughout the morning we watched firefights between loyal troops and insurgents. Through our alcoholic haze we heard the voice of Major Dimka who led the coup saying, "We the young revolutionaries are enforcing curfew and all persons seen on the streets between six A.M. and six P.M. will be shot." As anyone knows curfew is between six P.M. and six A.M. We knew that this was going to be a screwed up coup and it was!

Finis

A year later Dimka and the rest of the plotters were taken down to the beach in front of the Holiday Inn, tied to a post and shot. The British community brought their picnic baskets, governesses, children, and dogs and had a high old time of it.

Post Mortem

I wonder which one of my friends was in on the coup and asked the woman to call me for my own protection? I knew enough not to ask.

The Best Sales Job I Ever Did

Once again quick thinking saved me from disaster.

The period of 1980–1990 in Nigeria was not a continuous round of pleasure for visitors, or the general population, especially the Ibo tribes in the south of Nigeria. I personally experienced four coups and changes in the government and two assassinations. Three of the coups and one assassination occurred in Nigeria when I was there over an eight year span.

In one of my other stories I described my getting involved as a bystander in the assassination of General Murtala Mohammed in Lagos. One of the fears that many of us, who were not indigenous to West Africa had, was that we would get caught up in a mob scene at one of these coups and pay the consequences with our lives.

In many Anglo societies, college professors furnish the engine for rebellion, demonstrations, and sometimes ill fated coups. It is interesting to note that sometimes the forces that win the coups execute the fomenters of the coups, i.e. Ivory Tower theorists, media left-wingers, and the fiery orators who fueled the coup or revolution in the first place. So, instead of creating the idealistic socialistic state, they paved the way for their own deaths and disgrace as well as forcing more starvation and disease on the masses that supported them seeking a better life. Unfortunately, the mobs started by these elements had no mind of their own and wantonly killed those in their way, burned their fields and homes, without ever worrying about the consequences.

It was after Murtala Mohammed was killed that a mob, created by the professors at the University of Ibadan who tried to convince the people that the assassination of Mohammed was engineered by the U.S. CIA, (who in my opinion would screw up their own funerals). Consequently, mobs were incited in Ibadan and Lagos to assault the U.S. Embassy and to damage it by whatever means presented itself; namely to burn the embassy and its records and to kill or hold hostage anyone inside.

It was my ill luck to get swept along in such a mob action in Lagos. I saw the streets fill with students clad in leaves and branches (which were the symbols of war) being carried by trucks towards our embassy. I urged my driver to make a beeline towards the U.S. Embassy where I thought I would be safe. The U.S. Ambassador locked the gates to the embassy for some reason thinking he would be safe. As the mob beat down the gates, I crashed through them and jumped out of my car with my driver, ran to the main door of the embassy with the mob singing behind me, chanting "Death to the U.S. Kill the Americans!" At the door I saw, much to my relief, a U.S. Marine.

"Safety at last," I said to myself, but as I glanced behind me I saw the first phalanx of the mob prying stones as big as my head from the street. Closer inspection of the solitary Marine at the door showed he was about eighteen, had a can of mace in his hand and was scared shitless. The mob approached and now they had torches. I pounded on the door and showed the Marine my passport. The Marine shook his head and motioned "No!" I pounded until my hands were bruised and he, I am sure, got a strained hernia from refusing me, a U.S. citizen, from seeking refuge. The U.S. Foreign Service members, who never leave their enclaves overseas, scores again!

Finally, I faced the mob which then surrounded me. Not knowing what they would do to me, a white American, I put my arm around my black driver and said to the mob, "You see, they won't let us in because we are with you!" The student leaders of the mob felt that we *must* be with them, and hence should be accommodated, as no one would be crazy enough to be white and walk among blacks who were being whipped into a frenzy. The mob parted and my driver and I, fighting the urge to run, got into our car and slowly drove away.

Post Mortem

The Embassy was sacked, and records burned. The U.S. Ambassador was at his home when this as going on. What happened to the Marine and his can of mace I will never know. The whole incident illustrates the weak backbone and lack of what the real world is all about by our cookie-pushing, left-wing Ivory Tower liberals. I was spared by the mob—go figure that!!

Hell Lady

This story highlights the old saying "Hell hath no fury like a woman scorned."

Doing business overseas involved meeting all kinds of people: some were quite dangerous; others covered the whole spectrum of the human psyche including people from the seventh ring of Saturn.

I will always remember one particular husband and wife team. She was absolutely gorgeous, having been Miss North Carolina in the late 70's. No shrinking violet was she, about five feet ten inches, well endowed with nature's gifts, and in great physical condition. Her husband, who shall remain nameless, was strictly the academic type having taught at a well known University in the United States.

They had come to Nigeria as a result of my advising the Executive Vice President of a very large defense company in Washington that the easiest way to survive and save money in Lagos was to buy a houseboat, anchor it at the Lagos Yacht Club and live on it, thus saving hundreds of thousand dollars in motel or house rentals.

Furthermore, the person should have a small motor bike to beat the customary traffic jams which occurred continuously all day making travel among customer offices impossible. For up country visits, a Land Rover and driver should be available. With the usual lack of attention common to many large companies, something got lost in the shuffle, because one day serenely sailing into Lagos harbor came a two masted eighty foot sailing vessel with the college professor and his wife aboard. This was a hell of a different approach from my modest recommendation. They had sailed the boat non-stop from Annapolis, Maryland to Lagos. Nigeria. The professor anchored in an arm of the port close to a shore along which were a number of makeshift houses.

Apparently he failed to note that there was construction being started on the opposite bank of a bridge which would span the arm.

As time went on, we would frequently come over to visit and cool off on the deck of the professor's boat, admire his wife, and drink his scotch. The breeze from the harbor kept the bugs away, so all in all it was the idyllic life for "bounders" like ourselves. During this time, my dislike for "ivory tower" types grew because generally they are about as useless as tits on a boar hog in "hands on" situations in the field.

As the bridge was going up, we heard tales of bandits roving around at night in rubber dingies robbing the various boats anchored in the harbor. They made off with anything not tied down and generally scared the hell out of the boat owners. One day I went out to the professor's boat for a wee bit of coffee with a generous dollop of brandy to buoy my spirits. I found the professor in a state of profound hysteria. His story was that he had been awakened by a thumping along side of the boat and rushed up and in an act of courage drove them away.

Miss North Carolina, just sipped her coffee and smiled. My driver was waiting for me on the harbor bank when I returned from the boat and he asked me if I had spoken with "Hell Lady." Not having the slightest idea of what he was talking about, I went on to describe the heroics of the professor.

"No, no," he said, "Hell Lady, Hell Lady. She almost killed my friends."

After expressing my disbelief, he said, "Come, I show you." Whereupon he led me to one of the tin shacks along the bank and there sat three young men looking like they had an unfortunate meeting with the world's most grouchy alligator. These were the bandits!

One man had received several slashes on the head; another had a broken nose and was missing a tooth; and the third man was holding his crotch and was moaning pitifully. The one with the slashed head kept saying, "Hell Lady killed us," and begged me not to tell her where they were.

Finally, I got the whole story. The bandits all of whom lived close by had observed the comings and goings on the boat and decided to rob it while everyone was gone; but they had miscalculated because the professor and wife stayed on the boat after all of their guests had departed. The three bandits got into their rubber dingy and paddled out to the boat around midnight, and were halfway on board of their target when out of nowhere "Hell Lady" appeared from the hatch with a dingy paddle in her hand. With a piercing scream she advanced among the bandits, swinging the paddle wildly and screaming at the top of her voice. Apparently the spectacle of the screaming banshee with her hair all over her head suddenly froze them in their tracks. Transfixed with horror after getting wounded by the paddle in various tender spots, they leapt back over the rail along the deck and paddled away from "Hell Lady" as if the devil himself was after them. Interestingly, the Professor was not in attendance during the particular exercise. Enough said!

No doubt the three young men wake up at night with a picture of "Hell Lady" emerging suddenly in the darkness and chasing them over the rail.

In subsequent visits we all watched the progress of the bridge from the deck of the professor's boat, and every time a section was finished we would urge him to move the boat down to the Lagos Yacht Club located on the bay and use one of their plentiful docks. Each time he would pontificate about the energy wasted on rushing about doing things prematurely, and that there was plenty of time to move. As time went on, we started a betting pool as to when the bridge would be completed and the professor's boat would become a prisoner confined to its mooring place. The professor was blind to our entreaties to move his boat. Finally the professor was called to London to answer for his lack of success in creating business for his company in West Africa and, while he was gone, the bridge builder with a final burst of energy put the last span in place. I was enjoying the professor's best scotch when he arrived on site and although I was a guest and not supposed to laugh, I was having a very difficult time keeping my hilarity in check.

The professor was ferried across from the harbor bank and climbed over the rail whereupon, he viewed for the first time the completed bridge. He assumed the expression of a man having a very difficult bowel movement, and expressed rage that someone would dare to finish the bridge before he was ready to move his boat.

The bridge was too low for the boat to pass under, and the superstructure of the bridge was too high to allow the boat to be easily lifted over. The boat had two very large and very tall aluminum masts full of ropes and other hardware. Removal of these was a very difficult task therefore going under the bridge was not feasible. The Professor then determined, he would wait out the government and let them take care of the problem.

The next day the police served an eviction notice saying that to ignore the notice would result in seizure of the boat by the Nigerian government; he had twenty-four hours to move it.

He retreated into his normal state of withdrawal, and we began to feel sorry for Miss North Carolina. While the professor was whining and crying at the sight of his boat swaying in the wind, we arranged for the proper equipment to raise this eighty foot boat high enough to clear the bridge. This having been done at considerable expense to the professor, we later that week departed with Miss North Carolina, alias "Hell Lady," in tow. We got gloriously drunk on his credit card at the local casino, while I am sure he lay cowering in his bunk twitching with fright at the faintest "thunk." If you have a suspicion that I disliked this S.O.B., you're right!

The Great Bank Robbery

My two partners on a contract for the Ministry of Defense for Nigeria were Major General Alex Madiebo, former Commanding General of the Biafran Army, which participated in the Nigerian Civil war, and Chief Ralph Nwakaby who was Minister of Finance at the time Biafra constituted the southern, oil rich portion of Nigeria, and which in the early 1960's had declared it's independence from the rest of Nigeria. The war was a bloody one with over one million casualties, mostly Biafran, and was based on economic, tribal, and cultural issues.

One day I was having lunch in New York with an acquaintance, who was doing a small amount of business in Africa, when he threw out on the table one of the most colorful currencies I had ever seen with the comment, "Jim, what do you think you could do with this?"

The "this" turned out to be a Nigerian pound which preceded the Nigerian Naira, the current medium of exchange. Interestingly enough, the pound appeared brand new and almost fresh off the press. "How many do you have?" I asked my acquaintance, who rolled his eyes and said, "Oh, about one hundred fifty million in U.S. dollars."

Now the words one hundred fifty million certainly got my attention, and as it turned out, this money was stashed away in Zurich, Switzerland.

On my next trip to Nigeria I brought the one pound note with me, and knowing that one of my partners, Chief Nwakaby, had been Minister of Finance of Biafra, I showed it to him with the smug comment, "I know where there is one hundred fifty million dollars worth of these."

"So do I," he said, "in Zurich."

Having been thus deflated, I got the real story.

Alex Madiebo's troops, early in the war, had advanced to Benin City where Nigeria had what amounts to the equivalent in the U.S. of a Federal Reserve Bank. The Biafrans knocked over the bank, took the money, and transported it to Calabar which was the Biafran temporary capital. There they packed it in boxes, bags, wicker baskets and anything else handy, and flew it to Zurich in a rickety old transport plane under the supervision of a trusted Biafran whom I will call Sam Austin. Sam somehow got the money past Swiss officials into a safe storage area. His assignment was to buy arms and supplies for Biafra. He arrived on a Sunday, and on Monday he saw that the pound had dropped a point on the International Money Exchange (I'm not sure that is the right designator), so he decided to wait until Tuesday before converting to Swiss Francs.

Tuesday arrived and the pound dropped further; Wednesday and Thursday produced further erosion; on Friday Sam had decided that he'd better unload his one hundred fifty million that day! On Friday, one hour before the exchange opened, the Nigerian government announced that the Nigerian pound was no longer a valid currency, and the new currency was the Naira. Old currency would be exchanged one for one, but on any quantities over one million, the sources would have to be verified. So there today sits one hundred fifty million dollars of brand-new money which became worthless because of one man's ignorance and greed, and I feel was a major factor in the Biafrans losing the war.

Post Mortem

I think it might be fun, knowing the turbulence of Africa at that time and the intransigence of its governments, to approach the Nigerian government as representative, *bona fide*, of a smaller country and explain that while rummaging around in the vaults the Minister of Finance stumbled across one hundred-fifty million dollars worth of old currency which one of the former rulers of that country accepted in good faith for goods, but had never spent due to the confusion at the time. It certainly is a serious matter of honor to exchange the old currency for the new currency (Naira), for good relations between the countries...

Wild? Yes—but crazier things have happened! But, perhaps fortunately, I was much too busy at the time to make a mere one hundred fifty million dollars.

Gloria's Dilemma

Gloria was a member of our U.S. Ambassadors staff in Nigeria. Her solution of a delicate issue is an absolute classic.

When God was assembling women he must have been in a generous mood when putting together Gloria. She was tall, stately, and particularly well endowed in all the right places. She had a beautiful singing voice, and had the kind of hearty humor that only a miscreant such as I could love. She was *café au lait* in color, and up from the streets of St. Louis.

She felt she had seen it all, that is before becoming Deputy Economic Counselor at our embassy in Nigeria. Unlike many of our diplomats in the third world nations who stay in their compounds and never come out, Gloria got out amongst the locals and was respected and liked by most of the high ranking ministers and military who were ruling the country at the time. She was also aware that in addition to the government and military infrastructure, there were even more powerful, but unseen influences which overrode even the rulers' desires and commands. These were the religious leaders of the Muslim tribes in Nigeria such as the Sultan of Sokoto, or the Emir of Kano, whose words were sometimes life or death.

On one occasion when I dropped by for a cup of coffee she was in a state of agitation, the source of which was a meeting with the Emir at a government reception. It seems the Emir, being slight of build with bad teeth, was instantly attracted to Gloria and suggested that she become one of his wives (Muslims are polygamous). It seems that he became more insistent as time went by, and Gloria realized that offending the Emir could provoke some very negative diplomatic problems—but by no means did Gloria wish to be one of his wives.

She had spoken of this to the Ambassador who had no real solution to what could end up as a serious problem. This situation did not contribute to Gloria's peace of mind. Knowing that Nigerians have a sense of humor, unless of course they are the butt of the humor, I suggested to Gloria that the best way to deal with proposals of this and other less complicated types was the following:

If the proposer is fat you tell him you think the world of him, but you prefer skinny men; and if he would just lose fifty or so pounds, you would appreciate him more.

If the proposer is skinny, you reverse your reply and suggest he gain fifty or so pounds.

Since no one can gain, or lose, that amount in a short time, they know you are saying no, but in a nice and humorous way. As it turned out, the Emir was a skinny, old man who couldn't gain the fifty pounds if he ate all day, every day. The strategy worked like a charm. The Emir walked away chuckling and knowing he was turned down, but accepting the refusal with good grace. This, my first, and last venture into diplomacy ended successfully and Gloria went on to become one of the best Economic Counselors the Embassy ever had.

Innocence and the Roast Beef

I was a guest at the U.S. Ambassador for Nigeria's house for dinner and Innocence was a houseboy. I still laugh when I remember our very "proper" dinner.

If you have ever dined with an ambassador, be assured that all protocols are scrupulously observed to include consideration of proper seating by rank, conviviality, religion, and its connotations as to what is proper to eat. The State Department takes great pains to ensure that the United States shows a proper image. Usually the furniture, glassware, and silver are first class along with food and drink. Most embassies are well staffed with cooks, stewards, housekeepers, gardeners, and guards. The number of staff and how ornate the embassy was depended on the importance of the post. Since Nigeria, at the time, was the second largest oil supplier to the United States after Saudi Arabia, the U.S. Embassy received a lot of attention particularly in view of the instability of the government.

Somehow I was invited to a formal supper for a number of visiting U.S. oil company "hotshots" who were planning to invest more exploration dollars into the country, and the U.S. Department of Commerce wanted to be sure that these gentlemen were well looked after. The wife of the Ambassador and her staff consisting of the housekeeper, steward, and the cooks turned to and started preparations the day before and obtained for the main course, through diplomatic pouch, a real twenty pound roast beef. In a country where a roast beef on the table is literally worth its weight in gold, its importance was beyond measure. As the roast was being prepared the steward was caught with it under his coat making a bee line for the gate with the cook in hot pursuit. Obviously, the poor man had succumbed to the lure of the roast beef and unfortunately had to be discharged for his thievery. With only a day left before the party the Ambassador's wife, as the hostess, was hard pressed to find a replacement for the departed steward.

In desperation she went to the gardener as a replacement who was a boy of seventeen years of age and was an Ibo Tribesman. The Ibo Tribe is mainly Christian and were converted early on by the British missionaries, many of whom were what today we would call Fundamentalists. As a result of the conversion, many parents named their children after the virtues, i.e. Chastity, Temperance, and so forth. This particular boy was named Innocence. He was a very earnest chap and eager to please, but he had spent his life in the bush and was certainly not used to serving in an Ambassador's home. Nevertheless, the hostess proceeded to give him a crash course on serving in a formal setting and, with only a sliver of confidence, launched him into the living room to serve cocktails, which he did with a great deal of surreptitious prompting from the cook who helped pour the drinks in the kitchen. All went well and our appetites, stimulated by the drinks, were running rampant by the delicious odors of the roast beef.

With a great sigh of expectation we were led into the dining room, seated with great care, according to some grand plan by the hostess. As we sat down to address our prawn cocktails, Innocence very stiffly, but with great dignity, addressed the hostess with such serious mien that we all thought there might be another coup in progress. After all there hadn't been one for six months or so. "Yes, Innocence, what is it?" inquired our hostess. Innocence drew himself up and said, "Madam, a dog just sheet[11] on the rug." Cocktail forks clattered as the proper oil company ladies looked up in shock; the rest of us were convulsed with suppressed laughter. To her credit, the hostess recovered quickly and handled the situation smoothly as all Ambassador's wives should.

This incident was the opener for the series of events which made the evening a memorable one. The second course, which was the soup, was served without any further incidents and the tempting odors of the roast beef filtered through the door from the kitchen as it opened and closed while Innocence was clearing the table and serving the second course. As Innocence was entering the dining room in preparation to serve the anticipated king of all roast beefs, the hostess decided that the roast beef had to be served in the proper formal manner, that is through the "pass through" which was a hinged panel leading to the butler's pantry.

Satisfied that all of the protocols of formal dining would now be observed, she seated herself and engaged in a lively conversation with the

[11] shit

most important of the oil executives. I, on the other hand, sat with quivering taste buds anticipating the grand arrival of the roast beef. Suddenly my dreams of rare roast beef were shattered by a clatter coming from the panty. Abruptly the pass through door flew open, my beloved roast beef emerged on its silver carving plate followed by a pair of arms gingerly holding the plate—this accompanied by the head and shoulders of poor Innocence who followed the orders of the hostess to the letter. I watched in horror as he struggled to get through this opening which was much too small for his shoulders, and to my dismay my roast beef slowly slid off the plate and settled itself onto the dining room rug. While I was contemplating the ruins of the beloved roast beef and thinking, "Oh well, it can be washed off and still be edible," my last hope was dashed. Without warning the kitchen door burst open and the dog, who had been banished to the kitchen for his earlier episode in the living room, bounded through, caught the roast beef on the first bounce and ran to a distant part of the house. All efforts to disengage the dog and the roast were met with growls and baring of teeth discouraging even the bravest of souls from any ideas of rescue.

By this time the poor hostess was in tears which were dried with an extra strong martini. We joined her with a drink while waiting for the cook and for Innocence to disengage himself from the pass through and to set things right. Later the wine was served and we enjoyed a vegetarian repast. We raised our brandies and toasted the late, departed roast beef amid the contented dog like noises emitting from the other part of the house.

Doctor Harry Makes an Extraction

Doctor Harry was a microbiologist who was visiting Nigeria as a consultant for a large U.S. company seeking contracts in West Africa. Also, Dr. Harry was a card player of considerable skill, which in a hostile environment could be extremely dangerous.

To further complicate matters an attempted coup was underway, and a curfew was declared, making it extremely dangerous to be on the street at night.

My adventures with Dr. Harry were harrowing to say the least.

We had our own Dirty Harry long before Clint Eastwood, the actor, appropriated the name for his crime movies. In fact Dirty Harry was the main character in a whole series of very lusty, dirty jokes back in the 1970's. My particular Dirty Harry was Dr. Harry S, a very successful entrepreneur who made a fortune establishing a company in the microbiology field. He was in his best moments obnoxious to the max, not nasty obnoxious, just well-meaning obnoxious, in short, a pain in the ass.

Harry and I were caught up in one of the numerous coups in Nigeria where we were trying to sell a very large medical program to the Minister of Health. While all the shooting and accompanying hysteria was going on, I spent most of my time stabilizing Harry who would go off like a skyrocket at any sudden noise. In addition to his other characteristics, Harry was an inveterate gambler and would bet on almost anything no matter how foolish. Unfortunately for me, everybody had to be home before curfew. The penalty for not observing curfew was running the risk of being shot on sight by the army units patrolling the streets. Doctor Harry seized this opportunity by trying to teach me to play cards. Since my concentration notoriously wanders, I didn't make a very good student and as Harry's frustration rose, the more determined I became to do *anything* to get rid of this gadfly.

Desperately, I reviewed my options. Finally, I decided it was worth risking a bullet somewhere on my anatomy to run the gauntlet of the army patrols with itchy trigger fingers rather than suffer further torture at the hands of Harry. Upon my suggestion that we break the curfew and make a run to the nearby Federal Palace Hotel, which reportedly had a casino of sorts, Harry enthusiastically accepted and sprinted to the taxi stand outside our hotel and was waiting for me with the engine running. After a heated negotiation with the driver, we set a world speed record and arrived at the Federal Palace shaken, but exultant that we were still alive. I am no judge of gambling casinos, but this one had to be out of an Ernest Hemingway novel. We were greeted by a rodent appearing Lebanese manager and escorted to the tables which were manned by Nigerian dealers/croupiers with "observers" overseeing the play.

Harry and I parted at the tables with Harry salivating at the thought of cleaning up. I in turn headed to the bar salivating over the "observers" who were English girls whom God had not neglected in the mammary department. The players suited the whole ambiance of the casino. No Nigerian players, they were all home observing the curfew. There were Arabs in dirty sheets, Greeks, Lebanese, Chinese, etc. All of these were interspersed with a number of very scary looking Lebanese housemen. It was very evident to me that this was not a place in which to start trouble.

As I should have known, trouble appeared after my second drink when Harry suddenly arrived sweating, out of breath, and his eyes had that glistening look of someone who had just struck oil. Clutched, in his hand he held a large paper bag stuffed with money. "Jim" he said, "we will never have to spend a dime for the rest of our lives for expenses in Nigeria." Observing several sour looks from the Lebanese housemen, I shushed Harry and, asked him how much he had won and how had he won it. Harry in his excitement explained in a loud voice that the Roulette wheel was not balanced properly and that the ball was consistently falling in to the same quadrant and that he had won the equivalent of twenty thousand dollars, Naira (Nigerian currency). I finally quieted him down and informed him that if we wanted to be able to walk out unscathed he would be well advised to lose enough to allay any suspicions. Sighing a sigh of relief, I watched Harry disappear in the direction of the Blackjack table secure in the knowledge that Harry would dutifully lose as directed.

Another hour passed amid more sour looks from the Lebanese, and Harry suddenly appeared again he was flushed with excitement and holding a still larger shopping bag stuffed with Naira. Now the eyes of everyone were fixed on Harry and the bag. When I asked him about the details of the larger shopping bag and why he hadn't done what we had agreed upon, he shouted in his excitement, "The dumb sumofovabitches were only playing with two decks and I counted cards!" He had won another twenty thousand dollars.

With as much dignity as we could muster, we sidled towards the door in preparation for a quiet getaway. However, we were intercepted by the manager and his henchmen at the door. The manager commented on our good fortune and suggested that we continue our good luck by staying out of the casino. We both accepted his advice cheerfully and on our way out Harry shouted, "Your wheel wobbles, you dumb bastard!" With that parting shot, giggling like two schoolboys, we ran down the hall pell mell out to the taxi stand, back to our hotel, avoiding the street patrols and sprinkling the Naira along the way.

Epilogue

Although we lived lavishly during this particular stay, I never found out what Harry did with the $60,000 worth of Naira because he passed away shortly thereafter. I am sure that he is cutting cards with the Devil and winning!

A Close Call

A part of the bloody history of Nigeria was the Civil War between the Hausa Tribes of the north, who were Muslims, and the tribes of the south, which were Ibo and Christian. Major General Alex Madiebo, formerly the Commander of the Ibo Army, was my friend. This story was told to me several years after the war was over.

During my business dealings in Nigeria, I met and took on a partner for one of my military projects, the former Commander-in-Chief of the Biafran Army, which opposed the Nigerian Army in their civil war in the 70's. This was a particularly bloody war as it pitted tribe against tribe, Christian against Muslim, and in some cases, family against family. The casualties were well over one million.

My partner was Major General Alex Madiebo, who before the Civil War was Chief of Artillery for the Nigerian Army and was well known and respected by the military. More importantly, he was an Ibo Tribesman, which formed the bulk of the fledgling nation of Biafra. Ibos were primarily Christian. The northern part of Nigeria, which borders on the Sahara Desert was the home of Hausa and Fulani tribesman, all of which were Muslim. The western part of the nation was split between Christian and Muslims. Kano was the capital city of the northern part of the country—no spot for an Ibo to be in if the Muslims were on the rampage.

On the eve of the Civil War, Alex was in the Officers Club and, after an hour wait, had finally gotten to the pool table and was settling down to a long awaited game when he heard a tapping at the window adjacent to where he was standing. Looking up, he saw the face of a Hausa member of his staff frantically motioning to him. Reluctantly he lay down his cue and went outside. His staff member informed him, with tears streaming down his face, that the Nigerian Army was killing off all the Ibo officers and enlisted men in all posts in Nigeria, and Ibo civilians, including women and children. Apparently the slaughter of Ibos in Kano was to be underway immediately. Alex was kept from going back into the club to give the alarm because the staff officer who was Hausa, but loyal to Alex, was risking his own life, as well as that of his family who would be shot out of hand if seen with him.

As Alex was being led to a home which would act as a hiding place for the next month, the killing had started with the Ibos who had the misfortune of living as civilians, or as part of the government, or were part of the Nigerian Army. Huge bonfires had been lit and screams of men, women, and children being thrown into the flames could be heard. (Hausa seemed to believe that fire consumed the soul, this prevents the soul from coming back and seeking revenge of the person who had been killed in some other manner). Alex hid for over 30 days hearing the noises of killing and stories of atrocities, which must have been a living hell. Finally, he decided to make a break for Ibo lands, some 1,000 miles away, cross the Benue River which was the dividing line between Nigeria and Biafra and to fight for Biafra which had declared its sovereignty from the nation of Nigeria. Biafra contains the majority of oil wells in Nigeria and today is a world leader in that sector. Since airports, roads, and rails were being watched by Nigerian Federal Troops, Alex decided that going by rail to the Benue River would be less risky. How wrong he was. Biafra had not yet been invaded as the Federal Army, had not been fully mobilized, so there was some freedom of transport into Biafra and obviously the Ibo fled from the north by any and all means possible.

When the day to flee arrived, Alex disguised himself as a Muslim Imam (religious priest) and boarded a train headed south. Much to the horror of Alex the train was stopped every hundred miles or so, and the Ibos who had gotten on at various points were identified, taken off the train, and executed on the spot. This process continued day and night. Only the disguise Alex wore saved him. Imagine how strong his nerves had to be to withstand the strain of such constant fear for one's life!

Finally the train came to a halt at the last stop before crossing the Benue River where there were customary searches. At this stop the station master approached Alex and said in a low voice, "I know who you are, Colonel Madiebo, you are our savior. The Nigerian Army has set up another guard post in the middle of the bridge over the river, so you are not free. Your country needs you and I will help make your escape successful." Alex was then informed that the engineer and the fireman were Christians and could be trusted. Alex was taken to the cab of the engine where he exchanged clothes with the fireman and the fireman wandered off into the town. The engineer then reassured Alex that he would be safe, but, in view of the fact that the Nigerian Army had set up a trap on the bridge, he should take the precaution to hide in the water tank which was a square metal box, the access to which was a round manhole.

Thus reassured that the train had been inspected many times and no one had ever looked into the water tank, Alex immersed himself in the box full of water up to his neck and settled in the most remote corner. The train slowly left the station and ground to a halt halfway across the bridge, 100 yards from safety. The train was inspected in the usual way, with one exception, a fully armed soldier climbed in the cab with a flashlight, ordered the engineer to remove the manhole cover and proceeded to shine the flashlight into the box. Alex must have frozen in horror as the beam played over the inside. It must have seemed an eternity until the soldier was assured that no one was hiding there. Alex admitted to me personally that he raised the water level in the tank by adding large quantities of his own.

Alex made it safely over the bridge and became the Commander of the Biafran Army, which made a valiant stand against overwhelming odds and was eventually defeated. The country suffered horribly with total casualties well over one million.

Biafra was reunited with the Republic of Nigeria and its citizens have made outstanding contributions in the fields of medicine, law and commerce.

Swindlers I Have Known

Have you ever seen a sinister Confidence Man? No. That is the right answer! As a breed they are almost always either cherubic in appearance, or present a very dignified and almost stately carriage. There is an entire spectrum of swindlers in Wall Street, but I've never had the pleasure of dealing with them—at least to my knowledge.

A typical example of the cherubic type was the head of a U.S. construction company doing business in Nigeria. He was about thirty-two years old, a product of our Midwest, baby blue eyes and an aura of innocence. He was the darling of our State Department in Nigeria and was held up as a model of a successful entrepreneur who was projecting the U.S. image overseas and all of us budding business people should try to be more like him. His contract called for the construction of a number of bungalows to be built as part of a World's Fair in Lagos, then the capital. The contract called for a twenty percent mobilization fee and seventy percent more when the roof was put on the bungalow, leaving only ten percent to be paid upon completion.

I noticed that our hero was accompanied by a "knock dead" looking girlfriend from London; occupied the distinguished visitor suite at our hotel; and always seemed to have a fully stocked bar. The rest of us were subsisting on very poor food and limited supplies of beer. We should have wondered. We did notice that he commuted to London once every seven to ten days with just a briefcase. One day he failed to show up and his girlfriend was transported to the airport for a night flight to Europe. The following week, my friends at the Embassy shamefacedly confessed that their paragon of virtue had closed his headquarters in Lagos and had absconded with fifteen million dollars.

The way that he had gotten the money was to dig a foundation, place a few cinder blocks in the foundation to which he attached vertical supports giving the appearance of work done; to this rigged arrangement he attached a roof and collected his ninety percent of the contract price. In his haste to leave he left a team of very hard bitten laborers up country on the Sahara Desert without pay or transport. As they drifted down to

Lagos each man took an oath to hunt him down and kill him. I am not sure how soundly he sleeps.

One of the biggest and most successful scams to come out of Nigeria involves the following scenario.

A letter is received from Nigeria with an official seal and an imposing letterhead.

The letter informs the addressee that the writer is a member of a select committee formed by the current government to locate hidden accounts by members of the former government.

This group has located a slush fund of thirty million dollars which they wish to transfer to a U.S. Bank.

In order to accomplish this they ask the addressee to make banking arrangements for them and for this they would be willing to give you one third of the amount to be transferred, i.e. ten million dollars.

The "Marks" of course want to hear more, and they reply, "OK, here is what you do."

> Set up a separate account in a bank of your choosing. Obtain a signature card and an ID number for the account. This is necessary so they will be able to process the transfer—they need to show the Nigerian Officials that the transfer is legitimate and that its purpose is to develop export markets for Nigeria. The signature card and the ID number, plus your blank letterhead is almost enough to complete the transaction. All that is left to do is to show that the account is active, and since you are going to make ten million dollars for doing very little, the least you can do is put ten percent into the new account so a one million dollar deposit in good faith isn't asking too much, and after all no one can touch it except us.

The Nigerians then sign the signature card and use the letterhead with a forged signature releasing the one million dollars to another untraceable account. Sounds really dumb doesn't it? Well literally tens of millions of dollars have been lost as a result of this scam. Sometimes they will ask you to come to Nigeria and see for yourself and meet with General X who heads the Ministry of Finance. When this happens, the swindler dresses up his accomplice as a General, who as the Minister of Finance (it's a military government) will personally guarantee the safety of your funds. How could you resist? Sometimes the swindlers will take your passport under the pretense of protecting you from robbers then blackmail you to get it back. Nice guys!

The biggest swindlers of all, however, are the penny stock boiler room operators here in the U.S who buy and sell their own stock by creating a false market for their dubious stocks. One of our local swindlers made up to seven to eight hundred million dollars in this way. It took the government over ten years to make the charges stick.

I could have gone on and on about the subject, but enough is enough. I've seen it all at one time or another.

Take One Wart Hog Tusk and Call Me in the Morning

For those who have had the luxury of taking pills for everything from PMS to lack of active hormones, all forms of human inconvenience are remedied by some sort of pill or another. But those living out in the bush, or out of the reach of qualified doctors, have a different area of concern, sometimes a life or death proposition. In entering the world of "no pills" and "high fallutin'" doctors to magically cure you with impressive degrees, one has no recourse but to go back to nature for cures.

Most modern doctors pooh-pooh the idea of local medicine men muttering incantations over a sick person and giving him some sort of vile fluid to drink. But did the critics ever think about the very mysterious phenomenon of the power of the mind over the body? Don't some of our well-known ministers, as well as those dating back to Jesus, do what we popularly call faith healing? Isn't that what the Shamans and Witch Doctors do?

With regard to vile liquids, pharmaceutical companies spend millions of dollars sending chemical people into the bush to search for various properties in the local vegetation to lead to cures for diseases which native medicines can cure more readily than those developed in sterile scientific laboratories. One example of this is the native medicine for malaria, which exists in several deadly forms in Africa and probably other tropical places in the world. My Nigerian driver, Waudi, introduced me to the effect that native treatments had on the medical cures of the "bush." Shortly after I employed him, he informed me that he had a particularly severe form of recurring malaria and that he may be on his sick bed for a week or so. While in conversation with a Nigerian friend of mine who was educated in London as a Ph.D. in Medicine, I mentioned Waudi's type of malaria. He was aghast and exclaimed, "My God James, you had better find another driver. This boy will never survive." A week later Waudi showed up, clear eyed and vigorous, and obviously none the worse for wear. Upon questioning, Waudi informed me that his malaria returned every year, but upon the first signs, his old grandmother would visit with some sort of vile liquid, which he said was made of palm wine, bark of a tree, and a solution of various leaves pounded to a pulp mixed with the palm wine and boiled. It was served hot and minimized the symptoms which would be deadly if left untreated.

Later I was driving in Northern Nigeria, the part that bordered on the Sahara Desert, and since things were very primitive, i.e. no hotels, restaurants etc., we would always look for a Christian Missionary or white businessman in the small towns we would visit en route. In this particular instance as darkness started to fall, we entered the last village on this particular stretch of the road. Rolling into this village in our Land Rover, we asked in our Pidgin English for the local minister and were answered only by mute stares by the natives who surrounded us, spears and guns conspicuously handy. Finally, a small boy piped up and said, "White man here, there!" pointing down a narrow dirty street with ramshackle buildings. For the equivalent of twenty-five cents he agreed to guide us to the white man. I had a lump in my stomach the size of a basketball from apprehension; after all here I am fifteen hundred miles from Lagos, my home base, and I am being led by a small boy down a dark alley without a friend in sight. It was not a good feeling!

As we climbed up a rickety flight of stairs to the second floor of the building, I wondered what kind of person would live here in this squalor. As I stood there wondering, the small boy knocked, on the door and ran back to the village square where he met us. The knock was answered by a fierce looking African, complete with tribal scars on his face and lips red with betel nut juice. As you may know, the betel nut while a mild narcotic is not something to fool around with. I asked rather timidly whether or not a white man lived here being absolutely sure that no white man would ever live in such wretched conditions if he could possibly help it. The man at the door started shouting and waving his arms in an attempt to frighten us away. I was about to oblige him when I heard a quavering voice saying, "Jonathan, let them come in." As I entered, I saw an old white-haired man seated and wrapped in a blanket, shivering so hard that his chair rattled; his cheeks were sunken; and his eyes a glare with fever. I hastily apologized and prepared to beat a hasty retreat out to the Land Rover, and sleep in the Sahara if necessary. The old man indicated that he was undergoing his periodic attacks of malaria, but Jonathan was almost finished preparing his medicine and that after he took it, he would be OK.

Soon Jonathan returned with a boiling preparation to give to the old man who with every sip seemed to grow stronger, and in minutes it seemed, he cast off his blankets, stood up, shook our hands and, poured Palm wine for me. His transformation was almost miraculous—his eyes glowed, his grip was strong, and new vigor seemed to flow throughout his body. I asked what he thought was in the medicine he had just taken. His reply was that he only knew that one of the ingredients was Palm wine, but the rest was made from various herbs and barks picked by Jonathan in the "bush." Jonathan was unwilling to reveal his secret. After having seen this most amazing transformation take place, I have become a firm believer in native medicine. I have also attained great respect for "casters of spells," but I will cover my experience in that sector in another essay to follow.

In conclusion, you may wonder exactly what the old man was doing in a run down house in a remote village nearby to the Sahara Desert. The answer to this is a phenomenon, which sometimes happens to people who through various circumstances stay too long in the natural environment and "go bush" as the British call it . This results in a slow, slippery decline into the native mode of life and, once into that life, people many times find it difficult, if not impossible, to leave it. Such was the fate of the old man.

The Singing Cockroach

This was an English joke told to me in a bar in Lagos, Nigeria. I, in turn, told it to the Nigerian Minister of Communications. His response still sends me into gales of laughter.

There's the old story about the convict who passed away his time in jail by teaching the resident cockroach to sing diligently. For ten years he painstakingly worked to make the cockroach sing *The Star Spangled Banner*. Finally on the last day of his sentence, the cockroach sang all of the words while standing upon his hind legs and trilling out all of the verses The convict, seeing an opportunity in the singing cockroach, placed it in a matchbox, and took it with him as he left.

After ten years without even a beer, the convict made a beeline for the nearest bar, sat down, ordered a double whiskey. Thinking perhaps to cadge a free drink, he informed the bartender he could teach a cockroach to sing for a free drink. Meanwhile, as he was surreptitiously opening up his match box to release the cockroach, the convict then reiterated the bet that he could make a cockroach sing. As he was saying this the singing cockroach crawled on the bar and was on its hind legs getting ready to sing when the bartender seeing a cockroach on the bar said, "Like this one?" and with one fell swoosh smacked the poor cockroach flat. (The punch line is delivered with a smash of the hand on wood).

The reason that I am dragging the reader through this horrible joke is that it constitutes an occasion where I was rendered speechless, which is, indeed, rare. My wife and I were sitting at a particularly sleazy bar in the Bristol Hotel in Lagos, Nigeria where sanitation was at a lost word. Sitting on my left was an Englishman who had imbibed in several very stout "refreshments." On my right was Irene, my wife, who among other things had an absolute mania about cockroaches. As our drinks were served, a very large cockroach ran past her drink, whereupon she emitted a very shrill scream and springing to her defense, I flattened him with a sharp smack of my hand. The Englishman who had witnessed the execution of the monster bug shook his head sadly and announced in a mournful voice that I had killed his singing cockroach. I roared with laughter and together we composed a Requiem for the cockroach. I don't remember the exact words, but it was an imaginative limerick.

The next day I had an appointment with Mr. Lasode, the Technical Director of the Ministry of Communications, who unbeknownst to me, was a member of some sort of very religious sect of Christians.

I could hardly wait to tell this story to anyone who would listen. Since he was my first appointment of the day, I launched into my story with great enthusiasm and to my pleasure, he was listening intently to every word I said and nodded his head from time to time with a very serious look on his face. I was quite sure that I had made a new friend and that it would be smooth sailing in the future through the ministry. As I finished the story in a gale of laughter I was greeted by absolute silence—you could have heard a pin drop. Finally Lasode said in a very serious voice, "Tell me, Mr. Malony, is it really possible to teach a cockroach to sing?" I was speechless!

Hot Pants

One of the banes of my existence as a major player in the sales and marketing activities of several of my major communications clients was a certain Major General whom I nicknamed "Fat Jack."

Fat Jack was from Texas and being a "good old boy" he attracted the attention of the congressman from his state as well as one of our democrat Presidents from the same site. All of this attention made Fat Jack's ascension to the rank of Major General many times easier than one would normally experience.

To make matters worse in my eyes was that he was loud, abrasive, and fat, fat, fat—not only was he fat, but he was a Signal Officer, and in my Infantryman eyes, a Signal Officer is about as worthless as tits on a boar hog. Although during his active duty days, I had no reason to deal directly with him, I was a victim of some of the dumbest directives I have ever read; and in the matters of procurement, it seemed that to every stratagem I created, down came another policy decision which made my job all the harder.

When Fat Jack's retirement came, there was great rejoicing at various Signal Corps installations. My joy, however, was to be short lived. In the meanwhile, in Nigeria, I had embarked on a major Telecommunications project for AT&T, at that time the world's largest telephone company. A friend of mine whose company was the consultant for the Ministry of Communications of Nigeria approached me with an expression on his face which under ordinary circumstances might signal an oncoming orgasm. In excited tones he informed me that Fat Jack had agreed to join his company in Nigeria as a Project Manager. I smiled to myself at the news because Nigeria is one tough place. Dirt and disease were everywhere, and it is hot and humid in the dry season, and when the barometer drops and the winds come off the Sahara desert filled with red sand with the texture of face powder, craziness is always in attendance.

The arrival of Fat Jack changed a normally calm situation into almost instant chaos. First he demanded a refrigerator for his room—no one gets refrigerators, not even God. Next his air conditioning went down and he was reduced to a wet, soggy hippopotamus like creature—rolling his bloodshot eyes and whining so much so that even the employees who were greeting him as if he were the second coming avoided him like poison.

My friend got Jack calmed down enough to arrange for him to visit the, Technical Director of the Ministry on the basis of protocol meeting (all smiles and compliments). The Director was Muslim, and anyone with a brain in his head *must* acquaint themselves with their customs before making any official visit. Well, leave it to Fat Jack. Upon seating himself in one of the chairs set around the office, he crossed his legs such that the sole of his shoe was directly in the line of sight of the Director; this is a serious insult to any Muslim and the Director took it as such. Fat Jack then took it upon himself to lecture the director as to the failings of his telephone system and, in particular, its management. The Director excused himself to receive an "urgent" call and never came back. My friend later on had to face the consequences of this inexcusable outburst and it almost cost him his very lucrative contract with the Ministry.

Not finished with his days work, Fat Jack distinguished himself at a cocktail party given by the Ambassador for some leading Nigerian businessman and clergy. Fat Jack, like many a Texan, was a "hard shelled" Baptist and his tolerance to any other church was almost nil. West African clergy have much more lenient views on certain commandments which sometimes make for wide interpretations. Fat Jack had targeted one of the more prominent black clergymen of the Anglican Church to loudly impose his Baptist message—ending up his little speech with a patronizing comment that wasn't it wonderful that the Nigerians had advanced from their primitive beliefs to the modern level today? At that, the clergyman smiled benignly and gently poked Fat Jack in his stomach with the same expression that a housewife would view a plump chicken and said "Yes General, we have come a long way very fast. If we had seen you in my grandfather's time, we would have eaten you." Thus properly chastised, Fat Jack left the premises a shocked man.

The next day, my friend with great reluctance arranged to visit the Minister of Communication himself. He would have cheerfully canceled if he hadn't set up the meeting *before* Fat Jack arrived in Lagos. My friend, along with the Director of External Communications, arrived in an old French Peugeot to pick him up and take him to the Ministry. Fat Jack sat in the rear seat while the others sat in front. In Lagos the traffic, at best, is murderous and on the least occasion can back up for miles—and this day was one of *those* days.

The heat was stifling, the humidity was such that it was instant sweat as the traffic moved along at a snail's pace. My friend noticed Fat Jack squirming in the back seat and on many occasions shifting to a new spot on the rear seat. Finally traffic ground to a halt, and at that Fat Jack let out a blood-curdling yell and exited the Peugeot like a cannonball, grabbing at the seat of his pants, which was smoking furiously. Startled, my friend and the Director turned to see Fat Jack's exit accompanied by heavy billows of smoke rolling out of the rear seat window.

Traffic was further stalled when the offending backseat was placed along the roadside. Fat Jack's parts were charred and great blisters were formed on his derriere, accompanied by various whines and groans. Investigation by my friend revealed that the batteries, for the car were placed under the rear seat, which had metal braces framing it. When Fat Jack sat on the seat and the metal frame was pushed down by his weight, it closed the connection across the poles of the battery, this transforming the seat into a sort of a waffle iron with Jack's rear end being cooked.

A curious crowd had gathered around Fat Jack admiring the blisters forming on his rear end, and some were laughing uproariously while pointing at various parts of his anatomy The picture of a famous Major General standing in a circle of Africans with his pants down with other stalled motorists cursing him for holding up traffic is just too delicious.

Fat Jack was treated at the Embassy, issued a rubber donut to sit upon, and evacuated by the U.S., never to be seen again in West Africa. We all breathed a sigh of relief.

The Large Orange Serpent

My German wife Irene (alias, the Iron Maiden) has no fear.

She, being brought up under Hitler, had been a member of the Youth Corps, as well as being firebombed in Dresden. This was capped off by the Russian Occupation and an escape through the barbed wire, which was later replaced by the Berlin Wall. Well, I said no fear, perhaps I exaggerated a little—here was one fear, besides the disgust of cockroaches, and that was of reptiles in any shape or form ranging from geckos to alligators. In Nigeria we had all kinds of deadly snakes and various lizards of all sizes and colors. The smallest of the lizard family there was the gecko who were allowed to run free in homes as they were veracious eaters of mosquitoes and many other types of insects and bugs.

Early in our marriage I thought it would be interesting if she accompanied me to West Africa, Nigeria in particular, to see that part of the world. I had never seen her in any sort of confrontation with reptiles, except maybe those you meet at the Country Club dance, so I assumed she had just the normal reservations—same as everyone else.

Unfortunately, I have this evil streak in me which recognized an opportunity to put her "on," so I conjured up this story which went thusly.

As I was packing for our trip, I remarked in an off-handed manner that around the hotel where we were to stay, there were colonies of large orange colored lizards who were the size of a alligator. While not aggressive, they had the habit of seeking warmth in one's bed. The journey from the vegetation where they lived to the beds of the quests was accomplished by crawling up the side of the hotel into a handy window and into the bed in the room.

I reassured Irene that it was customary to make sure that there was no lizard snoozing away in one's bed by beating the bed covers with a broom, thus awaking the lizard who would then scurry back from whence he came! We arrived at our hotel in Lagos, Nigeria after an exhausting trip from London, and were escorted to our room overlooking some gardens. Our steward, whose name was Wilson and who was formerly a policeman under the British Colonial rule, came to check on us and to see to our needs, if any. Since it was bedtime, Irene, mindful of the orange colored lizard threat, asked Wilson to please bring a broom. Wilson, puffed up with indignation replied "But Madame, I have thoroughly cleaned the room personally and there is no need for a broom."

Irene in her strongest Teutonic manner replied, "Vilson, you vill get the broom right now!" Reluctantly, Wilson brought the broom and stood by. Irene resolutely approached the bed, raised the broom over her head, and with a resounding series of blows attempted to drive the non-existent orange lizard from the bed. Wilson stood frozen with shock of seeing a lady seized apparently by some evil demon beating the bed; upon each series of *whap, whap, whaps* his eyes got larger and larger. As best he could, he sidled out of the room and disappeared without a sound. For the rest of our stay, all of the employees of the hotel, undoubtedly hearing about the strange lady from Wilson, avoided her glances, and detoured in different directions upon her approach.

Finally after a day or so of this, I had to confess to Irene and Wilson about my little prank. For this I paid—the hotel help combined with the wrath of Irene had their revenge. I was subjected to watered down drinks at the hotel bar; brown shoe polish on my black shoes; coffee made with what seemed to be made of carbolic acid; buttons missing from my shirts back from the laundry; and gastronomical distress caused by fiery pepper strategically placed in my food. I finally surrendered by confessing my sins and humbly asking forgiveness to key members of the hotel staff, and life resumed its normal routine of coups, murders, and corruption.

Lions and Tigers

One of my classmates at West Point had started a small services company in Maryland and asked me, as a favor, to drop off his very modest brochure to the Ministry of Defense the next time I was in Nigeria, which I agreed to do. This particular company offered technical support services to Federal and Defense sectors and was made up of ex-officers and some civilian employees in the Defense community, and headed by my classmate, whose last assignment was to run Aberdeen Proving Grounds, the largest test facility in the world.

I had arrived in Lagos in the middle of Hamatan season. This period of the year is to be dreaded, as the winds from the Sahara fill the air with finely gritted red "face powder–like" sand, which fills every crack and cranny of a building, as well as one's lungs. The barometric pressure drops, which causes depression, short temper, and general craziness. This, coupled with the heat and humidity, make life very difficult. To make matters worse, Ramadan, the Muslim period of abstinence, usually coincides with this period—this means no food or water from dawn to dusk—obviously not a good time to try to do business with *anyone* of the Muslim faith.

On Friday of my first week back in Laos, as I drove past the Ministry of Defense on my way back to my hotel, where a shower and a very large cold beer awaited me, I remembered my promise to my classmate. I was tired, sweaty, and dirty but I remembered one of my own rules I tried to impress on my salesman when I was working for large corporations, which was to the effect that 2% is the difference between success (51%) and failure (49%); and that 2% is the extra effort which is extrapolated into such things as making that one last call late Friday afternoon when one is hot, sweaty, and tired and the easiest thing to do is to retire to the motel swimming pool, because that one last purchaser could be *the one* with the big order…

With this in mind, I gritted my teeth and climbed ten floors (the elevator was broken, but so what, everything else was broken in Nigeria). Huffing, puffing, and red-faced I staggered into the office of the Chief of Staff for the Nigerian Army, and addressed a solitary officer sitting at his desk, who, it turned out, was Major General Babangida, the Chief of Staff at the time (later the Ruler).

It was obvious that he was about to depart for the weekend. His briefcases were packed, and his desk was clean. Determined to make my exertions worthwhile, I launched into a very preliminary discussion as to what the Service and Support Company was prepared to do for him. I could see clouds of suspicion gathering as he inquired if I was a mercenary. I replied that we loved our country and our flag, which always comes first, but were always loyal to our customer otherwise. At that he asked what the difference was between loving a country and its flag. My reply was that our flag was a symbol of our country's history and character; but the country, led by President Carter at that time, left a lot to be desired. He then informed me that Nigeria was neutral, they buy equipment from Russia, U.K., and France—none from the U.S., and that he did not want to be placed in a compromising situation by bringing in the U.S.

At that he began to gather his briefcases and other paraphernalia and leave. Seeing that I was losing ground fast, I took one last wild shot. "General Babangida," I said, "you are probably getting ready to drive down to your village." (Many ranking government officials, as well as businessmen, traditionally return to their village on holidays and weekends.) "You will probably park, and walk the rest of the way down the path in the 'bush' to your house—along the path may be lions and tigers each on their own side. If you walk down the middle you are exposed to being eaten by one or the other; but if you walk down on one side, or the other, you are exposed to being eaten by only one or the other, but not both." The General broke into an ugly frown and I *knew* that I had overstepped the bounds of propriety and that I had let my classmate down. "Well," the General growled, "which one are you?"

I smacked his desk with the palm of my hand, looked him in the eye and said, "I am the Lion, Sir! I am King of the Jungle!"

Slowly his expression changed into a broad smile, "Well, Mr. Lion,' he said, "be here at nine A.M. Monday and we'll talk to my staff."

That episode ended in a key contract as Advisers to the Nigerian Army for my classmate's company, which teamed with the Germans for the needed financing. My partners were Major General Alex Madiebo, former Commanding General of the Biafran Army which bought Major General Babangida in the Biafran Civil War, and Chief Ralph Nwakoby former Minister of Finance for Biafra—strange bedfellows, but uniquely effective. The contract itself was all encompassing in scope and had the potential to make all of us very rich. Unfortunately, as time went on, the OPEC cartel fell apart, and the Nigerian Naira became too soft to make it worthwhile. Who would ever know that a last minute meeting with a person just walking in off the street would have this surprising result.

Our first tasks were:

1. Build twelve separate training ranges for small arms firing and tactical missions.
2. Build a central range for tanks, artillery, and other heavy weapons.
3. Oversee the training of the Nigerian Army on the range.
4. Set up and operate a Training and Documentation Command.
5. Create a Ranger School.
6. Create a test range for evaluation of various weapons of other Armies.

The other tasks to follow could have covered everything from Military Hospital upgrades to creation of ammunition factories. The potential was enormous.

Part V

Romping With Uncle Sam

Overview:
The U.S. Defense / Aerospace Domain

My participation in this sector was when it was at its height. A golden tide of funding was flowing for space exploration, as well as fighting the Cold War—good times were rolling for the technology firms and the champagne was flowing. While ITT was the main setting for these stories, I consulted for others to include Litton, Northrup Aviation, McDonnell Aircraft, Western Electric, and LTV all major players at the time. There will probably never be another period like this where the sky was the limit, but I certainly enjoyed it while it lasted.

My Italian Language Lesson

As part of my marketing duties for ITT Federal Systems, I called upon one of my classmates who was in command of Camp Darby near Livorno, Italy. Camp Darby was what we called a "spook" site. In other words, there were lots of intelligence gathering activities, etc. After a night of revelry at the classmate's villa, I emerged groggily the next morning. After bidding the classmate *adieu*, his wife drove me to Pisa to see the Leaning Tower, and from there to the train station. At her urging, I agreed to climb up the balustrades of the tower. After manfully agreeing to do this, I suddenly realized several facts of life. First, I had a raging hangover; secondly I am deathly afraid of heights; thirdly when I look down from a height, I have an urge to jump.

With my female escort watching, I started painfully up the stairs which, to my horror, had no railing. Crablike I held onto the tower walls, afraid to look at anything but the wall itself. Trembling, I made the summit, and on my way back I was drenched with sweat.

In this condition I was delivered to the station where I purchased my First Class ticket and approached my train with a sigh of relief. I was looking forward to a nice quiet ride and perhaps a chance to deal, man to man, with my hangover which by then had assumed gargantuan proportions. While approaching the First Class section of the train, I started to feel some twinges of guilt concerning traveling First Class and never mingling with normal, out of the cookie mold, working class Italians. A brief conversation with a very surprised conductor re-routed me to the Second Class section of the train. As I walked along the aisle, peering into the glass walled compartments, I drew up a list of things to avoid in selecting the ideal compartment. Pretty ladies like Sophia Loren were definitely out because I was sure that any vocal admiration on my part would surely result in her calling for the *Carabinieri* (police), and I would spend the rest of my life not in the jailhouse, but under the jailhouse.

If, on my search for the ideal compartment, I found two rough looking Italian fellows taking slugs out of a bottle of cheap wine, I should studiously avoid that compartment as I am sure that at some point, thirty minutes out of the station, I would have in some way gotten into an altercation. The safest way for me to be transported, along with my hangover, would be to find a compartment occupied by an old lady where my concerns over sex and violence would be put to rest.

With this thought in mind, I discovered a compartment with not only one old lady, but even better yet, two old ladies. They were dressed alike in shiny black dresses; a large bun of grey hair on their heads with a very long, sharp knitting needle thrust through the bun. This needle alone was menacing enough to make even the roughest character mind his manners. I and my hangover selected a seat next to the window and struggled to compose myself for the four hour train trip back to Florence (Firenze). In the meanwhile, I listened to the two old ladies chatting to each other in staccato Italian. While listening to their chatter I noticed they had between them a large wicker bag filled to the brim with what I assumed were clothes, accessories, and whatever; so I paid no heed to the bag. As time went on I heard the ladies opening the bag, and once again, I didn't bother to look up from the book I was reading. Suddenly a horrible smell permeated the entire compartment.

My gorge rose, my eyes watered, and the pounding in my head threatened to burst. The air was filled with the smell garlic, oil, onions, oregano, plus God only knows what else. Frantically looking up, I saw the two old ladies wolfing down one of the largest, nastiest sandwiches that I have ever seen. Gritting my teeth, I desperately tried to keep my breakfast down and addressed myself to my book through blurred eyes.

When at last the air cleared, I sighed a sigh of relief while congratulating myself on soldiering through the assault on my senses. Scarcely had the sigh escaped my lips when I heard the two old ladles who had finished up the offending sandwich, scrounging through the bag again. I half arose from my seat and prepared to flee the compartment in panic.

To my relief I saw the ladies pull out a bottle with a battered label which was falling off and capped by an old cork. The contents of this bottle was a sickly yellow fluid about the color of horse urine (a sick one). Old lady number one raised this awful looking bottle to her lips, pulled the cork with her teeth, spat it in the corner and took a slug and passed the bottle on to old lady number two who enthusiastically partook. My hangover once again kicked in and I sat looking out the window wondering how far to the next station as I was definitely going to escape and find a nice quiet pig pen in which to lay down. This would have seemed like heaven by comparison.

As I sat there feeling sorry for myself, the two chattering old ladies fell silent and I got the distinct impression that someone was staring at me. Slowly I looked up and there was old lady number one holding the bottle of "horse urine" out to me and speaking Italian, from which I deduced she was offering me a drink. In my condition a drink was just what I didn't need; but not wishing to appear rude, and being Irish which means I drink anything that pours, I retrieved from my briefcase my collapsible shot glass which I use for taking my malaria pills. Old lady number one poured a generous dollop of "horse piss" into my cup and passed the bottle to old lady number two who toasted my health.

Now I have drunk a lot of concoctions ranging from Carolina moonshine to Filipino coconut based *tuba*, a drink considered strong enough to impact on men's sanity and senses, but never had I ever tasted anything which tasted so vile. My lips, tongue, and upper olfactory canal were seized with instant paralysis; old ladies numbers one and two smiled approvingly. Immediately we toasted our friendship and this time it didn't taste too bad. I was informed that the "horse piss" was called *Grappa*, which I am sure can be used for many purposes such as varnish remover, rocket fuel, and household cleaner.

After the next toast, the two old ladies decided to teach me a "simple little song" and I was rewarded with another portion of *Grappa* if I got all the words right. By this time, we were all singing in full voice when the conductor entered our compartment to punch our tickets. Upon hearing the words, he shook his head hard, beat a hasty retreat without fulfilling his mission. It suddenly dawned on me that just maybe the "simple little song" might be a bit spicy. So, celebrating the departure of the unfortunate conductor, we calmed our nerves with a little more *Grappa.*

Feeling very Italian, I then suggested to the ladies that they could teach me a few simple phrases which I could use when I arrived in Firenze. These phrases ranged from how to say hello to a pretty lady without her calling the *Carabinieri*, to complimenting the head waiter on his choice of the meal, (which I always asked the head waiter to do) and the selection of wine. The rest of the trip was spent practicing my Italian and graciously accepting *Grappa* as a reward for getting the phrases right.

I arrived in Firenze with my second hangover of the day, and checked into a very nice small hotel in which there was, I had noticed, a very snooty *concierge.* A concierge to a humble person like myself is a godsend, and one whom I depend upon it to keep me out of trouble.

Four hours later after driving demon hangover from my body, I descended upon the *concierge* for advice on dining. I proudly presented my list of Italian phrases and informed the "snooty" one that I had spent hours becoming adept at Italian, but being *very* sophisticated, I wanted to make sure that my pronunciation and inflection was such that I wouldn't accidentally say anything offensive.

Saying this, I thrust the list in front of Snooty for his blessing. Accepting the list, he started to read the *Grappa* soaked paper and immediately dropped it on his desk, and assumed an expression that one's host gets when you have stepped in dog doo and tracked it into the house. He looked at me with a shocked expression saying, "Signore, you must destroy this immediately."

He then pushed the paper back as if it were contaminated and made me promise to destroy it. Normally when in a restaurant in a foreign country, I place myself in the hands of the *maitre d'* in matters of wine and foods and allow him to order for me. Upon completion of the meal if the food and wine were outstanding, I would pay my respects to the *maître d'hôtel* by complementing him on his selection as I paid my bill. I had requested the two old ladies to include an appropriate phrase for this occasion. Judging from Snooty's expression, the phrases which I had been given were naughty, to say the least, so I chose the one which I felt would be the least onerous, which was my thanking the *maître d'*. Snooty reluctantly agreed to translate this phrase, provided I promise to never, ever try to use the language on the paper anywhere else. I agreed. Here is the translation: "You approach the *maître d'hôtel* with the bill in hand, you smile and say, 'Signore, *you are breaking my ass!*' "

Today there are the two old ladies in Palermo, cackling to each other, wondering if the American they met on the train ever got out of the jailhouse.

Cocktails for Two

In the "Brass Knuckles" atmosphere of the race for contracts in the U.S. Aerospace environment, the stakes were high and anything went. This story illustrates my point.

One of the enduring mysteries of my life is, "Whatever happened to the guy on the cocktail wagon?"

I know that there are other deeper mysteries such a decoding human DNA and the origins of the universe, but even more mysterious to me, even greater than the mysteries of the engineering curriculum at West Point, was how a full grown man could completely disappear in a space of five minutes, or less, while confined in an eight feet by eight feet enclosure and in a shaft approximately one hundred feet deep.

Well, I guess I had better explain; maybe you can help me out on this.

In the 1970's, the Aerospace Industry was on a roll—the government was preparing to send a man to the moon, and spending dollars as fast as they could be printed on a full range of hardware for Defense. The marketing efforts were of a "no holds barred" nature; no trick or strategy went untried.

When technical symposiums or conferences were held, the Aerospace and Defense contractors would set up hospitality suites in the leading hotels, and no effort was spared to entertain important government customers and decision makers. The normal suite was complete with only the best booze, snacks, and hostesses of various persuasions. I remember one such "hospitality" formation which was touted as a "Trip around the World."

This certainly rang a bell with some of us as our overactive imaginations prevailed. I wrangled an invitation from a friend who worked in sales for the company and I attended with great anticipation as it was being held in a gym of one of the best schools in the area. My heart was beating with anticipation and not knowing what to expect, I entered the gym and there around the four walls were small bars each decorated with the decor of the country from which the "refreshments" were being offered—rum from Puerto Rico, tequila from Mexico, etc.

In the middle of the floor was a small Red Cross Tent manned by pretty show girls dressed as nurses in very short skirts. Every now and then someone would stagger up and disappear into the tent with one of the nurses attending. I found out later that the host had installed an oxygen producing machine; a deep breath or two of oxygen would revive the drinker who would then resolutely continue the rounds of the bars representing the various countries.

Alas, I seem to have strayed from my original premise that I am still haunted by, my unsolved mystery. At any rate you can see the tones of the times.

I was in charge of our hospitality suite (another place and another time) in Los Angeles. I had taken great care to have the prettiest hostesses, and to set up the finest bar and most luscious goodies on which to nibble (the hostesses were off limits). Our customers were full of good fellowship, and I was licking my lips at the prospect of a golden year ahead with new contracts floating down like snow upon my desk, when suddenly my most hated competitor strolls into our suite, uninvited and starts to avail himself of nibbles, booze, the hostesses and my customers.

Now there is one thing you just don't do in our business, and that is going into anyone's hospitality suite if you are a competitor, and not invited. I tried to ease him gently out of our suite, but he had consumed a number of refreshments and was adamant about staying. I summoned the hostesses and gave them their marching orders to get him drunk and fast, and put him into the adjoining bedroom.

The hostesses accomplished their mission and returned from the bedroom giggling, whereupon with the aid of one of my salesmen, we undressed the offender, placed him naked on a cocktail wagon and displayed him prominently much to the glee of our guests. After several times around the suite where various offerings were placed on his body, we wheeled him out to the elevator and pressed LOBBY on the control panel and stepped smartly back into the hallway; we watched the floor indicator indicate LOBBY and subsequently ran back, into our suite where we waited with bated breath for calls from hotel management.

Time passed and no message from the lobby, no shrill threats from the competitor company, and no appearance of a red eyed, sodden, hung over competitor at our door the next morning.

Discreet inquiries at the desk revealed that no cocktail wagon appeared at the lobby. He just dissolved into the air; and no one reported anyone missing. We decided that we would not inquire at the competitor's company for surely retributions would be extracted. Years later I had occasion to ask whatever happened to good old so and so (I have forgotten his name) from some of the old timers at the competitors and received a tired smile in return, implying something scandalous had happened several years before and that he was in politics and now running for State Treasurer of California. *Wow!* No one, but a politician could have gotten out of that one.

The Nose Knows

This story is one of the funniest situations in which I have ever been involved.

Ivory tower pontificators, button down collars, drinking tea with the pinkie extended, and Ivy League educations have never really appealed to me and although I went to a fancy prep school and had an athletic scholarship to an Ivy League College which provided such an environment, I went to West Point instead.

I have never missed an opportunity to show, and act out, my distaste for phony altruism—give me a good old country environment where we drink "white lightning" and refer to coon hunting and fishing and I will feel right at home. Unfortunately most of my career has been spent in Ivy Land, or in places where no one spoke English at all.

The capital of Ivy Land is either Boston, Massachusetts or Princeton, New Jersey. It was my misfortune to be a Director of Marketing for a small Aerospace company in Princeton, and as such I was exposed to the left wing liberal professors at Princeton, most of whom seemed totally out of contact with the world, occasionally would accept invitations for formal dinners which are okay once you get there, but which I tried to avoid if at all possible.

My first wife, Patricia, felt the same as I do, except she was a Southerner and every now and then the old "red clay" streak would show especially after a cocktail, or two.

We were invited to a formal party in Princeton where our Chairman, Chief Executive Officer, plus members of the Faculty of the Department of Engineering of Princeton University were in attendance. Our hostess was the wife of our Chairman, and a lady of obvious culture. She had unmistakably made a visit to a very expensive lady's wear store and had spent many hours in various salons having everything done from her toenails to her hair, which by quick calculations would add up to ten cents a share on our stock.

The husband, who always had the look of a deer caught in the headlights of an approaching utility vehicle, had clearly surveyed the damage to his checkbook incurred by all these services and reacted like an automaton to all that was, and was about to be, occurring around him. As the guests arrived in all of their finery, some of whom were sporting impressive academic beards, I began counting the minutes until I could be in my car and on my way back to the Jersey Shore.

However, fueled by several very stout Martinis joined by my wife "Petunia Blossom," I enchanted several of the academic wives with a lively discussion of the Sex Life of the Cotton Aphid. I was stopped in my tracks with a scrawny, pigeon breasted, academic wife with hair on her legs who archly informed me that the aforementioned aphid was asexual and probably so was I.

Having set the tone of social civility, I broke all records to be seated away from old "Scrawny Breast" and next to the hostess. Petunia Blossom sat next to a very dignified, fully tenured professor who had not said two words all night. The scene in the dining room was right out of the finest social etiquette books—candlelight, crystal, fine china, select wines, solid silverware, and *aperitifs* served at the proper temperature. There was a fire in the fireplace, and the family terrier, Sparky, was asleep under the table.

As we toasted the occasion to include the professor, who was the guest of honor, a strange odor arose from under the table, innocuous at first, but increasing in intensity. Being a dog owner, I recognized this as a dog fart. Most of the guests, not knowing that Sparky was asleep under the table, glanced hurriedly at each other, while stoically not changing their expressions. As the meal wore on more offerings from Sparky were forthcoming and being nearest to Sparky and the hostess, I would scarcely be recovered from Sparky's last contribution until another emission would occur from under the table. All the guests sat glassy eyed awaiting the next barrage and as dinner wore on Sparky's contributions overcame any efforts to carry on any semblance of civility.

Finally the poor husband said from the other end of the table, "Dear, I think Sparky is a bit indisposed; could you please let him outside." Sparky was led out completely confused as to the extent of his sins; the table fell silent as everyone looked, down at their plates thinking of something to say to break the tension. Suddenly Petunia Blossom looked at the guest of honor sitting next to her and said, brightly, "Boy, what a relief! I thought *that was you all that time!*" I wondered whether or not Sparky had left any room under the table.

Exploring the Moors

I swore to myself that I would never write this as I have always lived by the adage, "Gentlemen Never Tell." However, now that I have reached the tender age of ninety years and I am writing all of these essays for my own enjoyment, I guess it's OK!

First of all, for those of you who have never seen or been in an MG sports car—it is an excruciating experience. In the Army we had an expression for describing a Blivot, which in the vernacular, is two parts of shit stuffed in a one part bag. Well, the similarity is amazing when a normal sized person tries to fit into an MG and since the steering wheel is on the right hand side confusion reigns. While being slightly on the small size, the mysteries of the back seat were unfathomable; one had to be a contortionist to even fit. Well, since the MG is a key scene in this true confession of mine, I do have to dwell on details.

One of my professional experiences was as Assistant to the Chairman of the Plessey Company in England. Plessey, for your general information was one of the principal information technology companies in U.K., and it was one of my jobs to try to expand Plessey's interest in the U.S. Although I was fired later on due to a small disagreement with the Chairman, I commuted routinely to London, and in the course of things, I met an extremely attractive lady who was living with a boyfriend, who was a reasonably high ranking manager of Plessey. He was a sort of a "Veddy, Veddy" English person and was about as amusing as a turd in the punch bowl. We tolerated each other, and that is about all! *Au contraire*, the live in lady and I were quite attracted to each other, but propriety forbade acting out my very erotic day dreams, and even though I was single at the time I still nobly took cold showers when the flames grew too high. In fact, as a result of these showers I acquired a blue tinge and wrinkled skin. Occasional cocktails with her and the boyfriend were my limits.

On my next trip to London, the associate was scheduled to pick me up at Heathrow Airport and transport me back to a company facility about an hour from the airport. He agreed to put me up in his house for the night so I could complete my business and return to London the next day. Much to my surprise, the girl friend showed up in a sporty MG to drive me back explaining that the boyfriend asked her to pick me up and return.

I lowered myself into the MG with a sigh of resignation knowing that the English with all of their maturity and propriety would never, in their wildest dreams make love in an MG, and we sped out of the airport. After approximately twenty five miles the MG suddenly turned off the road into the moors. I guess a moor can be typified as a series of large fields and swamps covered by healthy gorse and other prickly kinds of growth. These moors were covered with ground mist giving them a threatening appearance, I fully expected to hear the howls of *The Hound of the Baskervilles* (Sherlock Holmes).

The silence was broken by the sound of my rushing hormones and feverish activity in Loin City. After much straining and acrobatics, I found myself in the backseat, *sans* most of my apparel, sweating like a horse, but thoroughly enjoying myself as well as spreading as much joy as I was able. In preparation for the departure to boyfriend's house, I groped about in the dark, put back on my apparel, which were completely soaked through by my efforts, and off we went back on the road to our destination. As we pulled up in the circular driveway, "boyfriend," who at six foot two and weighing in at about two hundred thirty five pounds appeared on the porch.

I intuitively reached down to adjust my clothing, and upon looking down I froze with sheer horror, because here I am with my pants on inside out normally no problem. One merely slips off the pants reversing them, and *voila* the problem is solved.

No problem? Are you kidding, this was the 70's style for slacks and the style was tight bottoms—you couldn't get them off until you removed your shoes. I said to myself, "What to do? Boyfriend is going to kill me and I'm too young to die!" Methodically, so as not to show my panic, I quietly opened the car door and went to the side away from "boyfriend" who was being distracted by tons of kisses by "girlfriend."

I was trying my best to slip my feet, with the shoes still on, through the legs of the pants, but instead, I was hopping like a one legged kangaroo taking ever increasingly higher hops. In the meanwhile, "Boyfriend" was inquiring, "Where in the world is James?" (me), and "Girlfriend" was saying, "Oh, he getting his gear (clothes) from the boot (luggage compartment), and he is preparing a surprise."

The surprise would have been me standing in my jockey shorts, with shirt, tie and coat, appearing like the hero in a 1929 stag film with my shoes in my hand, with my offending sex organ doing a disappointing act in my nether region from sheer fright!

After more hopping, and encouraging words to "Boyfriend," I finally got my pants turned around and my shoes on. Confidently, I stepped around the MG and walked slowly towards the couple with a nervous smile on my face, I glanced down just to make sure and here is the offending zipper again on the outside of the pants, but this time at half mast. While walking towards "Boyfriend" I give the zipper a quick jerk and the son of a bitch was stuck. "Keep walking Jim," I said to myself. "Remember what animal trainers say, never show fear to a hostile beast."

Well, this beast wasn't hostile yet, but if I failed the zipper test I was sure that I would be subjected to a violent and involuntary castration. Suddenly, while analyzing my dilemma, both legs without warning developed the worst cramps I ever had and I dropped to the ground with a howl of pain which could have been heard all the way back to the moors. It was obvious to me that my kangaroo hopping had taken its toll. I was carried into the home, moaning with pain and I must say relief as "Girlfriend," spying my zipper condition suggested that my breathing would be helped if I undid my pants. I was put to bed after a few libations and dropped off immediately. The next morning I woke up with a bad cold from my exertions in the, moors, laryngitis, a muscle pull in my back for the same reason and two very sore cramped legs.

This always reminds me of the English joke in which the teacher was explaining to the class about the virtues of abstinence of sex. She finished her impassioned plea by saying, "Now class, just think of the unfortunate results of sex without protection. Is ten seconds of pleasure worth a lifetime of sadness?" The class seemed quite impressed and the teacher asked "Are there any questions?" A boy in the back of the class raised his hand; the teacher happy that she had made a deep impression on the student, said, "Why, yes John, what is your question?" John earnestly replied, "Please Mum, tell me how do you make it last that long?"

In my case it took me two weeks to recover, and my nerves still twitch at the thought of my predicament. So you may ask, "James, was it worth it?" to which I say, "You're damn right!"

Breezez in My BVDses

At Page Communications in Washington D.C., we had an office pool as to who would be the next VP of Marketing. The progenitor of all of this was the President and was famous for his even temper—*he was pissed off all of the time!*

Word was out that if he was ever nice to you, the odds were overwhelming that your professional life was due for a sudden and rude halt. This esoteric attitude carried over to any VP of Marketing who failed to create miracles on call. Hence, our pool became the "Marketing Manager of the Month" exercise. The carpets leading to and from the office of the VP were becoming well worn.

This process produced many bizarre characters, most of them lovable, but just salesman, not marketing managers. There is a difference, a big difference, but I digress. The worst specimen to turn up was a dilettante; an egotistical, arrogant bastard named Mr. K. He came from IBM, which automatically meant that he didn't know our business. He had some sort of New Zealand accent, where he had once served. After thirty days I still had not met him, but boy I had heard a lot about him and all of it was bad! Finally, the other field managers and I were summoned to meet with him at 0900 sharp on a Monday for an important announcement of policy.

"All a-twitter" I flew down from Fort Monmouth, New Jersey where I lived, in a four-passenger plane in bad weather. Running after a cab at Washington National Airport in the rain, I felt a draft in my nether regions, which caused my jockey underwear to freeze. Upon looking for the source of the draft I was horrified to discover that I had ripped my suit pants from belt line to belt line, fully displaying what little manhood the cold draft had left.

As delicately as I could, I slunk into our offices in Washington, and got one of the secretaries in Marketing to locate a needle and thread to sew up my pants. I assumed my place behind my desk in my little office with coat, tie, and shirt, all in place, plus black socks and shoes. The only thing missing was my pants, which the secretary was feverishly sewing up. Following protocol, I called Mr. K's office to explain that I might be a little late because of my current condition. My explanation was curtly brushed aside and I was told to get down the hall NOW! At West Point I was taught to respond immediately to orders given by a superior officer—not that Mr. K was superior to anyone, so I marched out of the office area, down the hall, and into Mr. K's office without my pants. I am sure that I looked like a refugee from a 1920's stag film, but I "soldiered on" and took my place with the rest of the field managers around Mr. K's desk.

While I assumed a very casual air, I could see the shocked expressions of the other field managers, and Mr. K's lips working and a twitch in his left eye, which I learned later, was a sign of some sort of inner turmoil. Since I saw that he was completely off balance, I complimented him lavishly about his dedication to time lines and closed by saying that we should try to be more like him.

I was dismissed to go back and get my pants and return to the meeting. I read *Playboy* and oogled the secretaries until I was sure the meeting was over. It was the start of a beautiful friendship, the Marketing Department gave me a standing ovation. Later, he fired me after several other incidents involving my successful endeavors to irritate him. This forced me on to other endeavors by virtue of which I benefited greatly in the dollars and cents department over the years.

Mr. K got his in the end, see my story below about "Yahya."

Yahya

One of my antagonists gets *his!*

Yahya was a "blue" man from the Sahara Desert in northern Africa. A "blue" man was called "blue" because the Fulani tribesmen, a nomadic tribe of Africa occupying the Sahara adjacent to Libya, Morocco and Algeria, traditionally wore robes dyed very dark blue.

This blue dye would run where exposed to sweat and heat, and stain the skin of the wearer blue—the color could not be easily washed off. Yahya through a history of "power plays," good marriages, and so on, became a power behind the throne of King Idris and later Mohammed al-Gaddafi. Like many powerful men who became power brokers, he remained relatively unseen by the public, but he was extremely effective as an agent for many large corporations, several of which were U.S., British, and French oil companies. Besides being powerful, Yahya was an absolute "wild" man. Wine, women, fighting, physical violence; you name it, he either has done it, or is getting ready to do it, or will do it in the future. Yahya could neither read nor write.

During the later part, of the 1960's, I worked for an international telecommunications company called Page Communications Company, which was a subsidiary of Northrop Aircraft Company, a major defense contractor. Our VP of Marketing was an arrogant horse's ass named Mr. K and people did not wish him well.

Mr. K was also very proper, and as we used to say, "He wouldn't say shit if he had a mouthful of it." The expression was a bit nasty, but true. After six months of banging around and not doing very much, our President, who was just as choleric as Mr. K was arrogant, sent Mr. K on a worldwide trip to visit most all of our agents, one of whom was Yahya.

One word on our posture in Libya is necessary before going further. Page had a contract for Pipeline Communications for the Libyan National Oil Company (or its equivalent). This contract was extremely profitable to Page and it represented around twenty cents per share to the Northrop Aircraft corporate shares listed on the New York Stock Exchange. The loss of this income would be welcomed with swift and unpleasant action.

Mr. K arrived in Tripoli amidst the clarion of bugles and ruffles of drums. There he took the best suite in the leading hotel. He immediately called Yahya's office and informed his secretary that he wanted to see Yahya in the morning; and that he should bring his sales forecast for the forthcoming year along with his sales plan. The next morning two old ex-U.S. Air Force Colonels appeared and informed Mr. K that they represented Yahya, and that Yahya wasn't coming. Mr. K then flew into a rage and informed the Colonels, who incidentally had retired at Wheelus Air Force base nearby, which was part of the U.S. Strategic Air Command (not a pantyhose outfit!), that if he didn't get the forecast plan he would cancel Page's contact with him.

The next morning, promptly the two Colonels appeared with the following message:

- Yahya don't make no f—ing forecasts.
- Yahya don't make no f—ing plan.
- Yahya has his private car parked outside. Yahya says be in it in thirty minutes or less. You're going to the airport and take the first plane out—no matter where it goes—and we're here to see that you're on it.
- Yahya says if you don't get in the car, he is going to kill your f—ing ass.

Mr. K got into the car.

I had come down from Fort Monmouth to talk with some of our engineers. I was taking the elevator up to the same floor where the president's office was located, when Mr. K stepped into the elevator resplendent, believe it or not, in a black suit of crushed velvet. No one had learned of his hasty retreat from Yahya and Libya, so I secretly wondered how high up he was on the arrogance index that particular day.

He curtly nodded and acknowledged my presence as we strolled Indian file past the president's office. Suddenly an arm shot out of the door grabbing the lapel of Mr. K's crushed velvet suit. With as much casualness as I could muster, I peered into the room and saw Joe's secretary, a nice old lady, in a semi-swoon. A fast sweep of the room showed Mr. K with his eyes bulging out like hard boiled eggs and Joe, whose complexion was all colors of an angry sunset, his voice choked with rage, spitting out, "Twenty cents a share, twenty cents a share you *stupid* son-of-a-bitch."

Chuckling to myself I ran down the hall to impart that to the downtrodden sales and marketing troops. I knew that Yahya had made the Mafia traditional "ten cent phone call." Yahya had struck! Mr. K was fired on the spot and as the sun sank over Washington, D.C., we all celebrated and drank to Yahya, our hero. As the two Colonels told Mr. K on the second day of his visit, "Yahya don't take no shit!"

Post Script

What price arrogance?

The Jakarta Giants

My West Point classmate, George, had cut his teeth before entry as a member of the Stage Hands Union in Philadelphia, and as a result, acquired a collection of burlesque jokes which I found hilarious. Early in his career he developed a baseball team while serving in the U.S. Embassy in Jakarta, Indonesia, a very critical spot in the U.S. concerns in the Far East. He named the team the Jakarta Giants. This account traces George's relations with the Ruler of Indonesia, Magssai, and how he became known as "The Green Giant" (like our Paul Bunyan).

Part I

My classmate George Benson became, at least in some defense circles, an expert in Southeastern Asian affairs; particularly in Indonesia, and to a lesser degree in Pakistan; not because of a degree in International Affairs from Georgetown, not with a Master's Degree in Business administration from Harvard, but due to a pick-up baseball game. Since a number of years have passed since he recounted the story of his success to me, I may have overlooked some points, but to me it is placed at the top of stories which appealed to me the most.

George was a product of the Irish section of Philadelphia and his uncle was a Shop Steward of the Stagehands Union, some members of which worked in the leading burlesque theaters there. As a result, George, while he was growing up, did odd jobs for the strippers. I'm not sure, but I think that he might have filled in now and then for the crooners singing *A Pretty Girl Is Like a Melody* under the baby blue spotlight in the wings. He was a natural entertainer and like myself, a free spirit. Only a good Catholic upbringing kept him from joining my select group of incorrigibles. We kept each other amused with a store of very poor burlesque house jokes such as, "I just flew in from Berlin, and boy are my arms tired!"

I had left the Army leaving George to fend for himself when I learned that he had been assigned to the U.S. Embassy in Jakarta, Indonesia, as

Assistant Military Attaché. If there is a more lowly position in the diplomatic chain I can't envision it, unless it's the man who cleans the toilets in a Bombay public restroom. In this lowly position George was in charge of the cooks, buglers, etc., anything no one else wanted—including opening and routing the incoming mail.

One day while dispirited sorting out the mail, he came upon a letter from the president of one of Indonesia's national universities. The letter read as follows:

> We understand that baseball is your national game—we too at the university play baseball. We would be honored if you could come and play baseball against us.

To George this was like manna from heaven, a chance to get out of the damn Embassy and do something, just *anything* as a relief. The university in question was a significant distance up country so, George could anticipate at least a day away from the monotony of "dog robbing" around the Embassy. George replied to the letter informing the president the day and time that he expected to arrive.

Upon arriving, George was greeted by the president formally attired as if for a formal meeting, and here was George clad in khakis. Knowing George, they were probably baggy. After the exchange of greetings, the president asked him if he wanted to see where the game was to be played. George expected to see an open field laid out like the sandlot fields we played on as kids.

Instead, he was lead to a large stadium built for soccer. I don't remember the exact size, but if I remember correctly it held maybe fifteen thousand people, or more. George was planning on just a pick-up game with no spectators and players coming from the Embassy. It suddenly became apparent that the situation was quickly acquiring some diplomatic overtones. When the president assured George that he anticipated that the stadium would be filled, little did George realizes how dark these overtones would become!

A preview of coming attractions occurred when George was explaining to the president the American custom of raising their flag and singing the national anthem. The president thought that this was a terrific idea and enthusiastically informed him that the Indonesian team too would raise *their* flag and sing *their* national anthem. Both seemed delighted with the arrangement until a small matter was brought up as to which flag would fly over the other. The discussion was heating up and headed for disaster when George performed what would be the first of a number of diplomatic gestures in his career. The whole issue disappeared when he suggested that they have two flagpoles, one for the U.S. and one for Indonesia, and that Indonesia be allowed to raise their flag first and sing their national anthem. The date of the game was set for ten days hence, and George departed probably with a sense of dread I know that I would if I had been in his place. Faced with a prospect of finding nine players, plus a pitcher or two, he promptly found enough in the Army and Marine contingents to make up a team.

But there was still the matter of uniforms as the Indonesians had been invaded by the Japanese during WWII and, further having been mistreated by their own Army, reacted violently sometimes to uniformed presence. This seems to have left only commercial baseball uniforms as the safe way to go. George collected enough cigarettes (currency) and sought out a tailor in the Jakarta marketplace and selected the uniform material from roll of bright green cloth with various figures in the background.

The day before the game George picked up the uniforms and was proudly walking down the main corridor in the Embassy when he passed the Ambassador, who hailed him with, "What's in the boxes, George?" Reply, "Uniforms for the team, Mr. Ambassador." "Oh, that's for the game with the national university I've been hearing about, let's see what they look like." As George happily displayed the uniforms the Ambassador's eyeballs assumed a startled look, somewhat like a deer caught in the glare of the headlights of an oncoming car.

"My God George," he gargled "you can't wear these; these uniforms are made from sacred cloth—all of these figures are sacred. If you appear in these, people will come out of the stands and literally tear you apart!" Having been forbidden to wear the sacrilegious uniforms, George reluctantly proceeded up country to the site of the game dressed in Army fatigues, but he took the forbidden uniforms with him. As they approached the stadium, they could see that it was absolutely packed; the field was laid out, but because it dimensions were for soccer, the left field fence was quite short from home plate.

The team had practiced some comedy routines for the warm-up and as they trotted out onto the field in their fatigues, the crowd grew sullen. Their warm-up tricks brought on even more sullen hostility and George had an ever increasing feeling that they were about to get into real trouble. The prevailing logic seemed to be either make a run for it, or take off the fatigues and put on the sacrilegious uniforms. Since the sight of Americans running for their vehicles and unceremoniously leaving is just not acceptable, out came the boxes, and on went the uniforms.

The team came out of the dugout for the rest of the warm-up and were met with a shocked silence—you could have heard a pin drop. As the players nervously looked at each other, a loud belly laugh was emitted from a very fat Indonesian seated in the center field stands. He was laughing so hard that he fell off his seat. Slowly laughter spread around the stands until everyone was laughing uproariously. I suppose the sight was as outrageous as Southern Methodist University football players showing up at Notre Dame in priests' cassocks.

Well, the tension was broken and the crowd started creating nicknames for the various American players. George's name (since he was over six feet tall) was "The Green Giant." That day the Green Giant parked four home runs in the short left field stands. Later he learned that the Indonesian legendary hero was called the Green Giant, who was the equivalent of our Paul Bunyan.

When the team returned to Jakarta they received and responded to many other invitations to play exhibition games. Their team name became the Jakarta Giants, and the Green Giant continued to hit home runs and he became a well known sports figure among the ordinary citizens of Indonesia.

During this period and after Indonesia had not really recovered from the ravages of WWII: the infrastructure was in disarray; the Army was ragtag; and the Red Chinese were just starting to get political control. One day the Ambassador received an invitation from Sukarno, the ruler, to attend a very major reception, but there was a pointed remark that he would like to meet the famous "Green Giant"—George.

George's boss, the Military Attaché, was furious over the fact that his assistant was invited but he wasn't. Little did anyone know the importance to the U.S. later on that George attended.

As the reception progressed, George was brought over to meet Sukarno who, after a few pleasantries, pulled him aside and asked him his opinion as to why all of his people hated their own Army. George answered him directly by pointing out that the Indonesian Army was behaving worse than the Japanese Army did when they were occupying the country—and in turn the people were reacting as enemies.

Taken aback by George's frankness, Sukarno asked him for suggested remedies, all of which involved using the Army to rebuild the villages; helping treating the sick; building roads, bridges, sanitation systems, and, most importantly, treating the people as friends and with respect. Sukarno followed this advice and consulted unofficially with George on far reaching issues that couldn't be directed through the State Department channels. I suspect, even though George wouldn't admit it, he might have made it more difficult for the Red Chinese to make further inroads. George also formed a close relationship with General Suharto, Sukarno's successor, who was but a young rising officer at the time.

The last time I saw George he was the U.S. Representative of Pertimina, the huge Indonesian Oil Company. In the lobby of his office was a huge stuffed Bengal Tiger. I'll bet he charmed it to death.

There's more to this story.

Part II

As a result of the success of the Jakarta Giants baseball team, George Benson, erstwhile star first baseman and Assistant Military Attaché, became known as the Green Giant who had been breaking down fences with home runs. In the incident described before, he had become a trusted person in the eyes of President Sukarno and his senior officers, one of whom was General Suharto, who later became the successor to Sukarno. As a result George had achieved a rare position of trust within the Indonesian power structure, which could certainly not be duplicated in our diplomatic corps.

Unfortunately, all good things have to come to an end and George was reassigned to the basement of the Pentagon, only God knows doing what. It has been rumored that many a young officer has disappeared in the basement only to reappear as a gray-haired old man years later.

George's labors were interrupted by the news that Sukarno was planning to visit the U.S. soon to discuss financial support from the U.S. for his country. This was to be a critical trip for the U.S. as Red China was aggressively trying to buy his allegiance with a combination of bribes and threats. In preparation for his trip Sukarno requested, through the State Department, an aide be made available when he came to the U.S., and as a special request that this aide be Major Benson.

"No problem," said the State Department, eager to please a visiting head of state, "we will make sure that he is available." Department of

State then called the Department Of the Army requesting that Major Benson be available to accompany Sukarno on this critical mission. Department of the Army replied that it was an honor, etc. etc. "Fine then," said the Department of State, "we'll send you the details, and oh, incidentally protocol dictates that any officer escorting a head of state must hold a minimum rank of Brigadier General. Since the head of state specifically asked for Major Benson by name—you must promote him!"

I am sure that never in the history of the modern Army has anyone jumped three grades under *any* circumstances. For weeks the whole issue raged through the Pentagon, and George, who was caught in the middle, was about as popular as a "turd in the punch bowl." The State Department was adamant—Major Benson must be a legitimate Brigadier General. All the colonels with twenty five years in the service glowered; George, all six feet two inches of him, tried to blend into the woodwork. General Johnson, a four star general, was forced into the act and reiterated the Army's position with a thunderous "*No!*"

The situation was imaginatively resolved by the State Department informing Sukarno that the ruler of Pakistan, whom George knew and was a close ally of Sukarno, badly needed George to help solve an urgent problem. So, the whole argument was resolved. Sukarno got his Brigadier; George stayed in the basement; the Colonels smiled again; and that's why the stuffed Bengal Tiger George has in his civilian office is smiling too.

Double Trouble: Lloyd and Floyd

Officer twins escape trouble at Fort Huachuca.

At one period of my life I commuted between Fort Monmouth, New Jersey and Fort Huachuca, Arizona as the worldwide representative of International Telephone and Telegraph Company (ITT) for Army contracts. Although I diligently tried to be humble and respectful to all customers, especially the military segments who invariably were quite taken with their own importance, I sometimes found this difficult. Being an Infantry Unit Commander at heart, I found it troublesome sometimes to appreciate non-combatant Army officers, especially officers of the Signal Corps. Of course, there are exceptions to this rule, and this is how I got to know a set of identical twins named Lloyd and Floyd who had achieved the rank of Colonel: their similarity caused many an embarrassing moment among their peers and contractors doing work for their organization!

I quickly broke the code of "who was who in the zoo."

Lloyd was the wild twin and Floyd was the straight-laced one. Obviously, I gravitated to Lloyd who was also my customer. One day, as a gesture of goodwill, Lloyd invited me to his house for a cocktail, and as each of us had other plans we planned to have just "the one" drink and then go our separate ways.

I duly arrived at Lloyd's house at the appointed time and was met by Mrs. Lloyd, a very lovely, vivacious woman who promptly served gold fish bowl sized Margaritas to Lloyd and myself. Since it was over one hundred degrees outside, we gratefully relieved our dehydration by greedily lapping them down.

Let me take a short time out to describe for the uninitiated just what a Margarita is. I suspect that the Mexicans, after losing their war with the U.S., decided to exact some sort of very sophisticated revenge and invented the Margarita, which is brain numbing when taken to excess (usually after the first one). It consists of a generous helping of Tequila (distilled cactus juice), a less generous portion of an orange flavored liquor (Contreau), lime juice, and a little sugar stirred over crushed ice and served in a large glass rimmed with salt. The whole concoction is delicious and the lime juice offsets the taste of Tequila. In a word, it is *deadly*.

Mrs. Lloyd, being the solicitous hostess that she was, offered us both a second Margarita since she had apparently mixed too many. Well, "waste not want not" I always said, so we manfully downed our Margaritas. At this point the stimulation of the beverages consumed, plus growing pangs of hunger, overcame our plans to go our separate ways and we decided to visit a Korean restaurant run by the wife of a former Master Sergeant who had served under Lloyd in one of his former lives. This restaurant was located about fifteen miles out in the desert near one town, the name of which I forget.

At this point the Margarita score was me, two; Lloyd, two; and Mrs. Lloyd, two. Upon entering we were effusively greeted by the Master Sergeant and escorted to our table which was covered with a hot plate top, just high enough to sit under. A waitress appeared, and so that she would not have to make two trips (being the considerate people we were), we each ordered two Margaritas each (making a total of six). As six gold fish sized drinks were served, Mrs. Lloyd suddenly realized that she had to take a diabetes test the next day and that she shouldn't have had the two drinks at her house much less two more.

Now Lloyd and I were faced with three very large Margaritas each. Now the score was me, five; Lloyd, five; and Mrs. Lloyd two. Mrs. Lloyd then sailed into a description of *her* day and it was like the Hoover Dam breaking, nothing could stop the torrent which veered into all of Lloyd's failings. We downed our Margaritas in record time to at least try to immunize the pain this diatribe from Mrs. Lloyd was taking. By this time Lloyd was getting a little glassy-eyed, either from the torrent of words emitting from his wife's direction, or from the Margaritas. Fortunately, the waitress appeared, turned on the hot plate tabletop, and brought three more Margaritas courtesy of the Master-Sergeant.

Two were set in front of Lloyd, and one in front of me. Score, me six; Lloyd, seven; and Mrs. Lloyd, two. As we were struggling with the last unwanted drinks, the barrage of words from Mrs. Lloyd started again, this time punctuated with some very naughty expressions. While recovering from my shock, I smelled something burning. "Oh well," I thought, "the waitress has put some meat on the hot plate to cook." I turned around to inspect the appetizing prospect, and to my horror there was meat there all right. Lloyd had pitched face forward upon the hot plate with his chin, nose and forehead cooking away. We rushed Lloyd out to the car, absolutely passed out.

Mrs. Lloyd dropped me off at my motel and as she disappeared in the darkness I felt sorrow in my heart for poor Lloyd with his fate in her hands. The next day, somewhat worse for wear for drinking so much cactus juice, I called Lloyd's office to count the fatalities (namely, had the aliens from space carried him away?). The telephone was answered by a voice that sounded like it was scratched across sandpaper, the voice informed me that it was indeed Lloyd and that I should get my little Irish ass out there fast!

Not knowing what indignation Lloyd had suffered after he arrived home the previous night, I approached his office with some trepidation. His office was as silent as a tomb. His secretary, clerks and others noiselessly floated about the office like ghosts and upon entering the inner sanctum of his office I saw this very strange figure sitting at Lloyd's desk. This figure had bright red burns on his forehead, nose and chin and they were just scabbing over. Yes, it was Lloyd OK, but not, the bubbly bright-eyed Lloyd I knew. This one had red bloodshot eyes, the burns, a greenish complexion and palsied hands. He demanded to know what had happened last night to render him in this condition. He further said that his wife had left him last night to spend the night at Floyd's house and that she refused to speak to him.

Suddenly, I was seized by an irresistible urge for revenge against all Signal officers, so I casually asked, "Well, Lloyd, have the M.P.s (Military Police) contacted you yet?" Lloyd turned a shade greener and croaked out, "What M.P.s?" "Those," I replied, "that had to break up that fight you started with those civilians at the Korean restaurant—and boy they were beating the shit out of you before I intervened. The civilian swore out a complaint against you and the M.P.s will serve the complaint after the Post Commander reviews the paperwork. Your wife probably won't speak to you until she speaks with her lawyer in Tucson, at least that's what she said."

Seeing the devastating effect all of this was having on Lloyd's psyche, I convinced him to go to the Post Hospital to get some antibiotics for the burns, and from there to the Officer's Club to advise him on how to take care of his predicament. As we sipped our Margaritas once more, I told him both stories: the one I made up and the one which actually happened; but I didn't tell him which one was which. Fearing the punishment his wife was going to give him more than military justice, he chose the story I made up. I had to tell him that his choice was the wrong one. It took two Margaritas at the Officer's Club to make him smile again.

Bell Hop

Bell Hop was a racehorse who up until the time of his purchase had never raced, and seemed to have an injury or defect in his leg which would have prevented him from ever racing. This was the horse that my aunt Polly Lyman and her husband Colonel Charles Lyman, who had served over forty years in various Cavalry assignments, spent their entire life savings of five thousand dollars to buy.

The time frame was 1940 amid the depression triggered by the 1929 stock market crash which had not completely subsided so five thousand dollars was not chickenfeed. My stepmother, who was a thrifty minded Bostonian, was horrified that *anyone* would spend such a sum for a horse, especially an unsound horse. But what she didn't appreciate fully was that Aunt Polly and Colonel Lyman grew up with horses and they *knew* that the unsound condition of Bell Hop could be easily fixed. So while the original owner of Bell Hop gloated over his coup by selling this lame horse to Aunt Polly, she and Charles were gloating in turn over "stealing" a horse worth far more than the five thousand dollars price tag. My stepmother argued politely that spending all of a person's retirement pay on any kind of a horse was just too much risk. My father who had known all parties for years reviewed the odds against success, but Aunt Polly was adamant.

Six months later, Bell Hop was raced locally in Maryland, Pennsylvania, and Delaware, winning in Bowie, Pimlico, Liberty Bell and other regional racetracks where he paid off his acquisition price and earned Aunt Polly enough to buy three hundred acres of grassland in Chester, Pennsylvania. From the base of Bell Hop's earnings she raised thoroughbreds, including a Kentucky Derby winner, Kauai King, and a runner up, Cosmic Bomb, who was the winner of two of the three races, which make up the Triple Crown. She named her farm Maui Meadows and was syndicated by the prominent Weidner family of Philadelphia and Long Island.

Although she survived Colonel Lyman (Charles) by twenty years, she retained all of the old U.S. Cavalry toughness and minced no words. I took my daughter Angela, who was in her early teens, to the home of

Aunt Polly. Aunt Polly regaled her with all of her Regular Army horse stories, when she commented upon her winning the National Pairs Jumping Championship with some Army Colonel who was stationed at West Point at the same time as she and Colonel Lyman. She was enthusiastically praising her partner for his superb horsemanship and feel for the horse when she stunned my daughter and me by commenting that his talents in bed were far below his talents on a horse. We drove back to New Jersey with our eyes still bulging.

What she accomplished with a five thousand dollar lame horse boggles the mind. She built a three hundred acre farm, raised thoroughbreds and Arabians which she sold for a fortune. She bred a Kentucky Derby winner and a runner-up; rode and won in the Madison Square Garden Horse shows; and was a prominent horsewoman nationally, besides being the judge at the Devon Horse-show in Devon, Pennsylvania—one of the most prestigious shows on the East Coast. She retired a millionaire and her son and his wife are carrying on. Not bad at all, I would say, for an Army wife with no bankroll.

Part VI

One Never Knows, Does One?

Overview: "You Never Know To Whom You Are Talking"

It happens to everyone, usually under very embarrassing circumstances; some amusing, some quite serious. Listed below are true ones which happened to me.

Assassination

One of the enterprises I was asked to set up while in Nigeria was a joint venture bank between a U.S. bank and Nigerian investors. My choice of banks was the American Express Bank, which was arranged by one of my best friends, Jim Greene, and my choice of Nigerians was one Henry Omo, a well-connected Ibo businessman. My friend Jim was a brilliant banker, very polished, high business principles and quite dignified; after much persuasion he agreed to meet Henry Omo and myself in New York.

I was delighted at the prospect of setting up this joint venture and it was with the vision of sugar plums dancing in my head that I met Henry Omo for breakfast at the Plaza Hotel in New York on the appointed day. Much to my surprise Henry appeared with another person whom he identified as one of the investors in the proposed joint venture. My surprise turned to amazement when he was introduced as Lieutenant General Theophilus Danjuma, former Chief of Staff of the Nigerian Army and the most powerful man in Nigeria. I had a most delightful talk with the General, both of us being ex-military. I reported to Jim Greene my conversation with the Nigerian side and spoke of the General in the most glowing terms. As a result visitations were scheduled.

That evening I found waiting for me a book written by Major General Alex Madiebo, formerly Commanding General of the Biafran Army which opposed the Nigerian Army during their civil war. This book traced the events leading up to the assassination of the first ruler of Nigeria, Major General Aguiyi-Ironsi, and there on the first page of the book was a passage that made my blood freeze.

> A group of soldiers seized General Aguiyi-Ironsi at his headquarters, spirited him into the bush near Abeokuta, whereupon he was ordered to dig his own grave by Lieutenant Theophilus Danjuma and was summarily executed thus laying the basis for the civil war which cost a million lives.

Well, you never know to whom you are talking; I introduced an assassin to my best friend on a crucial business deal. Suffice it to say the deal was killed.

The Phoenix Project

Classified counter terrorism by the U.S. in
Viet Nam.

Although much concern and care was directed toward the Vietnamese people in the early days of the Phoenix Project, as is the way of war, there was much misdirection that evolved through the program giving it a reputation for stepping way beyond originally directed bounds.

The Phoenix Project was one of the bloodiest covert projects in the history of U.S. combat. It was implemented during the Viet Nam War and very little has been known about it to this day. Generally its activities could be classified as murder of various target enemies; terrorism; intimidation; ambushes; and wholesale killing of the enemy when met. In other words, giving the Viet Cong a dose of their own medicine. Obviously, this was a very high-risk type of business and took a special type of person to carry out these kinds of missions—choirboys they were not!

One of my friends was a Division Chief for Transmission Systems, part of the Information Systems Command—a very high-up organization within the Department of the Army. As one of his staff, he had this very innocuous seeming Staff Sergeant whose acquaintance I had made over the years; was one of the most self-effacing, gentle guys I had ever met. One day my friend, the Division Chief, was asked to notify the Sergeant that he was to attend an awards ceremony the next day in which chosen personnel would receive awards for various accomplishments. Where upon the Sergeant refused to attend not only that ceremony, but any other similar formation. The Division Chief argued, but without success as to why the Sergeant should attend.

Namely, the Commanding General would have to know of his refusal and a sure result of this would be that he would not only get his ass kicked, but he might be court-marshaled if he refused a direct order from the General. The Sergeant was adamant! He did not care who gave the order, he wasn't going to any award ceremony and that was that. My poor friend, the Director, approached the General who was known for his explosive temper, and upon being informed that a Staff Sergeant had in effect told him to "stuff it" didn't disappoint by exploding into an Olympic class fit. In spite of the Director's pleadings, he called for the Sergeant's records jacket, which always bodes bad news for the owner of the jacket. He dismissed the Director until he called.

Ten minutes passed. The Director's phone rang, and the director's eardrums were almost pierced by the General's shouts. "For Christ's sake! Get your ass down here!"

The Director gingerly stepped into what he considered a viper pit and braced himself for the usual torrent of colorful language issued at a high decibel level. Instead, here sat the General with the records jacket of the Sergeant in front of him, which he tossed at the Director to read. As it was being read, the General said, "The Sergeant doesn't have to attend any ceremony—*ever*—if he doesn't wish to attend!"

Long story short, this quiet, modest Sergeant was a highly commended leader in Phoenix and had numerous citations and medals for bravery in the dirty jungles of Viet Nam. Once again proving that you never know to whom you are talking, regardless of their demeanor or appearance.

Recently, I was telling this story to my friend "Jack," an ex-Colonel who served in Viet Nam in the quiet of a northern, Virginia outdoor restaurant. While making the point of never knowing to whom one is talking and citing the above story, he grew very quiet. He said, "Well, Phoenix wasn't a bad operation."

He took another drink and ten minutes later he said, "It started out as a good clean operation; it's too bad things got out of control." I agreed and we both sipped on our drinks and he grew silent again. Time passed without either of us speaking before he said, "Yeah, everything was okay until a number of 'cowboys' came in and liked what they were doing too much."

I ventured that he, being in Viet Nam for a number of years, probably had heard all about this kind of stuff. After more silence he said, "Jim, I do know about that stuff—I was Director of all Phoenix Operations in Western Viet Nam and Cambodia."

Well, like I said—you never know to whom you are talking.

Golfing With the General

There comes a time in every athlete's life when the light bulb turns on and he discovers the secret of success in a particular activity. In baseball maybe it is to hit a curve ball; in basketball how to hit a fifteen foot, three point shot, etc.

In my case, it was the secret to hitting a golf ball over two hundred fifty yards as a fifteen year old kid. It happened one day when I was playing alone on the course at Fort McNair in Washington, D.C. The second hole on that course was about two hundred forty-five yards, which I had never gotten near. As I teed up my ball, I saw a man and his wife standing on the green getting ready to putt out. Thinking to try a few changes in my swing, and much to my horror, the ball flew like a rocket. I stood transfixed as the ball went on a beeline towards the man who had bent over to tie his shoe, my shout of "*Fore!*" was too late as the ball hit the green and shot forward hitting the man square on his posterior.

With a shrill cry of pain, he jumped straight in the air and started making little bunny jumps around the green. Knowing if my father was told that I had driven into an officer and his wife I would be banned for several weeks from playing—for a true golfer even a day away from the course is a veritable life time. I gathered up my clubs and set a new record for the two hundred forty-five yard dash to where the man stood rubbing his posterior vigorously. As I babbled out my apologies, he asked me who I was and did I always hit the ball that far. Well, of course I wasn't going to admit that I had a break-through shot, I did not discourage the thought that a two hundred and fifty yard drive was a common occurrence (although later on, before I went to West Point, I could drive that distance regularly). I didn't get his name in the stressed condition of my mind, but he was a Major "something or other" and he suggested that I play through before I killed somebody. Years later, as a First Lieutenant, I went over to the Pentagon to visit my father who was on the last assignment of his career. As I was standing in one of the many hallways around the corner came a Four Star General, flanked by two, each Two Star Generals, who in turn were flanked by full Colonels. Suddenly the Four Star General stops and calls to me, "Lieutenant, come over here a minute—what is your name?"

Wondering if I had left my fly open, or stepped in dog droppings, I dispatched myself to his presence, whereupon he said, "Your name is Malony, eh?"

"Yes, Sir," I replied desperately trying to control the quiver in my voice because now I knew who he was. Smiling broadly he turned to the Two Star Generals and said, "Gentleman, this little guy can hit a golf ball further than you ever dreamed." The Generals started to glare at me and the Colonels joined in with their glares. I was still groping for an explanation for all of this when the General said, "Jimmy, I was the guy you hit in the ass with a golf ball at the second hole at Fort McNair! Let's go out to the Army-Navy club this afternoon and hustle the Navy."

I had to refuse because I had to fly back to Fort Sill where I was stationed, but he gave me a standing invitation to call him for golf if the occasion arose—what a career opportunity that could have been. The Major whose butt I had bruised with a golf ball as a kid was General "Tony" McAuliffe, the hero of Bastogne who when asked by the German *Gruppenführer* to surrender as he was surrounded and cut off, replied "NUTS" and endeared himself to the Military and the American public forever.

White Feather

My friend and business partner turns out to be the leader of a major portion of the Ibo Tribe in Nigeria (25 million).

Just as I was putting the finishing touches to my modest collection of stories, I remembered possibly one of the major examples of my uncanny ability to either put my foot in my mouth; or as an alternative to run into, quite by accident mind you, the most bizarre situations.

In some of my former stories, I have described Nigeria at times in the bloodiest terms, and it took me almost eight years to "break the code." To old hands like the British colonials, it was all "duck soup," but to us from the "Colonies" really understanding and dealing with West African culture at a Rubik's Cube with being there from New York, I felt that I was starting to learn. After all I learned that my business associate, in one of my ventures, had been the commanding General of the Biafran Army during the bloody Biafran War which incurred over one million casualties: didn't I also learn never to discuss families, secret societies and colleges which many Nigerians had attended, etc.? Well, yes I did! So now that I was aware of the many pitfalls which await the unwary, I was on the same level as the old veterans from the U.K. How little did I know!

On the competition for one of the large microwave projects for the Nigerian government, we had a very competent business partner named Chukwema (Chuks) Onianwa who ran a Nigerian construction company. He had been a physicist in the Nuclear Science Department at a well-known German University and had married the daughter of one of the professors and had brought her back to Lagos. He was a very mild mannered man, although he was very intelligent, he didn't strike me as the usual butt-kicking tough construction guy who usually ran construction projects. I had tried to involve him in other business ventures, but his outlook was passive and not very entrepreneurial. So while I enjoyed his friendship, I didn't place him in a position of great importance in the overall Nigerian power structure. He was from the Ibo tribe, which had been slaughtered by the Hausa in the Biafran War, and most Ibos were not looked upon with very much favor by the winners (Yoruba and Hausa tribes).

As a matter of professional courtesy, I invited Chuks and his wife to my penthouse flat for dinner and instructed William, my steward, to spare no effort to make sure that everything was ship shape to include wines and food. William was also an Ibo and was a real jewel. There was nothing he could not do including pest control, carpentry, top grade cooking, and of course supervisory skills over the houseboy and various clerks who controlled the household budget. He was important and acted important, so visiting "big shots" did not impress him too much. When I informed William that our guest was a prominent Ibo businessman, his reaction was "ho hum."

Right on time Chuks arrived with his wife. He was spectacular in his silk brocade, robes enhanced with gold thread throughout. I was impressed because I had always seen him in a business suit, where he looked like everyone else. William came out of the kitchen with ice and an array of drinks and when he saw Chuks standing there, the ice and bottles crashed to the floor as he prostrated himself on the floor in front of him kissing the hem of his robe. Chuks patted him on the head and told him to get up. William rushed back into the kitchen with me hot on his tail. He was still trembling when I grabbed him by his shirt and hissed, "What in the hell is going on, are you nuts?"

William said in an uncertain voice, "Master, that is the Chief with the White Feather." Not wishing to leave my guest standing there with ice and bottles over the floor, I returned and asked Chuks what was going on here. What is this White Feather stuff? I was informed that the two most powerful figures in the homogeneous Ibo tribes were the White Feather Chief and the Red Feather Chief. Each represented certain areas of allegiance. And these areas interlocked, thus creating a whole infrastructure. I asked Chuks how many people were under his domain and he answered, "Oh, only about twenty-five million." So here I had invited what I thought was just a business associate who turned out to be a behind the scenes ruler of twenty-five million Ibos. Once again, I have had impressed upon me, *you never know to whom you are talking!* You Never Know Who You are to a King!

Jack the Roofer

Left the British Army in North Africa in WWII and sold tin roofing in Nigeria, ended up selling tin roofs and siding in Nigeria and West Africa, later owned shipping lines from UK and Europe to deliver to building trades in Nigeria. Owned estates in United Kingdom and Switzerland. I mistakenly treated him without respect. His appellation was Jack the Roofer.

A typical American, is one not ever having been involved in the old Colonial atmosphere attendant in the former British and French colonies and is basically unfamiliar with the cast of characters found in the typical colony. Nigeria was such a colony, complete with "old gin bag" wives who hung around the "oh so proper" British military and exclusive civilian club bars soaking up gin until they fell off their bar stools. In addition there were all sizes and flavors of colorful and also sinister characters.

One characteristic of colonial inhabitants was that many of the women who came down from the British Isles sometimes wilted under the heat and aged rapidly into wrinkled up old prunes. Some of the men, if they stayed too long in a particular tropical colony, sometimes "went bush" meaning they grew careless of their dress, drank to excess, and started to take on mannerisms and habits of the natives. We termed these people as "old coasters," some of whom left government or commercial service and lived off the local economy. Every now and then we could find someone who had become fabulously rich and these people always had a very colorful story behind the acquisition of their wealth. One such person was "Jack the Roofer."

The story starts in the bar at the Frankfurter Hof Hotel in Frankfurt, Germany where I sat "calming my nerves" after a three week sojourn in Nigeria, part of which was spent coping with the curfew brought on by the assassination of General Murtula Mohammed, the ruler of Nigeria. Since I had witnessed the assassination my nerves needed a lot of calming. Above the normal hubbub of the bar, I heard a loud Cockney voice from a drunken Englishman on the opposite side of the bar turning the air blue with a stream of curses among which were references to Nigeria. Assuming that this individual had been in the same boat as I, I ordered a drink for him and asked if he had been involved in the attempted coup.

His answer was that no he hadn't been there lately, but that he had done business there in the past. He obviously did not want to get into particulars. He did volunteer that everyone in Nigeria would know his name—Jack (no last name), just "Jack the Roofer." Having turned down his offer of more drinks and a trip to the "Red Light" district, I retired early and forgot my encounter with Jack.

Several years later in Lagos, Nigeria, the English director of Barclays Bank of Nigeria and I were discussing the phenomena of people staying too long in the tropics and going "bush." He brought up some of his remembrances of a few of the old free booters who made millions in Nigeria and other British colonies. I recounted my meeting with "Jack the Roofer" in a Frankfurt bar and offered him as a typical loser who stayed too long in Africa.

The eyes of the Barclays Bank Director widened in surprise at the mention of the name and he started to question me. "Was he coarse and loud? Was he filthy mouthed? Was he drunk, and did he want to go to a prostitute?" I nodded my head and answered all questions affirmatively. The Director then said yes that was the real "Jack the Roofer" all right and that he had a huge estate in Switzerland and a country place in the United Kingdom. "Furthermore," the director said, "Jack is so rich that he could buy and sell the local Barclays if he so chose."

The Director then went on to recount the life of Jack which I found fascinating. It seems that Jack deserted Montgomery's Eighth Army during World War Two in the middle of one of the desert battles with the German General Rommel. As the war progressed and Rommel was defeated, Jack drifted down the West Coast of Africa and found employment selling sheets of corrugated tin which the Nigerians used as building materials. They were used mainly for roof construction, hence the name "Jack the Roofer." Jack worked very diligently and used a bicycle as his main source of transportation, Jack, being a vicious sort, eliminated his local competition by many methods, most of them violent. In time, he became the exclusive agent for his supplier. The corrugated tin manufacturer was within the United Kingdom, and as his financial strength grew he bought out the manufacturer.

Remember the population of Nigeria is over one hundred million people—that's a lot of roofs! Jack topped off his operation by purchasing several freighters to transport the tin from the United Kingdom to Lagos Port, thus ensuring a vertically integrated supply chain to support his near monopoly, and the cash rolled in! He retired to Europe as a multi-millionaire and I am sure that he bought off any charges of desertion from the army. Thus a lowly army deserter and petty criminal who peddled around on a bicycle in the dusty streets of Lagos rose through the ranks of millionaires selling the most common commodity, corrugated tin. I am sure that he worked hard to get there! I am also sure there are many such stories like this one in far off colonies such as Hong Kong, Macao, Manila, etc. In today's competitive business climate and culture these odd type entrepreneurs would be looked upon almost as prehistoric men, but in my book they are the stuff from which fortunes are made through endurance, single mindedness and sheer toughness—my kind of guys! And so for Jack, he justified my old adage: "You Never Know Whom You Are Talking To."

Part VII

Tidbits

The Little Rag Doll

This story about my mother, who as a little girl grew up on the Cavalry Posts in the West in the 1800's. When the Major Military Units moved to new areas, they moved *everything*, and many times through Indian territory, at a danger to themselves. As can be imagined, the scouts, enlisted men who lived in the West, had to be tough as nails to survive.

My mother was Fanny Hunter Lockett before she married my father, Harry James Malony, a First Lieutenant stationed in the Canal Zone in 1915. Her father, Colonel James Lockett, was a well known Cavalry Officer who graduated from West Point in 1879, and whose father was Samuel Lockett who also was a West Point graduate 1854. Samuel Lockett was first a Union Officer, but later resigned to accept a commission in the Confederate Army and built the Confederate defense at Mobile, New Orleans, and Vicksburg.

As you can see my mother was a third generation "Army Brat" and as such followed her mother and father on various assignments throughout the world. It's hard to realize that while she was growing up in current states like Arizona, Montana, Utah, Wyoming, Oklahoma, the Dakotas they were *Indian Territory* and not states at all! These areas were populated by *some* friendly, but other not so friendly Indians, such as the Apache, Shawnee, Sioux, and Blackfoot tribes. So when one crossed Indian Territory they did so at pretty high personal risk, unless they traveled in groups large enough to defend themselves against Indian attacks.

When I was a kid our games were based on the concept of Cowboys and Indians in which we would fire at each other with cap pistols or rubber bands.

When Army detachments were sent to provide protection for settlers or Army encampments, they usually traveled in large groups, and if Army households were being transferred from one Army post to another across Indian Territory it was a movement "en masse" with hundreds of women and children in covered wagons and armed escorts to protect the wagon train. The following true account dealt with such an occurrence.

Upon the occasion of the initial Apollo landing on the moon my father and step mother and I were having a quiet Sunday supper at the Army-Navy Town Club in Washington D.C. As we seated ourselves at our table, we were approached by a distinguished old gentleman. Upon seeing him my father, who was a two star general at the time, had sprung up from his chair and embraced him, and introduced him to my step-mother and myself. "Colonel Johnson," he said, "knew your mother and grandfather very well, and was stationed with them in Indian Territory." Colonel Johnson, after commenting on how much I resembled my birth mother, gratefully accepted a cocktail from the waiter and seated himself and said to me, "Jimmy, I remember your mother well, I knew her as a little girl when we were along the Mexican Border." He then told us this story:

"Your grandfather's regiment was due to transfer a detachment of which I was a Junior Lieutenant from our location near the Mexican border to Fort Reed in Montana which was Blackfoot Indian Territory. The route was through territories inhabited by some very hostile tribes, not, the least of which were several maverick sub-tribes of the Comanche. The greatest threat to anyone leaving the border was usually encountered during the first week when any movement north could be sure to attract the attention of the Chiricahua Apache whose activities it seemed was to kill and scalp all males and to capture all women and children and to subject them to God only knows what atrocities.

"Prior to the departure of the party being transferred to Fort Reed, your grandfather, Colonel James Lockett, who was in command of the party, called the officers, non-commissioned officers, and several senior civilians together and explained the dangers ahead and the absolute necessity to stay with the wagon train at all times. The Colonel added to the seriousness of his instructions by saying that *if* anyone did stray he would court martial the violator and if the violator was a woman or a child, the husband or father would be the one to be court marshaled.

"Lastly, he said, because of the danger of being ambushed by Indians no one, under any circumstances would leave the wagon train to search for the person who turned up missing as if they did the same provisions of the court martial would be applied. Well, after several days travel, the wagons circled as usual at the end of the day and the roll was called, and all were accounted for, except a senior enlisted man who was a First Sergeant and a key person in keeping all aspects of the wagon train order.

"After several efforts to find the First Sergeant failed, it was assumed that he had somehow been spirited away by the Indians and was probably dead. The appreciation of the danger they were in settled like a pall over the camp. Several officers and men volunteered to go back over the days route to find his body or some trace of him, and there were tears in the eyes of those who knew him, but the answer from the Colonel was still a firm 'No!' We posted the guards around the perimeter of our encircled, wagons and settled in for the night with apprehension knowing that our chances to beat off a Comanche attack without receiving casualties in our soldiers, children and wives, were not good.

"Early the next morning, just before dawn, there was an uproar at one of the guard posts; the noises of the yells and cheers roused the Colonel who sat on the edge of his cot rubbing his eyes; suddenly appeared before the startled Colonel was the First Sergeant charging in like a wild man on his horse which was covered with lather and which was on the verge of complete exhaustion. The First Sergeant reached under his shirt which was in tatters and pulled out a rag doll. He dismounted, saluted the Colonel and said, 'Colonel, I know what you said, and I know what you're gonna do to me, but I want to explain to you why I did it.' The Colonel got up from his cot and without a word tore the stripes of his rank from the First Sergeant's shirt and said, 'All right, Private, let's hear it!' The new Private then said, 'Sir, I've spent twenty years here on the frontier and I've seen and done some bad things. I've got a lot of blood on my hands too! This rag doll I have here belongs to your little girl, Fanny, who was playing with it as she sat on the tailgate of the wagon. I guess she didn't know that it had been jolted off the gate until we got to camp last night. When she saw that she had lost it, she started to cry, and Colonel, I can stand a lot of things but I just can't stand to see a little girl cry.'

"The Colonel took the doll to give back to Fanny and dismissed the demoted First Sergeant. Can you imagine in today's society, anyone riding back in the darkness through a territory populated with Indians who would gladly kill you if they caught you, just to find a rag doll for a little girl?"

As he finished his story, I asked Colonel Johnson if the First Sergeant ever got his stripes back. With a twinkle in his eye, he replied, "Well, I guess the old Colonel found a way to make sure the First Sergeant *earned* those stripes the second time (meaning yes)."

I reflected on this story with fascination, for here I was speaking with someone just two generations back talking about Indians and covered wagons, in a time when we landed a man on the moon. The wonder of it all!

Russian Diamonds: The Tax Man Cometh

I don't know why I always seem to get involved with diamonds, I have never made even one dollar from any precious stone, much less the most precious of them all. I suppose it was while I was a twenty-two year old Second Lieutenant in Japan, when I commanded the guard detail at the Bank of Japan in 1945 when we started to discover caches of jewels and precious metals, stolen by certain members of the Imperial Staff. It would have been all too easy to become an instant millionaire which, fifty-five years ago, would have been beyond the reach of all but a few people, but I guess it just wasn't my style.

Several years ago, one of my colleagues called to ask if I knew of a source for yellow diamonds; apparently he didn't realize that yellow diamonds aren't worth very much; but it started a chain of events which still haunts me to this day, and would be a classic marketing case for a master course in International Marketing. As it turned out the whole structure of the diamond industry is so complicated it almost defies logic. I'll go into all of this in a minute.

While tracking down sources for diamonds as a favor for my colleague, and in following the thread leading from mining to final retail, I learned that there were many sources for diamonds other than South Africa, and one of the largest was Russia. Coincidentally I had assisted a female Russian friend in becoming employed as Administrator in the Moscow office of a large transportation firm which could become useful in identifying highly placed Russians if I decided to initiate a project there. Obviously, I had a lot to learn, but I felt that with the proper connections I could do business in about any field.

I was mulling over whether or not to initiate a project in Russia, I casually mentioned the crazy yellow diamond call I had received to another acquaintance who indicated that he had access to the "Diamond District" merchants in New York which were located side by side along two square city blocks 46th and 47th Streets and 6th Avenue. I was told that this area did over sixty percent of the world's wholesale trade in diamonds; and the merchants themselves were Jewish and sometimes Orthodox Jews who act more or less as a closely networked group—one does not casually walk in off the street and try to do business with these people unless you have been sponsored.

The largest members of this group were called "Site Holders" and they did hundreds of millions of dollars in business per year. To appreciate the privileged status of a Site Holder one must realize that they are so designated by De Beers Company and only *they* are invited to attend the auctions which De Beers holds for rough (uncut and unpolished) diamonds the sources for which De Beers holds as a virtual, worldwide monopoly. To maintain this monopoly De Beers plays a very dirty and rough game. Errant Site Holders who disobey De Beers "rules" may be barred from the auctions; if they have no constant source of rough diamonds, they quickly go out of business. Workers in the mines who attempt to smuggle diamonds concealed in various parts of their bodies, are beaten and sometimes killed. People who try to smuggle diamonds out of the territory in larger quantities are trapped and shot on the spot. As one can see, not just anybody can play the game.

After taking a look at making our project viable in Russia, I decided there was enough potential and solicited a major Site Holder who was indirectly related to my acquaintance and secured a contract for a five percent commission on sales for a five year period. His estimated sales volume for Russian diamonds was one hundred million dollars per year once we got started based on, of course, an agreed upon discount from wholesale prices. We avoided the wrath of De Beers by buying only cut gemstones, not rough diamonds.

Well, it appeared to us that we had the sales end of the project pretty well tied up, now to get the source of supply identified and arrangements made to procure and pay for cut and polished diamonds. "No problem," I thought, "The Russians should be falling all over each other to sell to us." How wrong I was! The omnipresent De Beers was ingrained in the government to the extent that Russia had to sell approximately eighty percent of the output of the mines which were located in Siberia to them. Only twenty percent was left to make available to the outside world, but since Russia had at least as much output as South Africa, even that amount was significant. One interesting thing about the Siberian diamond mines was that due to the extreme cold, the carbon monoxide fumes emitted from the mining machinery could not rise and be distributed into the atmosphere, so in the winter operations could be only three days or so during the week.

This of course affected the output. To make the situation even more confusing, there was a continuing contest between central government authority and regional authority as to who would receive the revenues gained from selling the output from the mines located in a particular region. The end result of this situation was a flow of diverted diamonds to sources within Russia and also outside of the country without passing through Central Government Channels. To make things even more confusing, Central Government throughout the Stalin regime, and possibly before that, had been warehousing huge quantities of raw and cut diamonds as a natural asset, in the same manner the U.S. does with gold at Fort Knox. People who were in power were accessing this warehouse, thus creating another flow of diverted diamonds into the world market. There was no doubt that there were enough diamonds available to sell through these channels, but the diamond business is such that secrecy is the order of the day. A person must become known and trusted, *then maybe* they will sell to that person.

So as can be seen, the whole process of just buying large quantities of high quality diamonds is not easy. The process of paying for, or accepting, diamonds makes the acquisition process even more complicated.

In a nutshell this is how the system works:

1. Buyer is made aware of the availability of a specific lot of diamonds.

2. An expert in the employment of the buyer examines the lot.

3. Buyer makes an offer.

4. After negotiations seller accepts.

5. Buyer creates an irrevocable confirmed Letter of Credit from his bank to the seller's bank which confirms the Letter of Credit. Without this confirmation, the Letter of Credit is invalid.

6. The Expert witnesses the packaging of the lot and signs the acceptance.

7. An accredited courier signs for the package which contains the lot, accompanies it through customs and places it in the safe of the carrier on the plane. The plane lands at the destination; and the safe

is opened by the accredited courier; and he delivers at a designated bank vault at the buyer's bank.

8. At this point, the package still belongs to the courier and the courier can't release the package until the buyer examines the contents of the package and accepts it; the bank furnishes a certificate showing the funds to pay for the lot have been transferred by wire to the seller's bank.

It may seem that this process is overly complicated, but the dollars involved are so substantial that a small inattention to detail can cost millions of dollars. One last complication, the Russians generally speaking have no real working capital and to fill certain special orders, they would have to buy the raw diamonds, and pay the diamond cutter before they can deliver. This gets one into a situation where the Russian seller seeks capitalization to fill the buyer's order and the buyer may be at risk in advancing millions to a seller he doesn't really know. My suggestion that the seller could use the buyer's Letter of Credit at the seller's bank as collateral was greeted with complete lack of comprehension.

In spite of all the obstacles, I soldiered on. The female Russian friend recommended a former Deputy Minister of Mines to work with me as an agent; he was a very nice old man who did not speak English at all—but he knew the right people! I made my first trip to Russia strictly an exploratory expedition and the agent certainly brought some interesting people to the "party." One was a Russian woman, Sophi, who had been expelled with her English journalist husband—who I suspect was engaged in a bit of espionage; she was readmitted, he wasn't. She even more than the agent, knew *everybody*.

I returned from Russia very encouraged and made arrangements to return to Moscow as soon as possible.

This time I brought with me the authority to buy one and a half million dollars worth of diamonds as a trial order. I made arrangements to have an expert flown up from Israel to examine the lot which we hoped to locate and buy. I was greeted by the agent and Sophi and after several days of discussions, plus three Russian holidays, we agreed to visit the potential seller the next day.

I forgot to mention that the highlight of my initial trip to Russia was upon my arrival at the hotel while getting out of the car which had brought me from the airport outside of Russia. I saw a number of Russian workers on their hands and knees at the entrance scrubbing the area with hot water and soap removing some reddish brown stains. I inquired from the doorman, who spoke English, what the occasion was; were they expecting a distinguished visitor? The doorman casually answered that no, the American equity owner/manager had been shot with eleven bullets in his body before he hit the ground. When I asked who shot him, he shrugged his shoulders, and to my question "why" he answered, "Because he didn't listen!" My hearing became quite sharpened upon receiving this information.

I mention the above because Moscow was absolutely lawless; kidnapping and murder were quite common; hence, while not being afraid I was *careful!*

The next day Sophi and I awaited the potential seller who was going to send a car to pick us up. Sophi stepped back into the hotel for a minute when a long black Mercedes pulled up and two very large Russians jumped out, grabbed my briefcase and started to hustle me into the car. I yelled for Sophi and pulled away as quickly as I could; Sophi rushed out and much to my embarrassment introduced me to the representatives of the seller. As we left for our destination, one of the "Representatives" turned out to be the Chief of the Committee on Precious Stones and Metals.

He spoke excitedly about motor car racing, and indicated that he was building one to compete in the Darlington 500—a premier race for stock cars in the U.S.—he had done his homework well!

We arrived at a diamond cutting facility where Sophi showed another man the contract that I had signed, with her as a co-agent, with our ex-Deputy Minister of Mines. The second man then came over to speak with me, I thought he was an American, he looked like a good old freckled "country boy" straight out of our Midwest. He spoke "American" complete slang; but he wasn't, he was Russian through and through he was appropriately vague when I complimented him on his command of our language, since he had never visited the U.S. thus causing me to "wonder." Also, the eventual seller was not identified, but a meeting was scheduled with all parties in attendance for the next day.

Our expert from Israel arrived that evening under a cloak of anonymity. He informed me that under no circumstances was he to be identified except at the stages where the diamonds were to be purchased. He informed me further that these precautions were necessary, as the underworld, particularly in Europe, preyed upon experts as sometimes they had diamonds on their person. This whole enterprise was getting spookier and spookier as time went by.

The next day the expert and I were picked up by the same duo of Russians and were transported to a typical gray stoned monolithic building so common in Moscow. While we were waiting in a rather large conference room, the veil of secrecy started to be lifted.

The seller was a company called Ural Platinum and Gold Company, this was an old, established company headquartered in Yekaterinburg. The Russian who spoke perfect American ran their Moscow office. The Deputy of the Committee of Precious Metals and Stones was formerly KGB director of the Oblast (Region) where Ural had their HQ. I was informed that this committee also had access to the huge government hoard of diamonds to which I referred earlier on. If there ever was an interesting set up this was one!

However, when we asked to see the lot of diamonds we wanted to examine, they failed to produce. Out of patience, I decided to fly back to New York. The day of arrival in my office I was informed that the people in Moscow had descended on Ural with a three hundred fifty million dollar delinquent tax assessment—suffice it to say our negotiations came to a screeching halt!

Unfortunately such occurrences were common in Russia. In a Communist society taxes were treated casually, in a capitalistic *society*—you had better damn well pay up! I'm thankful we left Russia when we did.

Well that's the end of the narrative—we had a potential fortune in our hands and we lost it all at the last minute.

I Spy

I received a call one day from a friend of mine who does a lot of international security work with a seemingly innocent request to check into the backlog of a Belgian Arms company which suddenly had grown by an order of magnitude. "This was no big thing," I thought. "A brief phone call was all that was needed to respond to the request, probably five minutes at the most."

It was this phone call which started a web reaching out to almost four corners of the world, and included not only a list of unsavory characters, but murder as well. Here is the list of events as they unfolded.

An investigation of the Belgian company revealed that they produced small missiles and rockets. I then traced their shipments to Frankfurt, Germany, which is a notorious hub for transportation of goods to and from Russia, the Mideast, and Africa. My suspicion was that the Belgian company might be shipping weapons to Iran or Iraq; hence, their huge increase in backlog was due to the influx of large orders from either, or both, countries. Well, as far as I was concerned, that was the end of that as to the favor for my friend. However, there was much about the Belgian company that just didn't seem right, so I asked for more details, some of which just blew my doors off.

1. The Belgian company owned a medium sized military systems company in the U.S. doing classified work for the U.S. Department of Defense.

2. A former member of their board and a consultant was Sir John Bull, the inventor of the Long Gun, which can lob atomic shells hundreds of miles across country borders.

3. A member of the U.S. Company board represented the M family, which claimed to be closely tied to the Royal family of Saudi Arabia, but from my experiences in the past were really Lebanese and very shady indeed.

These inputs added up to some astounding conclusions. Sir John was shot down in the streets of London by an assassin. Since the Belgian company was selling weapons to enemies of Israel and the Long Gun inventor was on their payroll—it was possible that the killing was carried out by the Mossad, Israel's secret service.

This was bad enough, but M Family was angling to get control of the board of the U.S. Company through subversion of its members. So here we have a company doing classified work for the U.S. Government, possibly falling under the control of a non-friendly group to Israel; which was a subsidiary of a Belgian company; which was selling weapons to enemies of the U.S. What a mess!

I told my friend the whole story and asked what was behind the inquiry about the inventory. He asked me if I had ever heard of the Company X of Dallas, Texas to which I replied, "Who in the hell are they?" It turned out that they were stock brokers who specialized in "short sales" which are always triggered by bad news—well I sure had some real *news*.

Who would have thought that such a simple request would have such repercussions? The target company for short sale was the U.S. Company just mentioned.

Several months later the FBI led the top executives of the U.S. companies away on various charges.

Kidnapped

At one time I acted as assistant to the Chairman of Plessy, Ltd., an English company with a desire to do business in the United States. My counterpart was a very, very proper Englishman named Ken, who seemed to be typical in my own mind and soft. I was never so wrong. Here is his story about his kidnapping in the State of Bengal.

In the 1970's, I was assistant to the Chairman of the Plessey Co. Ltd., Sir John Clark, who had driven the company which specialized in military hardware and telecommunications in the U.K. and Europe, and was trying to gain inroads in the U.S. in competition with AT&T, GTE, and ITT, each of which was many times larger than Plessey which lagged behind GEC in its own market in the United Kingdom. In my area of responsibility I got to know the British on all scales of responsibility. This was before my introduction to the British colonies in West and East Africa, so I really didn't appreciate the environment in which the average British colonist was raised. In a word, it was *luxurious*—servants, polo, celebrations, nannies, etc.

One of my associates at Plessey was Ken who was typical of the "high born" British: he came with an Oxford accent; a disdain for all Irish who he deemed as some sort of poorly civilized savage; and surprisingly a very practical view of life honed by a year of captivity by one of the hostile tribes on the Indian/Afghanistan border.

Generally his story was quite simple: his father was Governor-General of Bengal and as such governed a province of tens of millions of Indians plus hundreds of thousands of square miles—in short more than the average Indian country. In short, not just a token Governor, but a real ruler. He was looked up to as such by the population of Bengal. During the British efforts of the colonization of India, which was second to China in terms of population there, was one particular group of Aryan people who stoutly resisted all efforts to subjugate them. Their efforts were such that the British tried on to keep the tribes of the "Northwest Frontier" at bay.

Their border was protected by the mountains and it was impossible to route wild Aryan bands from their strongholds. These bands would periodically raid the British controlled provinces; take hostages; shoot a number of people; seize whatever wasn't tied down; and disappear back into their strongholds. In this environment, the British had to take all precautions for themselves and their families, and usually employed bodyguards when venturing outside their compounds.

One day when Ken was going to the British School outside the Governors Compound with his younger brother and their bodyguard, they were attacked by the Aryans. The bodyguard was killed and Ken was kidnapped—the younger brother was left to give the alarm. Ken was taken to the mountains and a large ransom demand given to Ken's father, the Governor-General. Ken's version of his life among his kidnappers is quite interesting, as they immediately treated him as a member of the tribe. He shared their food, he rode with them on their horses, he played with their sons and joined in their Hindu and Moslem rites (the original Aryans were Hindu).

During his stay he learned the rudiments of their spoken language. Ken confided to me that this period of captivity as a boy was as much fun as he ever had in his youth and that he almost regretted the fact that the British came up with the 100,000£ ransom. When he returned after about nine months, his little brother expressed a keen desire to be kidnapped also and seemed quite disappointed that he didn't share his older brothers adventure.

Can you imagine the stink that our media in the U.S. would have raised? Congress would have mobilized the Army to go in and take Ken from the Aryans which no doubt would have caused him to be killed. Instead the British considered it the "cost of doing business" and Ken was treated with dignity by his captors.

Incidentally, these are the same people who defeated the Russians in Afghanistan in the 1990's—not a group to be taken lightly!

Hot Stuff

When I go to hell for all my trespasses in this life, I am positive that I will be transported to Fort Sill, Oklahoma where the temperature will be stuck at mid-summer temperatures of 110° F in the shade. Believe me this is no exaggeration! Oklahoma ain't no picnic in the summertime, ask anyone who has attended the Field Artillery School there and when I was stationed there, air conditioning was a space age concept as yet unheard of.

On July 3, 1948, a few junior officers, myself included, were told that Col. K our Commander had received orders from the powers that be in Intergalactic Headquarters located in the second quarter of the Universe 2nd Armored Division, Fort Hood, Texas had decided that a small Infantry Unit (meaning us) would present themselves on July 4 complete with band at Cache, Oklahoma and proceed to march down main street, thereby stirring up passions of patriotism among the spectators.

As an aside, Cache is an all Indian town occupied by members of the Shoshone Indian tribe whose home was originally in the mountains and Cache Valley of the area. Its main street, its one street, was a street made of black macadam, which absorbed heat like a sponge. This coupled with the mid-summer Oklahoma heat, the temperature stood around 105 degrees made actually walking on the black asphalt and raising the personal temperature by walking, all to the point of being unbearable. With this miserable prospect in mind, Col. K tried to raise our morale by informing us that we would attend a picnic to celebrate the 4th of July at which home cooked "goodies" would be served as well as unlimited "beverages." The idea of beer, wine, whiskey, etc., seemed particularly attractive after three or four hours in the sun. As we approached Cache in what seemed to be a cauldron, Colonel K urged us forward with promises of "beverages" of all descriptions so we rode on in our motley caravan.

As we dismounted, somewhat wilted and bedraggled, we formed up for the parade—it was hotter than hell! And we were soaked with sweat within 5 minutes; all the heat came up in waves from the black macadam; even the tar had started to melt. The Shoshone Indians lined the street watching us without expression. Now I knew how General Custer must have felt at Little Bighorn. Throughout this "parade from hell" we envisioned cold bottles of beer, and icy highballs of every description. Spurred by these visions, so "soldier" on!

Completely exhausted, we gathered around our vehicles after the parade and I, with Col. K led out our unit to the park where the picnic was to be held with our throats completely parched. As we entered the area, I noticed a pulpit and chairs laid out to form a chapel. Colonel K and I shared a nervous laugh that surely we weren't going to have a church service the attendance to which would certainly interfere with our consumption of drastically needed beverages. Such a thing would be ridiculous to the extreme!

Guess what? We had the church service, which went on interminably, finally ending up with the Indian women setting up the serving tables. I looked wildly about trying to locate where the beverages were being dispensed. My panic and thirst increased proportionally as there appeared to be no beverages in sight.

Frantically, I signaled to Col. K my concern and he reassured me with a conspiratorial wink and indicated that since Cache is a "dry" town, the beverages were probably stored under the counter at the end of the line. Practically dying from thirst (no water available in the park), I eagerly joined the food line the first item to be offered was a leathery piece of meat with a woman serving the sauce that accompanied it. "Want sauce?" said the server, looking for anything liquid, I replied "you bet and plenty of it."

"It's a little hot," said the server. "It's OK." I answered bravely, "the hotter the better."

Thereupon she poured a liberal dollop on the paper plate I was holding. Several serving stations were passed in my haste to get to where the beverages *might* be stored. I arrived on my last leg. By this time, I was thoroughly dehydrated. Raising my eyebrows in a knowing leer, I requested a "beverage." The server replied, "Well, you really are lucky, you are getting the very last one." She reached under the counter into a washtub full of ice; my tonsils were doing the Tango, and I was saying to myself *oboy oboy oboy*!

The last *oboy* died on my lips as I was proudly presented with a large bottle of... strawberry soda. By that time, I didn't care if it was horse pee, I bolted to a chair between two mature Indian ladies and greedily swigged down the whole bottle of the vilest tasting stuff I had ever encountered.

I blew up like a balloon, and had created enough gas to float the *Graf Zeppelin.* There I was marooned between the two women, with my paper plate on my knee, trying to saw through the piece of leather, which passed for meat with a wooden knife and fork. Finally, in desperation, I reached for my pocketknife and sawed energetically on the unyielding meat (it turned out to be buffalo and I'm sure that it had died of old age).

Without warning the meat gave up the struggle, and my knife cut through the meat, soaking the sauce right through my trousers, and cutting a large gash in my leg which promptly started to bleed copiously.

To cover up my confusion, I grabbed my leg and thrust the meat soaked in the sauce into the nearest receptacle, which was my mouth. Simultaneously I was struck by two of the most painful experiences of my life: one was the pain caused by the sauce, which was liquid fire and had flowed from the soggy paper plate into my wound; and the second was from the meat, which I was chewing, which in turn was soaked in the sauce. The strawberry soda in perfect harmony with the sauce was doing its work. This breaks up the party!

In the most diplomatic terms I could muster, I hobbled over to Col. K and told him that I was grievously wounded, I had burned the inside of my mouth with the sauce, and if I had to "pass" that damn sauce I would be permanently injured.

On the way back to Fort Sill, I must have consumed a gallon of water, but my mouth was so swollen that it was tough to put out the fire in my "nether" regions. I never did bring up the question of the "beverages" to Col K, but he did assume a more deferential attitude thereafter.

Taps

In 1945 my father's division, the 94th Infantry Division, after much bloody fighting cracked the Siegfried Switch position, the strongest part of the entire Siegfried Line, which protected the German Fatherland from invasion.

The Germans had worked for decades to make this line of defenses impregnable. Sometimes, up to forty miles deep they hid laced anti-tank ditches, dragons teeth, reinforced concrete pillboxes and bunkers so that there was not an inch of ground not covered with killing fire. The linchpin to this mighty line of fortification was the old Roman City of Trier. If Trier could be taken from the Germans, and the line broken, it could be peeled back like a gate, thereby exposing the entire German defense.

Facing the 94th Division were several famous *Wehrmacht*, German Army Divisions. One was a notorious SS Division which was accused of being responsible for a number of atrocities such as shooting prisoners.

Another was the 7th Panzer Division, called the "Ghost Division," allegedly because the Division Commander drove to Paris in 1938 to accept surrender from the French Garrison commander, who thought that the division was on the outskirts of Paris, when in fact they were a good fifty miles from Paris. When the poor Garrison commander looked around for the German troops after his surrender and upon being reassured that the troops were really there, he exclaimed, "They are like ghosts." The name stuck and they were known as the *Gespensterdivision*.

The fighting between the Ghost Division and the 94th was bloody and vicious with high casualties being sustained on both sides. The graveyards in Luxembourg are filled with bodies of soldiers, both American and German, from both divisions. During the bloody fighting the men of the two divisions gained a healthy respect for one another, and although they were enemies it lasted throughout the campaign and later on after the Germans surrendered, and lasts until this day.

The 94th Division took Trier and broke the Siegfried Switch position breaching the Siegfried line twice. As previously stated, the carnage was terrible. The Ghost Division was reduced to the point that it had to be withdrawn from battle to be re-outfitted. The 94th raced to the Rhine and the Remagen bridge and over it, only to be pulled back by General Patton so that the armored divisions could pour through.

The Division continued its drive until it reached the Czechoslovakian border with Russia where they met the Russian Army. As the process of establishing a peacetime environment in Europe was just beginning, the officers and men of the 94th had time on their hands while awaiting redeployment and discharge. One of the Captains of a rifle company and his men came up with the idea of a monument to peace—not to victory over the Germans; but to hope that the ultimate prize is peace, not big parades and flag waving, just the luxury of being left alone.

The first step was to take up a collection from the soldiers of that company to buy a huge slab of marble from a Czechoslovakian stone cutter with carved lettering, a message for peace. This stone was transported to the German battlefield where the drive to break the Switch Position began. Later the carvings honoring the 94th Division and the Ghost Division were placed on each side of the stone. The ground upon which the Peace Memorial was placed was donated by a German farmer on a hill overlooking the battlefields. The farmer promised to keep up the site, which he has faithfully done all these years.

Several years ago I was asked by members of the 94th Division to present a very elaborate wooden carving to the head of the German War Graves Commission. This carving was of an eagle with the symbols of the 94th and the Ghost Division. In each claw, and from his beak, was a ribbon with a peace message inscribed. I was to meet a representative from the Division at my hotel in Luxembourg, turn over the carving, and tour the battlefields, graveyards, etc.; and attend several affairs over the next few days. The representative arrived accompanied by a foggy drizzle which penetrated to one's bones. As we toured the cemeteries, the destroyed pill boxes and bunkers forty years later still haunted the battlefields. My spirits fell lower and lower after seeing the death and devastation which had visited that land so long ago.

I asked the representative to leave me at the Peace Memorial to reflect. So there I stood in the fog and drizzle looking out over the battlefield, sloping down to the Saar River which took so may lives when the 94th crossed it. I must admit I was a little teary eyed when I sensed someone else was nearby. Glancing out of the corner of my eye I saw an older man with his hat held over his heart staring out over the battlefield and saying a prayer, as was I. When it looked like he was about to turn away, I went over to him and said, "Sir, my name is James Malony, the son of Major General Harry Malony, the commander of the 94th Division." He replied in very broken English, "I am Colonel Thieme, Regimental Commander of the Panzer Grenadiers of the Ghost Division, and I have fought with honor against the 94th."

At that he placed his arm around my shoulder and in a choked voice repeated over and over again "No more, no more, shall we ever fight such a war. Let's pray to God everyday for peace." In retrospect it was almost a miraculous chain of circumstances which brought us together like that.

May the circle never be broken .... TAPS

Eddie's Adventure on the Eighth Fairway

At one time my friend Eddie and I were the only bachelor members of a very swanky country club in Middletown, New Jersey. A large percentage of the members toiled on Wall Street in New York City, hence usually came home late, dog tired, and four martinis to the wind. This work ethic left a number of youngish ladies with a lot of free time.

Eddie and I, having the same "base" appetites, licked our chops at the prospect of cavorting among them like satyrs among wood nymphs and one day while reviewing future prospects we came to the sad conclusion that under no circumstances, whatever, should we lure any wives of members away to view our stamp collections. Over a clicking of our martini glasses we swore a permanent oath that Never! Never! Never, would we even consider such a course of action. *But*, if we did, we would have to tell the other and suffer, a later to be determined, horrendous consequence.

Some time had passed when Eddie approached me with a hang-dog expression, somewhat similar to a pet which has stolen a twenty dollar steak from the outdoor grill just before the company arrived. Eddie indicated that he wasn't sure, but, he thought that he had violated our covenant. He related the following story:

"My date for a dance at the club was a very attractive daughter of one of the senior club members; we had a wonderful time plus a number of cocktails when, in a moment of blind passion, we strolled hand in hand down the eighth fairway (a long par three) bordering the entrance road. Feverishly we tore off our clothes, and sated our maddened lust on the spot. It seemed only moments later when I heard a loud clamoring and whirring sound. I opened my eyes and saw nothing but green and I panicked not knowing where I was or what I had been doing just a short time ago.

"Slowly it dawned on me that I was lying face down in the wet grass. As I was trying to orient myself, I painfully turned my head towards the source of the noise and was immediately blinded by the rays of the sun just coming up over the horizon. I finally cleared my eyes and saw, much to my horror, a mowing machine cutting the adjacent rough. I rose to my knees to get a better look and noticed that a milk truck had driven up to the entrance road and the driver had dismounted and was staring at me much in the same manner as a frog about to catch a fly.

"Suddenly I realized I was standing stark naked in the middle of the fairway adjacent to one of the most exclusive clubs in New Jersey amid a pile of clothes. In a flash of panic I remembered the circumstances of my unseemly presence and further remembered I might not be alone. I was right, about twenty five yards closer to the club house I saw another form also face down amid a pile of clothes; my poor date had tried to crawl back to the sanctuary of the club house and never made it. I crawled twenty-five agonizing yards an my hands and knees, aroused her, gathered up our clothes and together we made a break for the men's and ladies' rooms respectively. Unfortunately, we had to run the gamut of the milkman and the greens keeper on our way. The expressions on their faces was one of frozen surprise. We did, however, manage to clothe ourselves and drive down the entrance way with as much dignity as we could muster under the circumstances, considering we were both covered with chigger bites, had the beginnings of a nasty head cold, and sporting monster hangovers."

As Eddie was recounting his confession (because not just wives, but daughters probably would have qualified under the covenant), I spied the head of the Board of Governors who was the king of all Curmudgeons. I am sure that if he smiled his face would fall apart like two hundred year old parchment, and he would slice an errant member up like a berserk butcher with a meat ax.

So I informed Eddie that I felt it was my duty to report him to the Curmudgeon for his disgrace on our golf course, particularly since number eight was my favorite golf hole. In spite of Eddie's pleading look, I approached the Curmudgeon, who was nursing a rather large whiskey and innocently asked, "Sir, what would you do if a member was seen performing the sex act out on number eight, my favorite golf hole?"

Curmudgeon took a large drink of whiskey and put his glass on the band-aid, "Well, it all depends? Was it with another man, or with a woman?" "A woman," I said glancing over at Eddie who was busily engaged in preventing further soiling of his jockey shorts "Well, then," said Curmudgeon eying his whiskey glass hungrily, "that's OK then; but, if it had been otherwise, we would have had to expel him."

“Well, thanks,” I said glancing at Eddie who had just finished purging himself in his shorts. “It’s just a theoretical question anyway.”

The Sociological Survey

Jimmy tames Army Procurement.

During my travels in Europe for my clients, I set up my headquarters in the beautiful University City of Heidelberg along the Nekar River. It is favored by a very old, but intact castle—Heidelberger Schloss. In addition to the Red Ox Tavern, site of *The Student Prince* of operatic fame, Heidelberger Schloss has innumerable *weinstuben* (wine cellars); a five star hotel; a museum featuring the prehistoric Heidelberg man; and a small hotel painted bright engine red which was located just behind the U.S. Army Commissary.

This hotel was five stories high. I am sure that the color gave away its main purpose which was, simply, a grand "cat house" with each floor having its own specialties. The first floor was populated by the top of the line, each floor above had a declining set of standards of pulchritude ending in a total zoo on the 5th floor. I suppose that an ardent prospective customer who wanted to save money by walking up to the 5th floor might be too tired by the time he got there to fulfill his mission.

The interesting part about this particular cat house was that a husband sent by a nagging wife could walk through the Army commissary, out the back door to the hotel, partake of its services while his wife was sitting in the commissary parking lot, and return with a bag full of groceries, without blinking an eye. We called the hotel *The Supermarket.*

The reason I dwelt on *The Supermarket* is that it played a prominent part in an event personally conducted by me, which only selected customers could be invited to join. This event was called "Jim Malony's Sociological Survey of Heidelberg" and the agenda usually included a trip down river by boat and return to Heidelberg for a gourmet lunch at Hotel Europa. Fortified by a good German brandy, we would walk via a winding road lined by *weinstuben* and would stop at each one for more wine. More wine was had at the Schloss and from there we would wobble down hill where we would visit the historic Red Ox, see the Heidelberg man at the museum, and then wind up the day at *The Supermarket.* Now, I know that you will not believe me, but, the object of the visit to *The Supermarket* was not to indulge, but, to sight-see and determine if *The Supermarket* lived up its name in offering a wide variety of merchandise ranging from heavenly to bizarre. Such a visit would be boring to a European, but, to the naive American it was a trip to a cornucopia of vicarious thrills.

While my European base was Heidelberg, my U.S. base was in the vicinity of Fort Monmouth, New Jersey, a source of substantial business for myself and my clients. As in all my large customer bases, there are one or two people who are real 360° sons of bitches (360° means they are SOBs no matter which way you look at them).

I happen to have been blessed with two of them who I will call John and Joe. John was a program manager for one of my biggest programs, and Joe was a real shot-in-the-ass contract administrator. John was a self-styled sophisticate; Joe was hard shelled, born again Christian who loved to preach. One day while enjoying *La Dolce Vita* in Heidelberg, I received the wonderful news—John and Joe were coming to Heidelberg on business and I would entertain them during their two-day stop over. The prospect of John ragging my ass about some minuscule oversight, and Joe trying to reform me for a complete day (which I anticipated), would turn that day into what seemed like a decade.

Greeting them with a forced demeanor of gaiety, I found them in their usual state of mind. John in his usual foul mood, and Joe looking like the farmer in the famous picture, *American Gothic.* Merrily we embarked on our "Sociological Survey of Heidelberg" starting with many glasses of Moselle wine, chased by Asbach Uralt, a fine German brandy. Then from the river cruise to the Hotel Europa for a five star meal, more wine and several shots of clear schnapps, and, we were off to the castle and more wine and schnapps.

Our tour rolled on until we came to our next stop, *The Supermarket.* As we entered, the heavens burst forth with sheets of rain whipping against the building. While John and Joe were walking around the first floor goggle eyed, I ambled up to the second floor where I saw an "angel of mercy" clad in a leather suit. Scarcely concealing my elation at seeing a perfect foil for what I had in mind, I approached her and asked her to tell me her specialty. "Und for forty marks, I giff you a good beating," she replied. I then explained to her that I had a friend downstairs who loved P&H (pain and humiliation), but that he really didn't want to show it. After forty marks had changed hands, I explained that I would introduce them and then regardless of his protests she would give him the beating of his life. I then informed John, who's disposition seemed to have improved dramatically with each glass of wine, that someone on the second floor *really wanted* to meet him. Leaving Joe, who had started to preach to the girls on the first floor, John bounded up the stairs to meet his new best friend with me following in his wake to make sure that things went as planned.

As soon as the girl saw him she embraced him with enthusiasm and led him by the arm to her room. I stood outside and starting counting to 30 seconds—suddenly the door burst open, and out came John, his eye bugging out, and his face the color of last weeks grits, saying, "Jesus Christ, she got out the biggest damn whip I had ever seen, and said, 'Now liebling[12], I gift you vat you like.' "

I kept as straight a face as I possibly could under the circumstances and said, "John in all my years dealing with you and you ragging my ass, I have always resisted the impulse to beat the shit out of you—now this one is on me—enjoy!" With John in tow, and now completely sober, we headed for our car hoping to pick up Joe, who was conspicuously absent. We looked high and low for him, and I was feeling slightly guilty for having contributed to his downfall, when we heard a tapping at the window, and there standing in the driving rain was Joe soaked from head to toe. It seems that *The Supermarket* bouncer, upon hearing Joe preaching to the girls about the hellfire and damnation which awaited them for their wicked ways, bodily threw him out into the rain.

Thus, the Sociological Survey ended up with a very subdued John who never again gave me a hard time, and Joe who caught cold and got deliriously drunk from my medicinal remedy for a cold—hot tea liberally laced with Asbach-Uralt. Once again, as many times in the past, the Sociological Survey did not fail me, and I found that my relationship with John and Joe improved enormously.

---

[12] darling

We Ain't Got None

Lancey B, one of my business associates, and I shared a common character flaw which is an inordinate fondness for the sight of a scantily clad, nubile young lady displaying her charms in dancing on the bar, or any other media for that matter.

In pursuit of satisfying our flaws, we were on constant alert for opportunities to succumb to the temptations of the flesh. On an extremely hot summer day we drove from our home base, Fort Monmouth, New Jersey to Fort Belvoir, Virginia to deliver a technical proposal worth a considerable sum of money.

It was our intention to deliver the document, and turn around and drive back the same night. On the way into the gate at Fort Belvoir, we noted a promising looking road house/bar which an acquaintance had told us had "Go-Go" dancers (scantily clad), and made a note of it because, after all it was a hot day, and a cold beer, or so, after delivering the document, and before embarking on our return trip certainly would do no harm. The prospect of quenching our thirst, while ogling the dancers, made the idea even more attractive.

We thundered into the parking lot throwing gravel in all directions. Lancey dismounted immediately and rushed into the bar leaving me to lock the car. No sooner had I turned to go into the bar, when Lancey ambled out and announced that this place of business had no "Go-Go" dancers, but they did have beer. The prospect of a cold beer on a hot day overrode the loss of the dancers, so I continued into the bar when Lancey announced, "Be careful when you go in because there is a big snake just inside."

Now snakes as a group and I don't get along too well. I exercise a great deal of caution when dealing with the every day garden variety, so an encounter with one in a darkened roadhouse bar isn't my idea of a well spent afternoon. I gingerly entered the door and my worst fears were realized because never in my wildest dreams did I imagine a snake that big! It was a monstrous Anaconda and it looked hungry. Slowly and deliberately, it stretched itself out and crawled silently toward the dimly lit bar. Before my horrified eyes it slithered under a table where one of the ugliest, nastiest looking women I have ever seen was sitting. The shock caused by the snake was quickly replaced by the sight of the snake disappearing under the table of this cross between a grizzly bear and a skunk. I was caught between the desire to run for my life and sticking it out. My dilemma was solved by the hostile looks coming from a group of rednecks playing pool by the only escape route back through the door. These boys looked like they were the results of about six generations of intermarriage with first cousins. They were even uglier and nastier than either the snake or the person at the table, and like the snake, they were hungry; hungry enough to take offense with two city boys in business suits who might think they were too good for their particular social center.

Cautiously, Lancey and I groped our way through the haze to the bar to plot our escape. Looming through the haze behind the bar was a very large man. He looked like King Kong, smelled like King Kong, and was about as smart as King Kong. Without comment, he placed two very dirty, chipped, fly specked glasses in front of us and said, "Wadayuh want?" Once we got our gorges down which had risen smartly, we said, "Budweiser in bottles." "Ain't got none," he said. "Well, then, Millers will be OK," we responded with our confidence falling as fast as a barometer anticipating a Nor'easter.

"Ain't got that either," King Kong grunted. Just as he served something he did have, the person at the table jumped up screaming, "That f—ing snake just shit on my shoes." Even the redneck pool players seemed to show keen interest in the scene of her cursing the snake, which was the pet of one of the Rednecks, and yelling at King Kong, and graphically showing him the damage that the "F—ing snake had wrought on her brand new Reeboks.

As King Kong advanced from behind the bar towards the "F—ing" snake victim, and the rednecks unsheathed their pool cues, Lancey and I beat a hasty retreat to our car and roared off into the sunset, safe at least, or so we thought, making bets on whether King Kong had bested the woman or vice versa, and the fate of the "F—ing snake."

As we sped along 495 North towards our homes on the Jersey Shore our car started making noises like rocks in a cement mixer. The car, wheezing like a steam Calliope, finally staggered into a service center in a small Maryland town which had a sign reading "Mechanic on Duty." Gratefully we rushed into the service center office and asked for the mechanic as advertised.

"Ain't got none," said the manager, "but there is another place one turn down the road that always has a mechanic on duty." Lancey, who was a field artillery person, was not used to walking and I, the old infantryman set out on foot to walk the mile as the sun beat down on us amidst gallons of sweat and Lancey's incessant whining, we realized that the haven we sought was much longer than a mile. After the second mile we saw in the distance the next service center in the midst of the waves of heat from the road which caused a mirage and in large letters we saw the long awaited sign, "Mechanic on Duty—24 Hours."

Now soaked with sweat and Lancey's fancy Italian shoes much the worse for wear, we staggered into the manager's air-conditioned office taking in big gulps of cold air. "We've come to get your mechanic," we gasped. "Ain't got none," said the manager without looking up from his *Red Ryder* comic book, "but, come back tomorrow, maybe we'll have one then."

At that point, we decided to desert our expired car and strike out for home the best we could. The manager, upon being asked if there was a car rental place nearby, informed us that we were in luck because there was an Avis Car Rental place just a mile down the road, but it closed at 4:30 and we had just thirty minutes to make it. Wearily we trudged out on what was becoming an endless odyssey. As might be expected Avis was much more than one mile, but by forced march amid Lancey's complaints about his feet, we got in under the wire by several minutes. Between the "F—ing snake" incident, our car expiring, the mechanics on duty fiasco, the heat, and Lancey's shrill complaining, I developed a nervous headache, complicated by mild dehydration.

I knew that we had reached our Nirvana. "We would like to rent a car, any car!" we said with the proper note of pleading. "Ain't got none," said the fat lady on duty who must have been the sister of the woman in the bar. No amount of begging or pleading helped because she really didn't have any cars. Not to be denied, we called a cab to take us to the Baltimore Friendship Airport where Fat Lady informed us flights to Newark were scheduled. Gratefully we called a taxi driven by a driver who must have taken driving lessons from Teddy Kennedy. By this time we were really wrung out, but secure in the knowledge that we were close to being out of the world of "Ain't got none," to a saner environment.

As we dashed up to the American Eagle counter to ask for tickets we were informed, "Sorry, Sir, there ain't any." Faced with the prospect of a night at the airport, soaked with sweat to the skin, blisters on our feet, and other assorted aches and pains, we whined, cried, and begged our way to the front of the line for standby and much to our amazement we finally got on the plane to Newark. As we gratefully settled in our seats, congratulating ourselves on beating the "Ain't got any" spell that had been cast upon us and were relishing the thought of several airplane bottles of Tequila mixed with fruit juice when the stewardess graciously asked us what we would like to drink. "Tequila!" we shouted in unison knowing that every decent airline carried Tequila. "Sorry," she said, "we don't have any."

Upon landing at Newark, and having greedily drank most of the alcohol inventory of the small plane, we staggered up to the Avis desk, because of Avis being number two, they always claimed to try harder and it goes without saying that they have a car, any car, for two slightly drunk fine, young men such as ourselves.

As we approached the desk my heart sank, there stood a fat lady who must have been the triplet sister of fat lady numbers one and two, and she responded in the old familiar, "Sorry, we don't have any."

Upon locating a limo for hire, I staggered into the front door of my home and was confronted by my very angry, Teutonic wife who demanded to know where I had been all day, and why I had booze offending her senses. I recounted my adventures with "F—ing snake" and the "ain't got none" curse that was put on me. She expressed disbelief of my story and stormed off to bed saying, "You ain't got none and you're not going to get none!"

A Nose For Quality

On one of my frequent trips from London to Lagos, Nigeria I was privy to one of the funniest remarks I had ever heard in my travels through Europe, Africa, or the U.S. The seats just in front of me in Business Class were occupied by an older English chap and a younger man, since that particular flight wasn't fully booked, passengers conversations carried further than normal and with amazing clarity.

It was apparent that the older man was an "Old Coaster" which is the name given to people who have lived along the West Coast of Africa for decades and perhaps have a little bit "gone native."

The subject of communication ranged from snakes to black magic, murders, secret societies, banking, trading, etc. With each passing hour, the young man who was obviously being trained to take the place of the older man in Lagos and vicinity, grew more nervous and apprehensive. As the plane landed and the doors opened a blast of hot air from the open sewers around the airport hit us in the face.

As we staggered down the steps onto the tarmac, I heard the younger man exclaim in impeccable Oxfordian English to the middle-aged "Old Coaster." "I say John, what is that horrible, nauseous odor?"

"Well, Harry, that's shit," said the "Old Coaster."

"I know that," said the young man, "but what did they do to it?"

They left me doubled up in laughter.

A Moscow Welcome

A preview of mindless violence in Russia.

Ever since I walked into a bar on Rizal Ave. in Manila, Philippines, eagerly looking forward to my first beer in two weeks, and ran into the shooting of three U.S. soldiers by Philippino Irregulars, I have been very cautious about my activities the first day in a country. However, to those who will have read of my first day misfortunes, I may seem to be a magnet for some sort of disaster—if that is your assumption, you are right.

For example, with great care, I planned my first trip to Moscow, Russia. I chose a flight from New York which landed in Moscow in daylight. To make sure I didn't get ripped off by the customs people, or the baggage handlers, I arranged for an escort to meet me at customs. I then finished my arrangements with a private car and driver to take me to a hotel partly owned by the Radisson Hotel group and called the Slavinskaya.

All went as planned, every phase of my arrangements went as smooth as a schoolmarm's leg, and I arrived at the hotel in grand style. I emerged from my car right at the entrance in which stood an imposing doorman in full regalia. As I approached him, I noticed a number of Russian men down on their knees scrubbing the entranceway with stiff bristled brushes and hot, soapy water. I was certainly impressed by this show of cleanliness by the Russians and I exclaimed to the doorman, "Are you expecting someone important, like a Head of State?" "No," he replied, "We are cleaning up the blood; they just shot the part owner of the hotel."

"How did it happen?" I asked. His reply was, "Two men drove up to the overpass," and he pointed to a section of highway about 700 feet distant, "and they leaned over the edge and shot their automatic weapons. He had eleven slugs in him before he hit the ground, and the killers got into their car and drove slowly away."

I then asked, "Why would he be killed this way?"

The doorman smiled and said, "He just didn't listen!"

Later on, my curiosity led me to casually ask a few more questions which revealed 1) that he had four bodyguards with him at the time and none of them were hit; 2) the owners were the Moscow City Council (50%), Radisson (40%), and the U.S. businessman who was shot (10%); and 3) the businessman had gone to the media complaining about the interference by the City Council, etc.

Looks like the council put out a contract for the hit. This event was a "preview of coming attractions" for my Russian experiences.

Part VIII

Childhood Memories and Potpourri

Overview

Most of us, especially as we get older, reflect back on our childhood and sadly, for some there are more painful memories than happy ones. In my case it was just the opposite, so my reflections are of many of the minutiae which fascinated me—it has always impressed me that as kids we had no criminals among us—no one stole, or got violent—everyone bathed and wore clean clothes. These were the dust bowl days, the period of the greatest poverty in the history of the U.S. No kids had elaborate toys, or games. It has been surprising how much ingenuity children show by inventing games requiring no more than hands and rubber balls, horseshoes, trees to climb, a few marbles, and some pennies to pitch. With all of this around us, we didn't have time to get into trouble. During this period of time 1930–35 my father was stationed at the University of Oklahoma as Commandant of the ROTC there. I well remember the reception I got from the kids wearing bib overalls and sometimes barefooted when I showed up in high top "Keds" and corduroy knickers and although I had had more that my share of bloody noses, I still feel at the age of 89 that those years were the best of my life. The descriptions of games we played, and the overall feeling of the Dust Bowl are still in my mind.

Up a Tree

I love the South and its people. I love the Southern cooking, white lightning out of a paper cup, real Southern music, and their sense of humor which sometimes is dry, wry, and really laid back. This story didn't happen to me, but was told by a Southern raconteur who used to sell Ralston Purina animal feed throughout the South. His name was Jerry Clower and the following account illustrates what happens to us when we are in a heated negotiation with an unyielding banker, wife, or competitor (choose one).

"My uncle used to take me and my cousin, Don, 'coon hunting when we lived down in Mississippi. One afternoon we were walking through the woods with our dog, Old Blue, when all of a sudden we heard him *giving tongue.*[13] Uncle Ned called out, "Hurry up boys, Old Blue has treed a 'coon."

We got to the tree where Old Blue, sure enough, had treed something, but it had climbed up too high. We couldn't see it, but knew it was there. Uncle Ned turned to cousin Don and said "Don, shake that 'coon out of that tree." Don shook the tree as hard as he could, but the 'coon didn't budge. Finally Don informed us all that the 'coon just wouldn't come down. Uncle Ned suggested that Don climb the tree where he was and shake him off the limb. Cousin Don climbed and kept climbing saying he couldn't see the 'coon, and Uncle Ned kept says, "Climb higher, climb higher Don, he's up there, I know." Finally Cousin Don called down, "I think I see him, I'm going after him."

Suddenly we heard the most ungodly shriek you ever heard, and above the shriek we heard Cousin Don crying out, "This isn't a 'coon, it's a god damned wildcat, and it's tearing my ass off." Uncle Ned kept hollering, "Shake him down, shake him down!" Cousin Don yelled down, "Shoot, Uncle Ned, shoot."

Uncle Ned replied "Ah can't, ah can't, I might hit you."

---

[13]Hounds don't bark, they howl, colloquially called *giving tongue*

"Shoot amongst us, Uncle Ned," Don yelled, "and give one of us some relief!"

I'm sure that all of us have wanted an Uncle Ned with a shotgun sometime during our lives.

Spells

In some of the more primitive societies, there is a firm belief that spells can be cast on an individual by a witch doctor, or his or her equivalent. Just anybody can't do this, one must be endowed by a higher power to create events which lead to the accomplishment of the spell.

There are good spells and bad spells, as an example of a good spell is an ivory talisman I acquired in Japan, which could ensure fertility. This particular object was a very pregnant bear which when worn on the Obi of a Japanese woman would lead to pregnancy. The Obi incidentally is a wide brocaded very stiff cloth worn around the waist over the robe. The talisman was strung by a silk cord and was attached to the Obi.

An example of a bad spell, which I saw in Italy, was a dead fish, covered with its own blood lying on the doorstep of a home symbolizing the threat that the recipient would "swim with the fishes."

In West Africa, we called Black Magic *Juju* and I personally saw the effects of it work on an unfortunate house boy of a friend of mine in Lagos, Nigeria. The houseboy, Felix, was a strapping nineteen year old weighing perhaps 200 pounds and easily 6 feet tall. He was always happy and in good spirits, and energetically performed all tasks given to him,. Also employed in the same household was an older boy who in the pecking order of the servants, was senior and had more privileges to include higher pay.

One day, unfortunately, the senior boy was caught stealing a pair of shoes and was fired and Felix took his place as senior boy. A short time later Felix found a broken clay plate by the door of his quarters—the broken plate is a signal that a curse had been put on him and that he would wither and die. Some investigation on the part of Felix revealed that the discharged boy had gone to a *Juju* priest and had paid to have a spell put on Felix. Upon learning this, Felix went to my friend and informed him that he couldn't work for him any longer because of the spell. My friend laughed at the idea of the spell and, after much discussion, convinced Felix to stay, to which he reluctantly agreed.

From that moment on, Felix started to waste away—every week he grew weaker and weaker until he weighed only 140 pounds and he was barely able to walk. In desperation, my friend decided to let him go home to die, but only after physicians who examined Felix shook their heads and claimed that there was nothing wrong physically with him.

A year after Felix was sent home to die, my friend, while walking along a street in Lagos, spied Felix who was once again healthy, happy, and generally enjoying life. Felix indicated that as soon as he left the employ of my friend, the spell was lifted and he recovered almost as quickly as he had lost his health and he was good friends with the former houseboy.

When one looks at fire walkers in India, Fakirs sleeping on spikes, and other phenomenon involving physical self-abuse, trances, etc., it becomes apparent that the belief that the mind can control many aspects of physical well being. We have seen instances where people have seemingly recovered use of their limbs by force of will.

Therefore, one who is healthy can also lose the functions of the body if they *really believe* that they are going to indeed lose the ability to perform. So the power has both positive and negative results. In the case of Felix, he really believed that he was going to die, and believed just as strongly that with the lifting of the spell, he would live.

Coves

It's hard to believe that it took the Colonists almost one hundred years from the first landings in Virginia to surmount the barrier erected by the Great Smoky Mountains; and to explode into the rich lands of Kentucky, Tennessee, and later on Ohio and west. True, individuals had explored the mountains and beyond, but the trails which they made could only be traversed by foot. Wagons and housekeeping paraphernalia would never be able to make it unless a gap in this formidable mountain chain could be found.

The Cumberland Gap in Maryland was one such gap, as was one which was in North Carolina, west of the Asheville of today. One of the features of these mountains was a natural phenomenon called a Cove. Geologically, a Cove can be described as a very rich closed end valley almost inaccessible except on foot (until the modern advent of transportation).

As families moved west through this gap in North Carolina, families, or groups of families, would drop off into these Coves where they successfully farmed, but where they would be isolated against the outside world. I lived in North Carolina in 1948 and had heard stories about the modern residents of the Coves, and the stories were amazing.

These people were a throwback to the Elizabethan days of England: one could barely understand their English; they still wove their own cloth using spinning wheels and looms; they grew all their own food; and their musical instruments were typical of 18th Century stringed lap instruments. The music they played was the old Madrigal as played in England in the early 1700's and of course *always* told a story.

Some of this influence can be heard in some of our present country and western songs. It was obvious that the Cove residents had, in fact, entered into a virtual time machine, and due to their lack of contact with modern day environments had not changed very much. I am sure that fifty-two years later all of that is changed, but it was a real shock knowing that 18th century culture did exist somewhere in its purest form in 1948.

Their religion was Church of England oriented, but absolutely fundamentalist—every word of the Bible they interpreted literally. This led to a very interesting source of income, which they created for themselves, so it was explained to me at the time. The Bible says in effect: "...through God's gifts foods and sustenance grows upon your fields and you shall employ it as you wish." The very rich soils in the Coves yield bumper crops of corn, barley and rye, and from this, the residents made bootleg "white liquor," AKA, "moonshine," which they sold to very selectively chosen customers by the residents to be transported to North Wilkesboro, a town which boasts that it is the "Moonshine Capitol of the World," and then sent on to points north and west. The residents of the Coves claim that the Lord's law is above states' law and *that's* who they obey. Who can argue with that!

The Dust Bowl

The dust bowl was truly named. When our family moved to Oklahoma, where my father was assigned by the Army to be ROTC Commandant at the University of Oklahoma (O U). Oklahoma had only been a state for a little over 30 years, and the rich topsoil which had accumulated over the millennium had been farmed intensely using far from modern methods. The land was flat as a pancake and there were no windbreaks along the edges of the fields; so if high winds arose there was nothing to stop them for a thousand miles.

During the 1930's winds scoured Oklahoma, sweeping up the topsoil into a veritable blanket, which obscured the sun, turning the sky into a sickly yellow. All of this was exasperated by a prolonged drought, which baked the soil into a hard crust which defied any growing thing.

Poverty was king! Farmers, of course, were particularly hard hit and many left their farms, packed up their kids and wives, and headed west to California. This mass migration was the subject of John Steinbeck's famous novel of the *Okie* migration entitled *Grapes of Wrath.*

As a kid growing up in a University town, we didn't escape the effects of this bone crushing poverty, although we were well clothed and well fed. Our schoolmates in Lincoln Elementary School grades 4–7, probably had dehydrated peas, beans, plus grits, and little else for supper. Sometimes, there was bread soaked in cooking grease to put lead in their pants. This diet caused great volumes of bowel gas in the classrooms, which caused great merriment among the students and great distress among the nasally disadvantaged.

In spite of the poverty, the parents all tried to keep their children clean. In the absence of indoor plumbing, everyone got a bath at least once a week. Upon arriving at home, before sitting down for supper, they cleaned their fingernails and washed their body with soap and water. Their clothes were hand me downs from other family members, but were always neatly patched and sewn. There was no welfare in those days; every extra penny was saved for family use. These are the kids who formed the backbone of our nation in the 1940's and 1950's.

I think I received the best education of my life in that dust bowl school; the teachers taught the fundamentals—nothing fancy—which made learning easier in later years. And those teachers, boy were they tough! Punishment was all physical—you disobeyed, you got beaten—and when you got beaten in school, your parents were notified and you got beaten again when you got home.

The little kids in grades up to grade five got off with their hands being smacked with a ruler, but grades six and seven you got it right in the shorts, usually right in front of the class.

This being the case I was caught by "Birdie" Hicks, our strapping six foot, seventh grade teacher leaning over the underpass under Rt. 66, which ran in front of our school, dropping mud balls on the girls who emerged. "Birdie" took great exception to this insult to womanhood and after lunch, and all the class had assembled, jerked me out of my seat and frog marched me to the platform upon which crouched her desk like some evil frog creature; grabbed me by my favorite Indian scout belt all inlaid with glass beads of which I was very proud—I don't know how many coupons I saved from the box tops of *Wheaties* breakfast food. Straining my poor belt to the limit, I was bent ignominiously over the desk facing the class with my pants pulled up tightly around my private parts—the pain was excruciating and I am sure that "Birdie" was extremely unaware of the devastation she was wrecking on my anatomy. I could hardly wait for the beating to start so I could get some relief.

The reader should appreciate the fact that there are certain ground rules about being beaten in public. The first rule is the teacher's rule, which is the victim, must be beaten until he cries—if he fails to cry, he is beaten until he does cry. The second rule is the students' rule—if you do cry, you are a sissy, and get beaten up at recess—if they miss you in the morning, they get you in the afternoon, or after school.

My dilemma was that here I was in this very undignified position, bent over a desk, and facing my peers which was my choice—*The Lady or the Tiger?* "Birdie" was pulling out a suspicious looking thin rubber hose from the bottom drawer, and was flexing her ample muscles, when it came to me! As the hose descended, I yelled bloody murder, and was in a paroxysm of screaming and crying, while winking and making faces at the class. "Birdie" thinking that she had killed me promptly ceased and desisted. This was my very first marketing triumph. I became the underground hero of the seventh grade class of Lincoln School.

Confetti

Outlaws

The 1930's and late 1920's, in my estimation (it's now year 2012), had the most colorful characters of any period in our history.

We are all aware of the so called "Golden Age Of Sports" with Babe Ruth, Bill Tilden, Red Grange, etc., but there were others too, almost everywhere you looked. One of the products of the depression of the 1930's was the gangsters, each one more colorful and gruesome than the next.

As kids, we secretly used to cheer for the underdog, which in most cases, was the gangster. "Pretty Boy Floyd" would keep robbing the same bank in Joplin, MO., which is close to the Oklahoma state line. After every successful robbery he would return to his home to Noble, Oklahoma and pass out $10 to people who thought he was Robin Hood. He died in an ambush led by Melvin Purvis, FBI.

Others were John Dillinger, Public Enemy #1 who escaped from the penitentiary using a gun carved from a potato and colored with black shoe polish. There was "Ma" Barker and her boys, psycho killers every one of them. She died in a hail of bullets from Melvin Purvis, FBI; Clyde Barrow and Bonnie who also died in a hail of bullets in a trap planned by Melvin Purvis.

Alvin "Creepy" Karpis survived into the 50's; Machine Gun Kelly masterminded the Valentine's Day Massacre and last, of course, was Bruno Hauptman who kidnapped the Lindbergh baby.

There were many others, most of whom died violent deaths. My own take on Melvin Pervis was that he was indeed the penultimate executioner—in my memory there doesn't seem too many examples when Purvis took prisoners. In retrospect, it seems to be extermination in its rawest form. War on crime was a war, not a left wing porch tea party.

Other Characters

Sally Rand   Exotic Dancer

Sally Rand dropped her fan. Don't you look you nasty man.

This was schoolyard sex speak directed towards Sally Rand, the fan dancer at the World's Fair in 1936. By today's standards, she would be called a dumpy, chunky, platinum blond, but then, she was hot stuff, the epitome of sex.

Her act was centered around the movement of two very large fans while the males viewers developed severe eyestrain trying to catch just a glimpse of just any old part of her anatomy. I am sure she had more news coverage than Franklin D. Roosevelt, our President, at the time. She made all of us 12 year olds *very horny*.

The Marx Brothers and W.C. Fields   Comedians

The films made by these comedians are absolute classics in that in both cases one had to listen carefully at the rapid-fire jokes, which today are still hilarious. Example: Scene—The depths of an African jungle, the heroine to Groucho Marx, "I've never been so frightened in my life. Why last night I was attacked by a fierce tiger in my tent, but I shot my gun in the air and frightened him away." Groucho to Heroine, "That's nothing! Last night I shot an elephant in my pajamas! What he was doing in my pajamas I'll never know!"

W.C. Fields as a sheriff in a tough Western town, escorts a very buxom Mae West from the stagecoach. The cowhands sitting around on the saloon porch call out, "Hey Sheriff, is that your new bride?" W.C. Fields replies, "Ah, yes, she is so new I haven't even unwrapped her yet!" (It's the delivery that counts).

Jean Harlow   Movie Star

She, in my book, was absolutely gorgeous; hands down better than any platinum blonde before or since. The added beauty mark made her even more sensational. She died under mysterious circumstances.

Busby Berkeley   Dance Director

In the dust bowl, where everyone was poor, the dance routines in the musicals, were an opiate to the grinding poverty people saw every day. Men in white tuxedos dancing in a nightclub, the roof of which rolled back revealing the stars, showgirls in short dresses dancing in a row, filled with white leather furniture and a glittering bar. The dancers then doing intricate designs while laying on the floor and, of course, the high kicking finale. All of this transported us to a different world even if it was only an hour or so. In one of my narratives about "Using The System," I mention building a nightclub and the largest bar in the Far East for our non-commissioned officers. This building was modeled after what I remembered from the Busby Berkley routines I saw as a kid. We even had the rollback roof.

"Alfalfa" Bill Murray   Governor and Politician

"Alfalfa" was the State Governor of Oklahoma and was an unabashed tin horn politician—and he made no attempt to conceal it. He was a big man (but, of course, everyone looked big to me then, and they still do): and sported a droopy walrus mustache; baggy pants held up by well-worn suspenders; and a shirt, which had started out as clean as snow that morning, was reduced through the day to a receptacle for errant streams of tobacco juice.

"Alfalfa" stands out in my memory as the only governor that I know of who declared war on another state. In this case the state was Texas, and the cause of the dispute was a matter concerning a bridge over the Cimarron River, which separates the two states. "Alfalfa" turned out the Oklahoma National Guard and dispatched it to the River with an unofficial declaration of war. Washington got wind of it and stopped it before things got serious, which they well could as Texas and Oklahoma had no love for each other.

The second thing I remember about the governor was that he had a working oil well right on the front lawn of the State House, and that we all lined up to walk into his office. He asked us one by one "Did your daddy vote for Alfalfa Bill?" and this followed by his farewell to us all, which was "Don't forget to tell your daddies to vote for good old Alfalfa." My father received this message dutifully reported by me with a great deal of humor. Afterward, in other circumstances, they became friends.

Father Coughlin   Rabble Rouser

Some of the other characters were not quite so lovable, the least of which was Father Coughlin, a renegade Irish Catholic priest from Detroit. He basically preached violence and forced redistribution of wealth. Once a supporter of the New Deal, he came to support and rationalize some of Hitler and Mussolini's policies. To those who had nothing, the lure of taking by force from persons who did have things appealed to many people. He was on radio and in the newsreels in the movie house constantly; his appeal was universal. The Church wanted him to stop his politicizing. On May 1, 1942, the Archbishop of Detroit, Most Rev. Edward Mooney, ordered Coughlin to desist from his activities. With the threat of being defrocked, he was ordered to simply tend to his parish activities at the the Shrine of the Little Flower. He retired in 1966, but he did continue writing political propaganda blaming the Jews for Communism.

Father Coughlin passed, at the age of 88, in 1979 in Michigan.

Huey Long   Governor of Louisiana

A truly dangerous man, a red neck to the core, and of course a racist. Huey Long appealed to all of the impoverished South, not just Louisiana. His hatred for President Franklin D. Roosevelt knew no bounds. His most quoted statement about Roosevelt was "That damn cripple, sitting up there in the White House eating fish eggs (caviar), and drinking champagne, while we're living off of grits and water here in Louisiana."

The large block of rural votes controlled by Long through out the South gave the Roosevelt Democrats a real heartache. I am sure that Roosevelt breathed a sigh of relief when Long was assassinated at the State House. Huey's brother, Earl Long, took over Huey's power base and for many years afterward governed with comparative moderation.

(See my story about Biff Jones.)

Movies

Today, the movies of the 30's and 40's must seem incredibly "corny," but they transported us to a different world. The world of *Charlie Chan*, played by Warner Oland, took us to the fog bound streets of London, where a gruesome murder awaited at every corner. The world of *The Thin*

Man, a urbane detective addicted to Martinis, with the beautiful Myrna Loy as his wife.

Who could forget Wallace Berry, who played in every role imaginable from the *Champ* with Jackie Coogan as the little kid to *Tugboat Anne* with Marie Dressler. However, for we boys, the kings of all the movie stars were the cowboys. Now these weren't the insipid singing cowboys who kissed girls and all that sissy stuff—these were real men who drank straight liquor, beat the crap out of anyone who looked cross-eyed at them, and maybe kissed their horses, but never forgot the new schoolmarm in town. Tom Mix, Hoot Gibson and particularly Buck Jones remain my icons.

Radio

Eddie Cantor, Fred Allen, Jack Benny, *The Shadow*, *Green Hornet*, etc. To me, radio was, in its hey, day the absolutely perfect medium. Television today dictates what you see, and the narrative has to match the picture, thus the input to the viewer is controlled in every aspect. On radio one could form their own visions, which were driven by the audio narrative.

My version of the characters portrayed on the Fred Allen show, I am sure were different than others listening to the same show. *The Shadow*, and *The Green Hornet* were just great in that respect—it was like going to the movies, but you made your own pictures. Incidentally, most of the leading radio comedians had worked in burlesque and were really funny.

Sunday night was always the big radio night and most families gathered around the old Philco console type radio and could tune in to a wide variety of broadcasts, ranging from symphony to comedy. Today, with multiple TV sets, everyone scatters to the four winds to see their own programs. The single radio was a great contributor for family bonding.

War of the Worlds

I was a student at Episcopal High School in Alexandria, Virginia when Orson Welles broadcast *The War of the Worlds*. It started Orson Welles on a fabulous literary and acting career. As I mentioned above, Sunday evening was a time when all families gathered around the radio for their favorite programs. Everything went along smoothly with the normal programs of that particular hour, when suddenly an excited voice interrupted the program to bring a news bulletin from "News Headquarters."

The listener was then switched to a broadcast site where Martian spaceships had landed in New Jersey. The narrative, complete with sound effects, described the mass slaughter of police, national guard, and bystanders by death rays from the Martian ships that then started to crawl towards New York and Washington D.C., their progress punctuated by screams, and the collapsing of buildings and bridges.

Complete chaos reigned throughout the U.S. People were fleeing in their cars to god knows where; others were barricading their doors and windows; and breaking out weapons to repulse the Martians. I am sure that half of the U.S. believed that the world had been invaded, and the other half just wasn't sure. This chaos lasted several days before everyone realized that it was just a radio program, which conjured up images that our TV could never duplicate.

At Episcopal High School, we were trained to be Southern gentlemen, and one of our rites was to call upon our Headmaster and his wife. We took turns doing this so that we would share the pain equally. Our school was *really* Southern—no Confederate flags, etc., but very notably mounted over the fireplace in the living room were crossed cavalry sabers—they could have been Confederate, but that wasn't important at the time.

As we entered the living room, the Headmaster's radio was tuned in to the initial account of the Martian landing. The Headmaster became frozen by the radio, and as the account grew more gruesome, he could no longer restrain himself and called out, "Come on boys, get out the students and defend the school if it takes all of us." In the meanwhile, he was brandishing one of the sabers and headed out the door; perhaps remembering when the cadets at Virginia Military Academy (VMI) defended the hill upon which the school stood against the advancing Union Army. Fortunately the Headmaster's wife who didn't buy the "Martian" idea at all, managed to head him off and shortly restored order. At sixteen years old, I was more than relieved that I didn't get the glory of defending it to the "last man." It was nice of the Headmaster to volunteer us though.

Years afterward in 1945, some soldiers assigned to our Special Services Radio in Tokyo, Japan, remembering the Orson Welles program in the late 30's put on a *similar* program using a gigantic sea monster that rose from the depths of Tokyo Bay and started to eat everyone he could see.

Once again, the narrative was gruesome, and the Japanese reacted the same way that radio listeners reacted to Orson Welles a decade before.

I was the Officer of the Day when the sea monster program came on. Shortly after the program started, I received a call from our Regimental Commander ordering me to double the guard along the sea wall because there was a monster loose. I choked down a gale of laughter, and good soldier that I was, agreed to follow his orders. He was Irish, so he probably was drunk at least I *hope* he was. If he wasn't, I want to look him up and sell him a bridge I know about in Brooklyn.

Gambling

Sometimes in business situations, I gamble; but never ever do I walk into a card game, or a Casino dead set to gamble my hard earned money trying to beat "house odds." My education into gambling was painless, and didn't cost me a dime, as my teachers were gamblers of the lowest order—basically I would call them "street gamblers." In the 1930's, times were tough, and a private in the Army made $20 base pay—but he got his room and board free, so his $20 was basically unencumbered. On payday, the card games and dice started, and as the winner in a certain barracks was established and everyone cleaned out, games would start between the winners, until only one was left. I would guess that the eventual payday winner may have won $5,000 or more, and in the 1930's that was real money! This then attracted professional gamblers who enlisted in the Army just to gamble.

Somehow or other, I forget the circumstances, I met an old enlisted man who was a professional gambler who knew all of the tricks of the trade, and through it all was trying to impress me that gambling was something I should never do. Here are some of the things he taught me.

Never roll dice on a blanket

There are men who practice for hours on end, who by manipulating the dice when they pick them up to roll, leave certain numbers up. They then hold them just a little loosely so they click in their bands as they are ready to toss them on the blanket without allowing them to turn over. They then know which numbers are face up before they roll. They can roll the dice on the blanket, and with practice, they can control the number of times the dice turn over, and the probable average of numbers. To do this, however, one has to release the dice in a certain way, which is to clasp the dice as previously described, turn your palm downward and release all five fingers simultaneously, thus making the dice roll straight and tumble evenly end over end.

The blanket helps you control the number of times the dice turn over, and if you have manipulated the numbers upon picking up the dice, your chances of avoiding "snake eyes" (two ones), or craps, which is seven, or any roll after the first, are improved. This is why players insist you roll the dice against a wall, or some soft backstop as a condition of play.

The Mechanic's *Grip*

This grip is used by dealers who wish to deal cards from the top and bottom of the deck, depending on whether he needs the bottom cards, which he has previously put there when he picked up the cards from the previous deal.

The grip is obtained as follows:

1. Put high point cards from previous deal at the bottom of the deck. Shuffle the deck without disturbing the high point cards.

2. Place the deck flat on the table, in a normal manner.

3. Place the hand palm down on top of the deck.

4. Leave the palm in place, put the thumb over the bottom card.

5. Having done this you will notice that the thumb can move the bottom card easily from back to front.

6. Hold the deck out in front of you the palm on top of the deck with the fingers extended together.

7. To deal, pull the card to be dealt from the deck between the thumb and the forefinger of your dealing hand. You will now see that with the Mechanics Grip, you can push the bottom card with the forefinger underneath the deck, or the next card on top with the thumb. This then controls the flow of high point cards into your hand. The old gambler claimed that some even amputated forefingers at the first joint so that the movement of it could not be detected.

Bicycle Cards

These are old time cards, but still used. These cards are easily marked because of their rather complex layout.

Marked Cards in General

There are all kinds of ways to mark cards: ranging from marks, which can be seen with special dark glasses; to puncturing cards with a finger ring with a small sharp protrusion on the palm part of the ring. A dealer can feel the puncture while dealing, thereby knowing the value of the card. These are obvious and crude, certainly not used in Las Vegas, but on the street they are no doubt still used. There are other tricks such as signals from watchers, slight defacing of cards with such as bent edges, etc.

I could go on and on about the street tricks I learned, but the above is enough. Suffice it to say *I never gamble.*

Prohibition

Now those were the days! Prohibition spawned the crime lords, which grace our television screens and other media-today. Al Capone, Bugsy Moran, Machine Gun Kelley, Frank Costello, Joe "the Boss" Marcella, and innumerable others all of whom got their start selling, transporting, and making liquor. Surprisingly enough, Joe Kennedy, father of President John Kennedy, created a monopoly of bootleg Scotch Whiskey along the eastern seaboard. He made enough money to make even a dogcatcher President—so John and his brother, Bobby, were easy. Incidentally, President Roosevelt sent Joe to England at the beginning of World War II as an Ambassador. Unfortunately, Joe after having made expressions of admiration for Hitler before being an Ambassador, developed a case of fear and trepidation after he arrived in the UK. So he was a great bootlegger, but about as useless as tits on a boar hog after he got there—probably the worst Ambassador the U.S. has ever had during a time of crisis.

I will always remember my father, and my very proper New England stepmother, bringing to the house an unusual number of #1 Mason Jars, which were usually used for preserving cooked vegetables, fruits, etc. These jars were put in our basement and the fruit mashed and allowed to ferment in a large tub; the odor from whatever my father was making was odoriferous to say the least.

Later we all noticed that the Mason jars were filled, and that a manual capping machine for bottles had been introduced. We kids used it to cap bottles of Hires Root Beer, the syrup of which we could buy for 35 cents, and when mixed with yeast and sugar made a gallon or so of root beer. As the yeast did its work in the bottles, so did the Peach White Lightning which my father had made.

The result was nightly 4th of July right in our basement when corks forced upward by the gas formed in both the Root Beer bottles and the Peach Brandy containers. It was literally World War I for weeks on end, with the loud sound of corks popping and the combination of Root Beer and Peach Brandy spraying on the ceiling, and the floor of the basement. For the rest of the year we kids spent our leisure hours cleaning up the debris. The memory of the smell of Root Beer and Peach Brandy combined still makes my gorge rise! So much for homemade alcohol!

As for Prohibition, I will always remember the old Army tradition of Breakfast Rides. Everyone who could ride a horse would be expected on Sunday mornings, when the frost was on the ground, to get up in the darkness when it was freezing cold; stagger out to the stables; mount your assigned horse; and gallop out into the darkness with your horse who was probably as angry as you were at the ridiculous idea of doing *anything* at such an hour. All the adults seemed "bright eyed and bushy tailed" at the idea of riding out into the darkness and freezing their asses off; at the idea of riding out to some distant point on the horizon; having breakfast cooked over a campfire; and then galloping back over several miles "hell for leather" back to the stables.

Kids notice things that grownups might not notice. For example, everyone seemed much happier when bottles of what appeared to be elixir from Mason Jars (#1) were poured into their coffee cup—good fellowship seemed to radiate from everyone, except we kids who were consigned to drink lukewarm tea (coffee was considered a stimulant, much to dangerous for us kids unless it was laced with Carnation Condensed Milk). Little did I realize the joys of Prohibition, which made the Breakfast Ride so exhilarating. In retrospect, one of the social highlights of Regular Army was diminished by the repeal of the prohibition law.

Henry the Bootlegger

After WWII, most of the Regular Army officers from the 1920–1940 era were company grade officers and had risen to the top of the ladder. Many were two, three, and four star generals. One of the most influential, but unknown, people with influence in the three services was "Harry." During the prohibition era, Harry had performed a meritorious service at the time, which was to act as unofficial bootlegger to the officers stationed in and around the Washington D.C. area, which included Fort Myers, Fort Belvoir, Edgewood Arsenal, the Army War College, Fort Meade, etc.

By performing this invaluable service, "Harry" became well known throughout the services as a discreet, and dependable friend. Formerly milk was delivered by a milkman who would drive up in his delivery truck, pick up the empties, read the instructions placed in a folded paper stuck in the top of the bottles, which instructed the milkman what to deliver from the truck. "Harry" performed the same service, minus of course the empty bottles. His orders, of course, were taken by phone.

After WWII, Harry opened a very grand liquor store in southeast Washington which displayed a number of autographed pictures that covered a large wall of just about every major player in the three services, including the President Dwight Eisenhower. The word was that if you really needed to see an important officer for an urgent reason, you could use Harry as a "back channel." This proving that perhaps the way to a man's heart is not through his stomach, but through his bootlegger.

Miscellaneous

The 1930's saw the rise and fail of all sorts of social and religious phenomena some of which were:

The *Penitentes*

Every summer our parents took us to various places, one of which was to a spot near Las Vegas, New Mexico, not to be confused with the other Las Vegas. How our parents found this place, I'll never know, but it was at a camp called *El Porvenir* located in the mountains among lakes and mountain streams full of trout, and other sporting fish. Surrounding this area were a number of Hispanic peoples who made their living from the soil, or from odd jobs locally. They were an extremely religious people, but I suspect, retained the superstitious beliefs of their native Indian forefathers.

The *Penitentes* were one such sect about which I heard from some of the Hispanic workers at *El Porvenir* which made my hair stand on end. I was told that the *Penitentes* would choose one among them to be Jesus, and throughout the year they would treat him as Jesus. However, on the day of the Crucifixion, their Jesus, would carry a wooden cross up a nearby sacred mountain, followed by all of the Penitentes to include women and children, and there to be crucified until dead. That part, if true, is understandable if one reviews the customs of the forefathers of the *Penitentes*, namely the Aztec and Maya Indians who sacrificed many people for many reasons; but prominent was the custom of choosing a young man of the tribe to be sacrificed to the Sun God after a year of special privileges. I do know that the ceremony did take place annually and that a young man was generally tied to the cross and taken down after a period of time, as such the custom did survive until the 1930's. I doubt that the custom still exists in that form.

The Silver Shirts and the German-American Bund

The Silver Shirts were the American version of the Nazi Bund. The roots of the organization were started in Ashville, North Carolina by William Dudley Pelley, the day Hitler took over, who claimed that a "psychic near death experience," as well as messages from the cosmos told him to support Adolph Hitler. At the height of their membership in 1934, the Silver Shirts numbered about 15,000 and were spread across several states.

As Hitler's influence spread throughout Germany and the U.S. movie goers were exposed to the sight of massed German supporters cheering the marching Nazi brown shirts, more and more people were drawn towards the hypnotic effect of these displays. For such reasons, some also joined the German-American Bund which began in New York, and spread training camps through New Jersey and Wisconsin.

One must remember, these were the days of our deepest, deepest depression and anything, just anything, which offered hope was eagerly embraced.

Although by 1939 the membership of the Silver Shirts was down to about 5,000, its members joined the German-American Bund in a rally, complete with Nazi flags and insignia, torchlight and all, at Madison

Square Garden in New York City on February 20, 1939. The *Fuhrer* of the German-American Bund, Fritz Julius Kuhn, gave a vituperative speech against Roosevelt. There was an outbreak of violence between the Bund Brown Shirts and protestors, and many came to feel these groups were un-American and membership diminished.

Kuhn was found guilty of embezzling money from the Bund.

With the invasion of Poland, September 1, 1939, the Silver Shirts and others were declared illegal. The New York District Attorney's Office made life miserable for the Bund, as did the House Un-American Activities Committee. With our entrance into the war, December 7, 1941 the activities of this type of group moved into attempted sabotage, especially in New York, New Jersey, New Orleans and other port areas; spies were rounded up, attempted espionage thwarted.

Communists/Left Wing Radicals

As post-WWII Communists, in government investigations, revealed the greater portions of prominent people as working Communists who were recruited during the 1930's—and that period of course was during the depths of the depression—I would almost be inclined to call it our "crazy period" politically as you may surmise from my previous narrative.

When my father took over as Commandant of the University of Oklahoma ROTC, he was met by campus radicals passing out leaflets banning war, and petitioning for the abolishion of ROTC. My father, and then Governor "Alfalfa" Bill Murray, had a few "confabs" about the situation. Alfalfa Bill wanted to shoot them all, but my father recommended more peaceful solutions. These radicals were to become the first critics of the military for the disastrous Japanese attacks at Pearl Harbor.

Obviously, the Communist ideas of taking from the rich and giving to the poor would affect a lot of people who sympathized with the poor, but unfortunately, most of them, but not all, were naive academic types, not the average underfed person. The damage the Communist spies did to our country, during and after WWII, is immeasurable, and they should have been shown no mercy. Today we see Communism as a badly flawed concept when put into practice, but then it looked good on paper and of course no one knew what Stalin was doing to his own people.

It is sad, but true, that the first people the revolutionists kill when they seize power are the college professors; student leaders, radical union heads, etc., which put them in power in the places like Cuba, Russia, China etc.

Games

With all the computer games, and with all the bells and whistles available today, and a surfeit of talking toys, I am sure that kids today would wonder why *anyone* would want to spend time playing simple games requiring a minimum of equipment; and no radio or TV to interfere with the competitive character of children's games where dexterity was king.

There are no end of games children and adults play. Bruegel, the famous Flemish artist, once painted a picture in which one hundred games were being played simultaneously, and that was over 300 years ago. Most games we play as kids usually required manual, athletic, and some mental skills, coupled with a lot competition

Some games were sedentary: Checkers, Monopoly, Parcheesi, etc. Some were strictly for imaginary environments, such as Cowboys and Indians, usually played in the woods.

There is no end to the variations of these games, which varied in accordance with the geographical location of the people playing them.

For example, with touch football played in the streets of large cities, one used parked cars, trolley wires, fire plugs as obstacles, besides the opposing defenders to overcome. A typical play might be to the end run out to the telephone pole on the right hand side of the street; cut left over the trolley tracks; and then I'll throw the ball over the telephone wires to you. In the country, one would draw a diagram of the play in the dirt with a stick and command, "Run out to that big rock on the side lines; cut left over the small ditch; and I'll throw the ball to you—and don't slip in the cow dung!"

Other games we played were:

Baseball

Of course! It's our national game and any *vacant* lot was the place for the diamond to be laid out, sometimes with big stones at the bases. Sometimes, if we had it, we would stake chicken wire back of the catcher so that we didn't have to chase so many passed balls.

During the depression, there was no such thing as a new ball. Gradually the seams would break, and the cover would fall off. This was replaced by black bicycle tape, which when new and sticky allowed the pitcher to add all sorts of fancy curves to bewilder the batter; but as the tape hardened the ball took on the characteristics of a rock hard sphere which, when received as a hard hit ground ball on the shins, or other tender parts of the anatomy, caused welts, bruises, and incredible pain. Obviously, we played with our gloves well in front of us.

The situation was the same with the bats. All had been broken and tacked together and were bound by black bicycle tape, or piano wire. You could have killed a Mastodon with those war clubs!

All of the games were played usually on dirt fields which were rocky and uneven. A ball hit on the ground would bounce. Sometimes when your pitcher was having a bad day, playing the infield was almost suicide.

Later, as we became older, there were rivalries between towns and villages where everyone turned out. There was no TV, and not everyone could afford radios, so town baseball was the main source of entertainment. Passions would run high and rivalries were intense; some towns would import "ringers" from some of the lower professional leagues to play in a single important game for the princely sum of 10–20 dollars. Usually these players would try to disguise themselves, with mixed success; usually word would get out, and people would flock to see just anyone connected with professional baseball, as it would be the closest that they would ever get to the major leagues.

I was assigned to Fort Sill, Oklahoma when I returned from three years in the Pacific Theater, and was encouraged by my Commanding Officer to play on the post team, which was probably equal to Class D professional baseball. We not only played other service teams, but also in the small towns in the surrounding areas in Texas and Oklahoma, where baseball was the main source of entertainment.

The baseball diamonds in those towns were bumpy, full of stones, and if we played at night, there was not enough candlepower to light up a closet, much less a ballpark. The poor soul who had to catch a high fly ball took his life in his hands, as the ball would disappear above the lights, and suddenly swoop down like an avenging missile towards the startled player. The crowds would toss coins out of the stands, and the visitors and home team would gather them up, and the winners would take 60% and losers the rest.

Some of the Service teams we played had former professional players from Triple A and Double A League Teams. Most were marginal players, who either got too old to play, or fell victim to booze. We faced a Black player who played for the Pittsburgh Pirates and had passed himself off as an American Indian, before he was discovered and banned (Black players did not play in Major Leagues in the 1940s/50s).

The tricks I saw in those games were incredible, some of these were:

Shine ball The pitcher rubs one side of the ball surreptitiously against his uniform, thus one side of the ball was lighter in color. When the ball was thrown, the batter saw a kaleidoscope effect, thus confusing him.

Cut ball In this case, the button on the glove of the infielder was sharpened. When the ball was thrown routinely, the infielder would nick the ball with the sharpened button on his glove, and upon the return to the pitcher he would dig his fingernails into the cut to make the ball flutter and dip.

Loaded ball On one occasion, the opposing pitcher seemed to have an uncanny curve, which was impossible to hit. We quickly came to the conclusion that someone was "doctoring" the ball, but as try as we did, we couldn't detect anything suspicious going on. We did notice, as time went on, that the ball which the home team was using was always returned to the dugout after their half of the inning was over. After the game was over we managed to steal the home team ball and found steel phonograph needles driven into the cover in a spot about the size of a dime When the ball was thrown it wobbled like a balloon in a strong wind.

Sandpaper ball On other occasions, we would find a ball which was rough on one side, and smooth on the other; this is a sure sign that the pitcher had sandpaper somewhere on his person. The result was the ball made exaggerated moves. Well, there were other tricks the other teams pulled, but we won our share games and had hell of a time to boot.

Today there are so many sports events available on TV and the newspapers that one's attention is spread over such a wide spectrum, and the so-called sports heroes seem to be externally identified as rapists, felons, or fathers of illegitimate children, so that what used to be a purely idyllic view of sports, is despoiled almost daily with spoiled low IQ athletes and greedy insensitive owners.

I remember sleepy afternoons when both women and men would sit on the front porch listening to baseball broadcasts and making hieroglyphics on a printed scorecard. Announcers like Arthur Godfrey, Red Barber, et. al., would paint a word picture of the batter and pitcher, coupled with interesting observations and stories about various players. One would picture in his mind their favorite player taking his stance in the batter's box or fidgeting on the pitchers mound, taking the signal from the catcher; or upon occasion the flight of the ball as it disappeared over the wall with the elation that followed.

Since most of us were not living near any Major League ballparks, we had to contend ourselves with knowing the batting averages, or won/lost records of our favorite teams. Even today seventy-five years later, I can still name many of the outstanding players on most of the teams of that era.

My favorite team was the Detroit Tigers—don't ask me why—and I rushed to get the sports page from our daily paper to see if my beloved Tigers had won.

I think that my favorite series of all was the 1934 St. Louis Cardinals and the Tigers. The Cardinals were a colorful hell for leather team, which featured the colorful Dean brothers. "Dizzy Dean" was a flamboyant braggart, with a blazing fastball and a wicked curve; Paul was as quiet as Dizzy was loud, and while not as skilled as his brother was more than adequate.

At the beginning of the season Dizzy bragged to the sportswriters that "Me and Paul are going to win over 40 games between us."

Everyone laughed, but together, I think they won 43 games that year. The Cardinals were nicknamed "The Gashouse Gang." The gang leaders were Pepper Martin called "The Wild Horse of the Osage" with his "take no prisoners" type of base running. It took a brave man to stand up to the flashing spikes of Pepper.

The other leader was "Ducky" Medwick who was named after his duck like walk. Ducky had a mouth as loud as Dizzy, and he backed it up with his bat. He was the perennial 300 hitter who could take your head off with his screaming line drives. He played left field, and as such, he was always stationed close to the left field bleachers. In one of the series games in Detroit, he heckled the fans in the bleachers until they filled his part of the field with showers of garbage. The Commissioner of Baseball, Judge Kennesaw Landis, who was in attendance, stopped the game and had Frankie Frisch, the shortstop and manager remove Ducky from the game.

My beloved Tigers were much less flamboyant, but were filled with a number of all time greats, many of whom are now in the Baseball Hall of Fame, in Cooperstown, NY. The pitching staff consisted of "Schoolboy Rowe," a real country boy from somewhere in the South. Eldon Auker, a submarine fireballer, threw in an underhand motion, which made the ball sink as he approached the plate—a very scary pitcher indeed.

Next on the staff was Tommy Bridges, a Hall of Famer, who was perhaps one of the all time curve ball pitchers. Alvin Crowder, a good journeyman type of pitcher, rounded out the staff. The forerunner of today's dependence on relief pitchers was a full-blooded Indian, Big Al Benton. Whenever any of the starters got into trouble in the game, there would come Big Al to put out the fire!

On first base was Hank Greenberg, a Hall of Famer, and the Home Run King of the American League. One year, he hit *58* home runs, just two short of Babe Ruth's record of 60. Second base was occupied by Charlie Gehringer, another Hall of Famer, always a .300 hitter and steady as the Rock of Gibraltar. "Flea" Owen was the third baseman, a light hitter, but a slick fielder. The left fielder was Leon "Goose" Goslin, the fourth Hall of Famer, and a consistent .300 hitter. "Goose" actually looked like a goose with a nose resembling a beak. Lastly, was the fifth Hall of Famer, Mickey Cochrane, a catcher. He was, I think, their playing manager. With this line-up, how could they miss? Well they did!

Dizzy Dean won two superbly pitched games, Paul won one game, and one of the other pitchers won the last one. The series went 6 or 7 games and Schoolboy Rower on an interview before the series started, staggered through a series of questions by the sports writers on the radio, and being the country boy that he was, as an aside said to his wife "How am I doing Edna?" The Cardinals never let him hear the end of it.

The fact that I can remember all of this seventy-five years ago illustrates the hold baseball had on all of us in those days.

Mumblety-peg

In the 30's and 40's kids loved to play with knives. These days kids use them to kill their enemies, and to cut up their friends. I am sure that we had some of that when I was growing up, but the inner city aspect of our demographics hadn't really taken hold at that time.

It was WWII, which caused mass migration to the cities to work in the factories, which supported the war effort, resulting in a population explosion in the big industrial cities. Well, enough demographics.

Most kids had a Boy Scout knife which you could buy at Woolworth's for 25 cents. They had basically two blades: a large one on one end of the knife, and a smaller one at the other end. We would throw knives at trees, boxes, and old doors; just anything that you could stick a knife into.

Our favorite game was called Mumblety-peg and the rules were very simple. A player would start by placing the tip of the blade on the little finger of his left hand (palm side up), and the knife vertical to his finger; then flip the knife with his right hand and stick the blade in the ground. The player is seated while doing this. If the knife blade sticks in the ground, he then goes successfully through all his fingers, then to his wrist, elbow, and shoulder. The winning flip is from the top of his head. If, at any stage, the player misses, he yields to the next player, etc. It always seemed to me that the best games that kids used play were those where you got down dirty—a happy kid was a dirty kid.

Marbles

Now, marbles, as a game, was supposed to be fun, but out in the dust bowl it was all business because we all played for "keeps." This meant that if you were a weak player and lost all of your marbles to your opponent, you either had to go buy more marbles, or if you couldn't afford to buy them, your marble playing days were over until you raised enough revenue doing odd jobs until you could afford them.

There were two kinds that we played at the dust bowl: one was "Bull Ring" which was played in a large circle drawn in the dirt with a stick; or "C Ring" which was a smaller sardine shaped ring. In both cases, the rules were generally the same.

The players decided the stakes, i.e. 5 marbles apiece, or more or less, depending on the decision. A straight line was drawn in the dirt away from the ring and all players lagged their shooters towards the line. The closest to the line got to shoot first. All of the marbles comprising the stakes were put in the ring and were grouped tightly in the center.

Before we continue about the game, I must go over the terms and definitions so that you may look at what ensues as an insider (we never, ever, let girls into our marble mystique). So let's go into Marbles 101.

Taw or Shooter The shooter is larger than a regular sized marble and is sacred to its owner—never disparage another boys shooter—it is worse than telling him his sister is ugly. The really top-flight shooter is made of agate and is particularly lucky if it has a bull's eye (ringed mineral layers).

Steelies Steel ball bearing, you can't use a steel shooter, it's illegal, but Steelies used as one's stake are OK.

Glassies Usually a clear glass marble, with some sort of design in the center. It's OK to use glassies as a shooter.

Saltpeter Agate Saltpeter marble with an agate marking. It tastes salty too.

Potsy Marbles made from clay, but glazed on the outside; not looked upon as legitimate stakes for "keeps" games.

Glassie Regulars Just plain old glass marbles of different designs.

Rules

First player shoots from edge of ring. If he knocks a marble from the inside of the ring to the outside and his shooter stays inside the ring, he keeps the marble and continues to shoot from the final position of his shooter as long as the shot hits another marble out. He keeps all of the marbles which he knocks out, but if his shooter leaves the ring, or he misses, he gives up his turn to the next boy.

At one time, I had a cigar box full of marbles, which I had won and my own beautiful blue agate "shooter" lovingly wrapped separately. This memorial to my playground skills followed me from Army Post to Army Post. My greatest personal loss in material things was unbeknownst to me while I was defending my country overseas. My mother decided that I was to old to play marbles anymore and gave the whole lot away, part of which went to my brother in-law, a Navy Captain to use in a Lazy Susan (a rotating server)—the *cad*, and my beautiful blue shooter disappeared forever. I still grieve!

Half Rubber

This is a great game! It is played usually with two teams of two people each, although it can be played individually by three individuals. All that is required is some playing space, a broomstick or an equivalent, and a solid rubber ball cut in half. The players are a pitcher, a catcher, and a batter. Various landmarks such as trees, bushes, stones, etc., are used as markers for various distances from the batter's box denoting singles, doubles, triples, and home runs. The score is kept like ordinary baseball.

There is a defined batter's box and a home plate so that balls and strikes can be called by the catcher, honor systems were used on ball and strike calls; also a spot was established from which the pitcher threw. No running was involved as the achievement of the proper distance to the marker by a pitched ball automatically placed a hypothetical runner on base, and this runner was moved along by other runners as hits to the markers were achieved.

Failure to hit the ball past the pitcher, or swinging and missing the ball three times constituted an out. Each side is allowed two outs before giving up the batter's role.

The rules are simple, but hitting the ball is extremely difficult as the ball will rise, drop, or swerve left or right depending on the way the ball is held by the pitcher. The normal pitch is with the flat side down and the pitcher sailing the ball side arm, the ball rises about two or three feet from the pitcher's shoe tops and to hit a rising half ball with a broomstick is no mean feat. I attribute my ability to hit a baseball in high school and college, and amateur league, to a batting eye honed by games of half rubber.

Rubber Guns

No kid today ever heard of a rubber gun, but those of us who played "Cops and Robbers" and "Cowboys and Indians" can vouch for the fun we had "pooping and snooping" in the woods. The gun itself was crudely carved in wood, usually a board cut, and shaped like a rifle. A clothespin was attached vertically to the handle, so that when you squeezed the handle the clothespin would open.

For ammunition one would cut up an old inner tube from a discarded tire, and from this a number of very strong rubber bands were cut. Armed with an adequate supply of these rubber bands, a boy was ready to go forth into the realm of cops, robbers, cowboys, Indians and assorted monsters. The gun was loaded by stretching the rubber band over the end of the barrel of the gun and securing it by pinching it at the handle of the gun by the clothespin.

As sides were chosen everyone scattered throughout the woods, and once hit by an opponent's rubber band, you were considered dead—it was considered sporting to attack an opponent before he could shoot you, disarm him and take his ammunition, and shoot him—all very sporting! These rubber bands really hurt too! The penalty for lack of vigilance was a red welt on whatever part of your anatomy was exposed.

In later life, as an infantry officer, I was an outstanding "pooper and snooper" thanks to my experience playing "rubber gun."

Jacks

Can be played on any hard, fairly even surface, with a small India rubber ball smaller than a golf ball, and about 12 each 10-pointed Jacks which were made of metal and painted various colors.

The first player would pick up the Jacks with one hand and the ball in the other. All players are sitting down. The first player tosses the Jacks on the ground from a kneeling, or sitting position, and tosses the ball in the air underhanded; the player must then pickup one Jack before the ball hits the ground after it bounces once. Having successfully picked up the first Jack, the player again tosses the ball, and must now pick up two Jacks before the ball hits the ground after the first bounce, etc. In this manner, he progresses up to twelve Jacks, and in doing so wins the game. It sounds easy, but remember that when the Jacks are tossed they scatter in all directions because of the ten points. To pick up more than three Jacks on a toss required the dexterity of a Riverboat card dealer.

Jackstraws

This game is played once again on a fairly even firm surface. The only things involved in this particular game are small metal straws, although the straws can be replaced by long wooden kitchen matches.

The first player holds the straws in his hand and tosses them underhanded into the designated playing area. These straws will settle in such a way that many will criss cross each other, while others will be gently touching. The first player then attempts to remove a jackstraw from the pile, without disturbing any other jackstraw in that pile, once a jackstraw is disturbed, the player loses his turn, but gets to keep the jackstraw which he has successfully removed. The next player has to deal with the jackstraws left by the preceding player; the one with the most jackstraws after the game is the winner. Once again dexterity is the key to winning the game.

Red Rover

This is a game that was strictly for boys, although the more athletic girls could probably hold their own. The game is played in a swimming pool. Any number of people can play. One person is the Red Rover: he stands on one side of the pool, the rest of the players stand on the other side in a group. The width of the pool is the playing area.

The Red Rover calls across the pool saying "Red Rover, Red Rover, won't you come over?" At that both sides jump in the water, and the players from the side opposite Red Rover try to swim under water to Red Rovers side without coming up for air. If they do, then they have to be on Red Rover's team. Red Rover also must swim under water and his mission is to grab as many swimmers as he can, and hold them under water until they come up for air. The swimmer is allowed to use any strategy to avoid a Red Rover, such as swimming along the bottom of the pool, or around the sides of the pool.

The game ends when Red Rover and his team have caught everyone. Pity the poor swimmer who now stands on one side of the pool and everyone else is on Red Rover's side with mayhem in their eyes. The game is quite physical and creates a tremendous amount of endurance.

Step Ball

This can be played almost anyplace where there is level ground and a set of doorsteps. It's played with almost any type of ball that bounces. The playing field can be almost anything; a yard, street, just about any sort of area which can be marked off in terms of distance or feature. In a city it could be a certain mailbox for a single, a sewer top for a double, and so on. Usually only two players can play at a time.

The first player throws the ball against the step, and the second player attempts to catch the ball before it hits the ground; or if it is hit on the ground, he must catch it before it reaches one of the scoring markers.

The game is scored like baseball: a single puts a man on first; a double puts a man on second, etc. It's a great game for reflexes, and the player who is throwing the ball against the step, the pitcher, can control the flight of the ball by the angle he throws it against the steps so it is also a game of strategy. It's an excellent low cost high energy game; all that is required is a cheap rubber ball and a doorstep.

BB Guns

I have heard a lot of stories about BB gun fights where kids actually shot at each other playing "Cowboys and Indians." The kids I played with were not that stupid; we spent most of our time tramping the woods, shooting at various targets to show off our marksmanship. There were various types of BB guns, one of which was quite dangerous.

There was a sort of pecking order of kids who owned the fanciest guns. These guns were manufactured by the Daisy Company in Michigan. The top of the line was the Daisy Pump, which held 1000 shots and had an effective range of about 150 yards or so. Only the rich kids had those. The most popular was the Red Ryder, a prominent movie and cartoon cowboy, 500 shot nickel-plated gun. One would load the weapon through a hole at the top of the barrel, and then close it by twisting the end of the barrel. The gun was modeled after the old Winchester repeating rifle where the round was forced into the chamber by a cocking mechanism integrated with the trigger guard. Oh, how I dreamed of getting that gun. If the devil had made me a decent offer I would have traded my soul for that Daisy Model.

After my begging, I finally got my wish for a BB gun. As the package arrived on my birthday, my heart leapt. Would it be the Daisy Pump, a gift beyond my dreams, or the Daisy Red Ryder model?

Excitedly, I tore open the wrapping paper, revealing a box just the size that a Daisy would be in. The box resisted my frantic attempts to tear it open and reveal either the Daisy Pump or the Red Ryder. My fingers bleeding from torn fingernails, I finally opened the box and there in its full splendor was a genuine Daisy—was it the pump? No! "Well then," I said to myself, "it has be the Red Ryder." No again.

Well, it was a Daisy all right, but a single shot model, which was loaded by pouring a single BB down the barrel. You could not lower the barrel for a shot below level or the BB would roll out on the ground, thereby startling the intended target.

Needless to say, I was darn happy to have even a one-shot Daisy, but pecking order wise, I was at the bottom of the ladder. The one good thing about the single shot Daisy was that you could not kill anything with it. The trajectory of the BB was a gentle arc with a range of about 30 yards.

I think I once stunned a robin when I bounced a BB off its head. It gave me a withering look and flew away.

The most dangerous of all the BB guns of my era was the Benjamin Pump which fired a pellet. To load it, one placed a pellet in the breech and pumped air into the chamber; pumping the air through a contraption attached to the breech gave the pellet incredible velocity upon discharge. It could propel a pellet through a 2" x 4" like a knife through butter. We all stayed away from those, although I think our counter intelligence agents may have used advanced versions because of the lack of noise and muzzle flash.

It is hard to believe that in eight years some of us would be carrying a rifle in WWII, looking for real targets while "pooping and snooping" through the woods.

Other Games

There were many other games, too numerous to mention all of them, which all kids played. They included hop scotch, jump rope, dodge ball, tree tag, and one played in the Southwest where stockyards were located in cattle raising areas.

There, one had to balance oneself on the fences which separated the cattle. The players all had to run along the tops of the fences. If you fell off a fence you became "it." The person who is "it" has to chase the players on the fence, and he is on the fences along with the rest of the players. If he tags a player, that player is "it." The same version is played with trees except there one would swing from branches, but the idea is the same.

All of these games developed high degrees of manual dexterity, and physical coordination. There is no end of games that kids can make up to keep themselves amused. Today's children who have everything imaginable furnished them for playing, don't have the pleasure of making use of imagination and original ways to occupy themselves.

Childhood Memories: Gloucester, Mass.

Being a child of the 20's and 30's, I grew up in a period of rapid change brought on by the boom or bust environment of W W I. It's hard to believe that when the family moved to Oklahoma, the state was only twenty-six years old. This was in contrast to what I experienced upon my introduction to Gloucester, Mass., about 300 years old, when I appeared in 1930.

I am not sure just how we were transported from Norman, Oklahoma where my father was stationed to Gloucester the first time. In subsequent years, we had two routes. The first was by Touring Car, which was my step-mother's LaSalle which was somewhat less expensive than a Cadillac, but unique in that it could hold 4 children ages 6–12 yrs, 1 rather large dog, 1 half grown Easter chicken, 1 college girl to help my step-mother, and the driver, my step-mother.

Sometimes the Easter chicken and the dog were not there, and although the trip was a long one, we always had games we would play which didn't require complicated boards, etc., so time passed quickly.

Mother would never drive over 400 miles per day sometimes much less. The air conditioning for the car consisted of a twenty-five pound block of ice in a dishpan placed on the floor in the front with the vent in front of the windshield, which could be manually raised to catch the air which would be funneled though the frame into the car floor and over the ice pan. This was a welcome relief, especially during the Midwestern leg of our trip.

Sometimes, we would drive north to Cleveland and drive aboard a Night Boat which would carry us all overnight to Buffalo, NY. We would then drive down to Boston and from there to Gloucester; other times it would be a straight shot from Norman to Boston and then down.

One of the highlights of *any* trip we ever took was a losing encounter with a bee flying into the car, and *always* into the back seat where four children would frantically scream and try to avoid getting stung. Inevitably, one of us would be victimized, either by sitting on the bee, or by missing a "swat" would be attacked by the enraged insect.

My first visit to Gloucester filled me with wonder. Our cottage, which was built and owned by my stepmother's father, Mr. Louis B. Fitch, was a wonderful collection of rooms, alcoves, closets, and a kitchen which probably had no improvements since the late 1880's.

To a small child, the closets held a melange of fishing poles, umbrellas of all sizes, foul weather gear, old yellow oilskin rain gear, board games of all descriptions, *almanacs*, and books of all kinds.

A particular set of children's books, which today are worth a fortune were *The Hardy Boys* plus the *Nancy Drew* series. Ironically, the granddaughter of the author and I play tennis together once a week.

The cottage was located in a section of Gloucester named Bass Rocks and was located right on the Atlantic Ocean; it stood on the rocks above the ocean. The view was spectacular as one could see twin lighthouses situated on an island off shore to the left, and a whole unencumbered expanse of ocean to the front and right.

In the 1930's, Gloucester was a world-class fishing port from which hundreds of ships of all types would issue. Their main goal was the fishing banks off Labrador, which were probably the most productive in the world. It was a common sight to watch the two and three masted schooners sail by under full sail headed towards the "Banks" to fill up with codfish, pollock, haddock, swordfish, mackerel, and almost an infinite variety of other kinds. Perhaps once or twice a month, one could see down on the horizon, a four masted schooner under full sail. This was the sight of all sights—one of the most beautiful in the sailing world!

It was as much fun as anything I ever did: the feeling of a boat under sail cutting through the water under sail cannot be duplicated.

As we grew even older there were beach parties which, I must confess, involved some minor underage beer drinking. We would usually make a New England Seafood Roast which we would create after an afternoon of sailing. The procedure for this was as follows:

Step 1 Gather at least 5 bushel baskets of seaweed along the beach and make a bed about 8 feet square.

Step 2 Gather smooth small stones and heat them in a fire.

Step 3 Set aside what is to be cooked, usually clams, oysters, shrimp, and some kind of white fish, plus corn on the cob.

Step 4 Take heated rocks and place them on bed of seaweed.

Step 5 Put a layer of seaweed over the rocks and place all things to be cooked on top of seaweed.

Step 6 Pour cold seawater over things to be cooked and leave for an hour.

Step 7 Put beer in ocean preferably in a textile bag. Secure bag by pounding a stake in the sand; connect stake and bag by a rope. Leave for a walk, volley ball game, etc. Add cold water over seaweed occasionally. Upon return remove seaweed cover and remove the most delicious seafood ever made. Retrieve beer and pour.

Sometimes, I would sail in some of the Regattas held by other Yacht Clubs. This was true competition, us against all the rich kids. They had the best boats, but we were competitive. Sometimes we won.

The fishing fleets in Gloucester were manned by Italians and Portuguese and these people were *really* tough. They were devout Catholics, but they combined a lot of their religious ceremonies with the hardship they endured, especially in the winter when the lines were frozen; the ocean hostile; and one slip on an icy deck would send an unfortunate fisherman to his death in the ocean.

Besides the usual services, which included each lost soul by name, a wreath would be blessed and floated out to the sea which had claimed them. Back in the late 1930's, a film was made in which the great Spencer Tracy and Freddie Bartholomew, a prominent child movie star, were the principals. The title comes from Psalm 107:23–31. A lot of old timers remember this with tears in their eyes.

In the town of Gloucester, high upon a hill that overlooks Gloucester Harbor, is a church which has a very high tower on top of which is a lady with a fishing vessel under one arm and a torch raised in another. This torch has a very strong light embedded in it, which can be seen from 50 miles at sea. Fishermen returning from the New Foundland Banks know that they are safely at "home" when they see it. The church is named Our Lady of Safe Voyages.

Once a year the Italian and Portuguese hold a festival in honor of one of their patron saints of the fisherman. All of the ships are at anchor and the streets around the docks are brightly lit with multi-colored lights, as are the ships. Lots of wine flows and music and dancing ensues.

On one side of Gloucester Harbor stands the Castle of John Hays Hammond. It is a *bona fide* castle with many artifacts from the Middle Ages. Hammond was the inventor of the Hammond Organ, among other things. My stepmother remembered that he had developed a radio controlled small scale replica of a U.S. Navy submarine, and he used to sit in front of his castle and maneuver the model through intricate maneuvers, and this was pre-WWII! Obviously, he was well ahead of his time.

The rivalries between the small towns on Cape Ann, the Cape on which Gloucester is located, are intense; and are sometimes based on the most insignificant things. One of the most bitter is between Ipswich and Essex, both are located near rich clamming areas and are separated by 15 to 20 miles. Clams from these two areas do taste differently and both are delicious, but ask one about the other and one would think that eating a clam from the other is a sure ticket to the cemetery.

In Gloucester, there used to be two different summer societies. One society was the original people who came down from Boston and built modest dwellings along the ocean on the western side of Cape Ann. These people had enough "old money" to allow them to live comfortably in Gloucester in the summer and Boston in the winter. The other society was comprised of the *nouveau riche* mainly from Chicago and the Midwest.

Typical names were Dorrence (Campbell Soup), Swift (Swift Foods), Birdseye (frozen foods), and many others. These people built huge houses on Eastern Point which bordered the Harbor. I remember as a kid having a date with Harriet Swift who lived in a castle like home with a drawbridge, etc. These huge homes and the surrounding lands now stand empty, forlorn, and raggedy from neglect.

Typical of this group was the Dorrence family who drove to the beach in long black cars with the nannies all dressed in white, one for each child (3). The chauffeur was the bodyguard, and god knows what else they had. All of the protection was to protect the children from kidnapping. This fear was brought about by the kidnapping and brutal murder of the Lindbergh baby in the mid-1930's. I privately thought that if they were kidnapped, the men that kidnapped them would pay the parents to take them back after a day with them. The oldest discussed being a draft dodger in WWII.

The waters around Cape Ann, upon which Gloucester is located, are indeed treacherous. The entire coast is rock bound, and once a ship is dashed against these rocks in a high winds, it is reduced to matchsticks in short order.

There is a map on the wall of our cottage there, which indicates the location of various ship wrecks and the names of the ships involved. There are literally hundreds of ships named, and in most cases there were few, if any, survivors. One of these wrecks was immortalized in the poem *The Wreck of The Hesperus* by Henry Wadsworth Longfellow. The site of the wreck was a group of rocks on the western side of Gloucester Harbor called Norman's Woe.

Hurricanes were a common occurrence. Some were extremely destructive uprooting roads, flooding towns, and destroying houses. It's difficult to realize how powerful water can be when pushed by tides and wind. One of the movies made about Gloucester and its fishermen, the most recent one is about a true event called *The Perfect Storm* by Sebastian Junger which deals with a monstrous wave created under a number of conditions which could all occur simultaneously one time among thousands of possible parameters.

Opposite our cottage is a point which protrudes into the ocean with a number of very large houses perched along it. The last house on the end is approximately 200 feet above the ocean. When the "perfect wave" hit during the hurricane which spawned it, surf was breaking over the house. Naturally, it was destroyed.

There are the usual numbers of Art colonies about: some are excellent; some less than excellent.

More important are some of the historical significances of the area. For example, British Naval Vessels would put ashore and kidnap the local men to man their ships. The practice grew so widespread that certain townships were literally stripped of able-bodied men. In Rockport, a community about six miles from Gloucester, the women started their own town called Dog Town, away from the ocean in the wilderness between Gloucester and Rockport. This area is full of carved stones containing words of the Bible, which are now almost 300 years old.

Gloucester will always contain the mystery and sense of adventure for me, unchanged since I was a little boy.

Part IX

Appendix

Ancestors

Name	Year	Rank	Comments
James Barron	1804	Commodore U.S. Navy	Commodore was Highest Naval Rank. Campaign against Sultan of Morocco. Killed Stephen Decatur in a duel. My Great Great Uncle.
Samuel Lockett	Class 1854	Co. U.S. Corp of Engineers. Resign Commission for Confederacy. Col. Confederate Army Corps of Engineers	Married Daughter of Gov. Alabama. Constructed Fortifications, Mobile, Galvezton, Vicksburg. Chief Engineer for Rulers of Egypt and Columbia. Signed Declaration of Loyalty after Civil War. Became Prof. Engineering at LSU. Supervised Raising of Statue of Liberty.
James Lockett	Class 1879	Col. U.S. Cavalry	Commanded 11th U.S. Cavalry in Southwest Indian Territory. Served in Moro Rebellion. Distinguished Service in Spanish & American War. Distinguished Service Medal.
James McDonald Lockett	Class 1908 (Did not grad.).		Served Philippine Scouts. Moro Campaign. INF. BN Commander (WWI). Wounded. Decorated Gallantry in Action. Commander Washington, D.C. district. Regimental commander. Commanded Infantry School, Fort Benning, Georgia.
Harry James Malony	1912	Maj. General (Ex-Artillery)	Served Panama during digging of canal. Served Texas-Mexican border. Served as Ordnance Officer and attached to French Airforce (WWI). Served as Secretary to Army Artillery School. Fort Sill Oklahoma. Artillery Board, Fort Bragg. Instructor Army War College. Chief U.S. negotiating committee with UK 1940–41. Headed Army War Plans. Commander 94th Inf. Div. U.S./Europe 1942–45. Heading negotiations and planning first Greek free elections (acted as Minister). Member UN Discussion Indochina. Member UN Discussion Philipines.
James Lockett Malony	Class 1945	Capt. Inf.	Infantry unit CMDR. Svd 7th U.S. Cav. Japan, Philippine Isles. BN-S-3 2nd Armored Div., Fort Sill, Oklahoma. Started own Consulting Company, Classified Clearances in U.S. Served various clients in UK, Russia, Spain, Germany, France, Italy. Liaison rulers of Nigeria, Liberia, Peru. Visibility Mideastern officials.

Eire

As we come to the end of *Kaleidoscope* and *Stories My Father Told Me*, it seems fitting to finish up with a poem by my father, Major General Harry J. Malony about the protocols concerning imbibing adult beverages. So, I raise my glass to you, Dad, in salute to the service you gave to our country, and the love and example you gave to me.

Eire

Wanst there was a Yankee mon
His name t'were best fergot
From Belfast town ta Dooblin town
He came and saw a lot
And whin he'd gone to Galway Bay
They tell me thot he passed away
And now the folks who know him say
He niver could quite learn
In Ireland 'tis a sinful thing
A weary and a skinful thing
To buy drinks out of turn.

www.ingramcontent.com/pod-product-compliance
Lightning Source LLC
LaVergne TN
LVHW091028080826
845145LV00002B/403

* 9 7 8 0 9 8 5 5 9 6 9 2 7 *